HOW
BLACK
WAS OUR
SABBATH

HOW
BLACK
WAS OUR
SABBATH

AN UNAUTHORIZED VIEW FROM THE CREW

DAVID TANGYE

AND

GRAHAM WRIGHT

PAN BOOKS

First published 2004 by Sidgwick & Jackson

This edition published 2005 by Pan Books
an imprint of Pan Macmillan Ltd
Pan Macmillan, 20 New Wharf Road, London N1 9RR
Basingstoke and Oxford
Associated companies throughout the world
www.panmacmillan.com

ISBN-13: 978-0-330-41194-3
ISBN-10: 0-330-41194-2

3 5 7 9 8 6 4 2

A CIP catalogue rcord for this book is available from
the British Library.

Printed and bound in Great Britain by
Mackays of Chatham plc, Chatham, Kent

CONTENTS

ACKNOWLEDGEMENTS

I would like to make a personal dedication of this book to my ever-loving mother, Kathleen Tangye, who left this world for a better one on 23 March 2004.

I would like to thank everyone who helped in the preparation of this book, especially those listed here.

Very special thanks go to our guru and mentor Carol Clerk for her patience, wisdom and never-ending help and support. Also a very special thanks to our literary agent Lisa Eveleigh, for her relentless energy and dogged determination to get us this far.

To Ingrid Connell and all at Sidgwick & Jackson – thanks for all the kind words and hospitality, and the faith you have shown in Graham and me.

I would like to mention specially my sisters, Christine and Joan, and their families for their encouragement and support.

To Marie – extra-special thanks for the support, and being there for me.

Hello to Sheba (a better friend man never had).

Thanks and special credit to Geoff 'Luke' Lucas, Keith Jefferson, Spock Wall, Les Martin and Albert Chapman. Thanks, Luke, for the great recollections and unfailing support. Thanks to Keith for the notes on Mythology and Earth, and the great photos. Thanks, Spock, for your generous help when it was needed. Thanks, Les, and sorry about the tuna sandwich! Thanks, Albert, for all you have done for me over the years, and for all the fun we've had at the Elbow Room.

Extra thanks to Ian Walsh and Neil Marshall. Also to Geoff Sharpe and Don Mackay, Jezz Woodroffe, Malcolm Horton and Jim Ward.

Acknowledgements

Special thanks to Trevor Clements for the kick-start.

The final tribute goes to the band, Black Sabbath – Ozzy Osbourne, Tony Iommi, Bill Ward and Geezer Butler. We shall never see their like again.

DAVID TANGYE

I would like to thank the following Black Sabbath crew members for the help they gave in the writing of this book: Geoff Lucas, Keith Jefferson, Spock Wall, Les Martin and Albert Chapman. Thanks are also due to all the other crew members who worked alongside us during our years with the band.

A very special thank you to Carol Clerk for her invaluable help and guidance, to our agent Lisa Eveleigh and to Ingrid Connell and all at Sidgwick & Jackson.

Thanks also to Jim Ward and the Fields Farm gang – Terry Lee, Keith Evans, Malcolm Horton and Barry 'Spence' Scrannage – for sharing their memories.

A very, very big thank you to my wife Mikki and two sons Daniel and Bryan who wholeheartedly supported me for the couple of years it has taken to write this book.

I would like to make a personal dedication to my late parents, Albert and Mary Wright, who always encouraged me in everything I attempted.

To Ozzy Osbourne, Bill Ward, Tony Iommi and Geezer Butler – the greatest heavy metal band in the world – WE LOVE YOU ALL!!! Thanks, lads!

GRAHAM WRIGHT

FOREWORD

It was early November 1975, and Black Sabbath were on a tour of Germany. They'd played a storming gig in Ludwigshaven. Now they were in Dusseldorf, and they were in high spirits as they came down for breakfast at the Intercontinental Hotel.

The plush restaurant was full of English and American executives wearing suits. As the Sabbath entourage sat around a table looking out of place, as usual, they were amused by a bellhop who walked into the restaurant carrying a slate board in a wooden frame, with a small bell attached. Someone's name was chalked on the board, and he called it out loudly, ringing the bell at the same time.

Tony Iommi got up and left the table. A few minutes later, the bellhop was back in the restaurant with his board and bell, this time displaying the chalked name Harry Bollocks.

'Paging Mr Bollocks,' he announced importantly, in broken English. 'Mr Hairy Bollocks . . .'

It was a typical Iommi prank. For all of his serious commitment, his many hours spent alone playing guitar, the unofficial leader of Black Sabbath liked nothing better than a good wind-up.

And so the day began with a laugh, and it looked like ending with one too. The local promoter had invited the band to a party at a place called the Why Not club, situated in a seedy district of Dusseldorf not far from the city centre.

Sabbath drummer Bill Ward decided to pass on the party, but Tony, Ozzy Osbourne and bassist Geezer Butler were up for a bit of fun and they went along with three members of the road crew – Dave Tangye, Geoff 'Luke' Lucas and Albert Chapman. Also in tow were members of

Sabbath's support band, Streetwalkers, who were led by the former Family singer Roger Chapman. Their drummer was the larger-than-life Nicko McBrain, who went on to work with the Pat Travers Band and, famously, Iron Maiden.

The champagne was flowing and everything was going fine until about 10.30pm, when a fracas broke out at the entrance to the room where the party was being held. Dave Tangye remembers it vividly:

Nicko McBrain was in the middle of the bundle, and he was taking punches from all angles. We never did find out what caused the fight, but there were so many people battering Nicko, we had to do something.

Albert and I went over and pulled him out of it. Suddenly, this guy in a yellow and black striped jumper landed a punch on the side of my face. I chose not to retaliate, and we immediately named him Bumble, as in bee.

Things calmed down for a while as we picked up where we left off with the bubbly, but a heavy atmosphere persisted in the club. Ozzy was past caring. He lurched over to a table where a pair of lesbians were kissing and cuddling, dropped his pants and mooned at them.

He then staggered off towards the toilets, and I followed him, just for safety's sake. As he left the gents, someone intentionally bumped into him. Ozzy took a swing at him, and missed by a country mile.

The next thing we knew, Bumble was heading towards us, obviously fancying another go at me. I had to deprive him of that, so I gave him the old "one-two" and he went down like a bag of shit. And that's when the riot erupted.

There were bodies flying all over the place, Albert was knocking them out left, right and centre, Big Luke hung one guy up on a coat hook, someone hit Geezer with a chair, Tony was, as usual, in the thick of it – he liked to throw a punch – and Ozzy ran for cover. I think he went back to see how the lesbians were getting on.

It was real Wild West stuff. We literally had to battle our way out of the club, as these hostile crowds just kept coming and coming. There must have been about twenty people having a go at us; we were completely outnumbered, and I'm sure they'd planned it in advance.

When we eventually reached the bottom of the stairs, someone pulled out a 'gas gun' and shot Albert Chapman in the mouth, with a very loud bang. These guns fired hard plastic pellets, and it blew a hole right below Albert's bottom lip, knocking one of his teeth out.

Once outside, we ran up to the taxi rank in the central square with this mob in pursuit, and we all jumped into cabs. I asked the driver for the Intercontinental Hotel. He started yelling wildly in German, pulled a Luger pistol out of the dashboard and stuck it in my face.

All of a sudden, there were police cars everywhere; we were never so pleased to see a copper. We were all bundled into the back of a wagon and taken to the local precinct, where Albert had the chance to clean up his face. There was a doctor there who looked everyone over, and the police were really good with us. The promoter turned up to explain that we'd been set upon in the club, and after the band had signed some autographs for the arresting officers, we were released back into society.

It was just another day on the road with Black Sabbath . . .

Dave Tangye and Graham Wright, the authors of this book, belonged to the team of back room technicians better known as the Sabbath road crew, and for many years they were the closest people to the musicians, both onstage and off.

Black Sabbath were the band who put the 'heavy' into rock. The true godfathers of metal music, they would have loved to turn the amplifier up to eleven, many years before the world would hear of Spinal Tap.

By 1980, they had sold more than twenty-two million albums and ten million singles worldwide. And with successive generations of rock fans and musicians discovering the awesome power of the band at their best, Sabbath's influence thunders on, forcefully, into the twenty-first century.

1

THE CUMBERLAND GAP

Ozzy always said it was a shit-hole. And true, there was nothing that lovely about the rows of run-down, back-to-back, terraced houses that were built to accommodate the workers coming in to operate machinery and man the heavy steel foundries as the industrial revolution gathered pace after the First World War.

But the Birmingham suburb of Aston has three big claims to fame. It's the home of HP Sauce and Aston Villa FC. And it's the birthplace of heavy metal.

Here, among the factories, the grimy back streets and the corner pubs, surrounded by the grand buildings and gardens of a more affluent history, the four members of Black Sabbath made the first loud noises of their lives.

Anthony Frank Iommi came into the world on 19 February 1948, followed by William Thomas Ward on 5 May. John Michael Osbourne arrived in time for Christmas, on 3 December, and the bouncing bundle that was Terence Michael Butler was born the following year, on 17 July 1949. The boys who would join together to revolutionize the world of rock music were raised within streets of each other, closer even than The Beatles in Liverpool.

Leaving school at fifteen, Tony, Bill, Ozzy and Terence (known as Geezer) were individually drawn to music, the one great force that would bring them together as Black Sabbath and enable them to escape from Aston as soon as they had the time and the money.

The first great British pop explosion was transforming the lives of teenagers across the country. Every city had its own movement, led by Liverpool with the Merseybeat sounds of The Beatles, Gerry and the

1

Pacemakers and The Fourmost. The London scene was thriving, thanks to the likes of The Rolling Stones and The High Numbers, later renamed The Who, and Birmingham was not sleeping either. It had its Brumbeat and a whole community of young musicians who would eventually come to prominence in bands like The Moody Blues and The Move. Any kid who had an ear for music was hooked. Bands were springing up everywhere.

Most did not have the luxury of going into music full-time, and they had to take on day jobs. Tony, Bill, Ozzy and Geezer were no exception, although they were clearly hoping that luck and fate would deliver them from the mundane.

Ozzy would often joke that his first job in the music business was testing car horns at a local automobile factory. That was at the Lucas car-accessories plant. His mum, Lillian, worked there, and she had arranged the job for him. He was also employed by a plumber, a tool-maker and a mortuary. He was a mechanic and a house-painter, and he was rejected by the army.

But his favourite job, by far, was at Digbeth abattoir. A school-friend had made the introductions, and Ozzy was initiated into the workplace by being thrown down the 'blood and guts' chute, where the offal ended up.

Recovering from the initial shock of his new environment, Ozzy seemed to enjoy killing up to 250 animals a day. He described it as his 'forte' – and it certainly explains the casual way in which he later killed his own chickens. But even Ozzy could only take so much, and after a couple of months of the stench and hideous, large rats, the apprentice Prince of Darkness left the slaughterhouse. It was later converted, and today is the home of UB40's recording studio and offices.

In 1966, Ozzy would endure an early taste of prison, serving six weeks of a three-month sentence in Winson Green for non-payment of a £25 fine he had incurred for breaking into Sarah Clarke's clothes shop. While in prison, he went to great lengths to avoid the 'heavy' guys who vented their sexual frustrations on weaker male prisoners. One con tried to have his wicked way with Ozzy, but he escaped by bashing a piss-pot over the assailant's head. Generally, he used his natural flair for comedy to make friends. Ozzy gained his first tattoo in Winson Green, spelling his name across his knuckles. Shortly after his release he was also sporting smiling faces on his bare knees.

The rest of the band had a less colourful career. Bill Ward began his career delivering coal around the streets of Birmingham. Geezer Butler – always canny when it came to money – worked in the accounts department of a local factory in Aston, where he was constantly getting bollocked for his timekeeping. Tony Iommi went to work as an apprentice sheet metal worker, during which time he had an accident with a guillotine and severed the ends of two of the fingers on his right hand. It's unlikely that any of the four enjoyed the daily grind of employment.

This was a time of great social change and excitement. Suddenly, boys started growing their hair long, in line with the new 'long-haired' musical heroes of the day such as The Beatles and Stones. Mods and rockers made headlines and terrified respectable society with spectacular rumbles in the seaside towns of England's south coast. Rockers developed out of the motorbike gangs of the late fifties and early sixties. They wore leather jackets, studded leather belts and jeans, sported heavily Brylcreemed quiffs, and were into rock'n'roll music. Mods, the more sharply fashionable group with their cropped or backcombed hair and mohair suits, raced around on Lambretta or Vespa scooters and were devoted to soul music, including British 'Northern soul'. They championed bands such as The Who and the Small Faces and switched on to the sounds of Tamla Motown. At weekends they would pack out all-night clubs, take a load of speed in the form of tablets like Black Bombers and Purple Hearts, and run around like lunatics, dancing to soul music by covers bands until they finally crashed out in the early hours of Monday morning.

Ozzy later claimed to have been a mod. Today, it is hard to imagine him with the short haircut, the smart mohair suits and the Ben Sherman shirts.

The landscape changed again in 1967 with the advent of the hippie movement and the use of psychedelic drugs, sounds and imagery. Young men were growing out their moptop cuts, once considered so daring, and sporting seriously long or freaked-out hair. The availability and widespread use of cannabis and LSD resulted in a more serious and experimental attitude towards music. There was a sense that anything was possible and the prevailing credo was 'do your own thing'.

For some people, including the late, great guitar guru Jimi Hendrix, acid became a way of life. He took it every day, according to John 'Upsie' Downing, the guitar roadie who accompanied him to the legendary Woodstock festival. Despite the fact that Hendrix had Upsie on his payroll for four months, he never once managed to remember his name. He just used to call Upsie 'man'. Upsie went on to be tour manager for ELO and for Ozzy's Blizzard of Ozz on their first UK and American outings. Happily, they were not so addled that they forgot who they were talking to.

While psychedelia cast a very positive influence on the development of contemporary music, some groups took it over the top. Hawkwind – self-styled timelords – were a complete audio-visual experience, with their swirling soundscapes and light show created by a couple of projectors with revolving coloured discs attached to the front. Just as memorable was their impressively endowed girl dancer Stacia, who cavorted about the stage topless.

But for the future members of Black Sabbath, there were no such extravagant ambitions. It was simply a case of tune in, turn on and form a band.

✝ ✝ ✝

Their story really begins in the late 1960s in the English border city of Carlisle in Cumbria – or Cumberland, as it was then known. This was the home of a band called Mythology, billed as 'Cumberland's Answer to The Jimi Hendrix Experience'.

The founding members of Mythology were Neil Marshall (bass guitar), Mike Gillan (vocals), Frank Kenyon (lead guitar) and Terry Sims (drums). They were well connected locally, on the books of the CES

Entertainments agency and later Border Entertainments, both in Carlisle. They also had the support of Monica Linton, a booker who set up their gigs.

By the end of their first year together, they were a popular and respected act on the northern club circuit, as well as in Germany and Sweden. After one of their short European tours, in December 1967, Mike Gillan decided to quit. Mythology recruited a Newcastle singer called Rob and began rehearsing with him. A week later, Frank Kenyon also left, later joining up-and-coming Carlisle band Timothy Pink.

Frank's departure left the band in crisis – they had gigs booked for the end of January. CES swung into action, contacting other agencies in the search for a new lead guitarist. It paid off. Someone in Birmingham knew of a player called Tony Iommi, who had apparently declared that the music scene was 'dying off' in the Midlands and was keen to spread his wings.

Tony was a young guy in search of new experiences. Few amateur musicians had any management or direction at the time, so they were quite happy to travel and transplant themselves from their normal surroundings, to see how the other half lived. He was frustrated at not being able to find a band in Birmingham that suited his style, and the opportunity to join an established group in Carlisle would have appealed to him.

Tony had already played with several bands in the Midlands. One was The Rocking Chevrolets, who covered American classics by Chuck Berry, Bo Diddley and Eddie Cochran. He had also served some time with The In Crowd, the Birds and the Bees and, finally, a group called The Rest, who specialized in twelve-bar blues.

Arriving in Carlisle, Tony was accompanied by The Rest's singer, Chris Smith. They had come as a package, and they played an impressive audition. Mythology's Neil Marshall was left with the awkward task of telling newly appointed singer Rob – who had not even appeared live with the band – that his services were no longer required. Neil simply said: 'You've heard the guys in rehearsal; we'd be crazy to turn them away.' Rob packed his bags and returned to Newcastle.

And so Tony Iommi and Chris Smith joined Neil Marshall and Terry Sims in the second Mythology line-up. They spent the next few weeks gigging around Cumbria, gathering more and more fans with their blues-rock workouts. Although this was the lifeblood of the late sixties 'underground' scene, most of the bands in the local area were simply coasting, covering rock'n'roll tunes and hits of the day, so Mythology were embraced as a particularly progressive outfit. Their secret weapon was Tony Iommi, who was developing his playing skills at a phenomenal rate. He was a naturally gifted guitarist, but he kept on practising, improving, trying to make it perfect. His influence on Mythology was immense.

The group set up home and headquarters together in a flat in Compton House in Carlisle city centre, next to the technical college. They spent their days searching for songs to cover, listening to recordings by John Mayall and the Bluesbreakers, Buffalo Springfield, Cream and Art, a short-lived psychedelic band which would mutate into the more successful Spooky Tooth. Tony would quickly pick up the chords and riffs, the band would rehearse the songs, and they would slot them into their stage set without delay.

Local DJ Keith Jefferson, who became a close friend, recalls:

When Mythology first started looking for accommodation, they spent at least one night sleeping in their van in Bitts Park. They looked quite weird at first sight. Their boots were decorated with blue chalk flowers, and their hair was standing on end, but it didn't take long to find out they were really nice guys.

In the Compton House flat, they occupied the large attic room plus a first floor room and a bathroom. They were never any trouble, but there were a few occasions when they would come back in the early hours and play their music loudly. Not surprisingly, this disturbed the landlady's daughter, Amber, who lived in the annex of the building. Early one morning, Amber turned on every television and radio on the ground and first floors, which brought them all out of their rooms, wondering what was going on. She told them that this performance would be repeated each time she was woken by them coming in. From that day on, she never heard another squeak.

In mid-February 1968, drummer Terry Sims decided to call it a day. Tony and Chris drafted in Bill Ward – their old drummer from The Rest – and half of the band that would become Black Sabbath was in place. For now, however, it was simply the classic Mythology line-up.

Bill Ward made his debut appearance with the band on Saturday 17 February 1968 at the Globe Hotel in Main Street, Cockermouth. Neil Marshall still vividly recalls Bill's performance, not for what he played but because he adopted such a low position behind his kit that he appeared to have buried himself in the drums.

Mythology gigged around the region throughout the spring, playing a particularly memorable show at Chester's Clockwork Orange on 4 May, supporting a group called The Rain. This was an outfit led by Gary Walker, formerly of the Walker Brothers, now singing as well as drumming. The headline artists were so shocked by the strength of their opening act that they weren't particularly keen to 'follow that'. Mythology duly blew them off the stage and received a mere twenty pounds for their efforts.

Keith Jefferson recalls another favourite club memory:

In the middle of one number, Neil, Tony and Chris had just moved to the side of the stage leaving Bill to his showcase drum solo. He was really getting into his stride when from the rear, the curtains parted and a frumpy-looking lady appeared, undoubtedly connected to the hall management. She immediately started to berate the lads about Bill: 'They don't like drum solos here. Stop this at once!' Bill carried on as the rest of the band lost their cool in fits of laughter. Clearly, this ferocious woman in her woollens and thick tights was not too familiar with the sight of long-haired young bucks wearing suede and leather jackets.

By the beginning of summer 1968, Mythology's days were numbered, but they had no idea of what lay ahead as they carried on gigging. Keith remembers the first of two run-ins with the police:

The band were nearing the end of a short tour in the north of England when, in Hartlepool, their clapped-out group van died on them, and a replacement had to be found that day. They bought an ex-railway van, but because it was a Saturday and the licensing authorities' offices were closed, they couldn't get a tax disc for it – even if they had had enough money left over for one, which they didn't. The ever-resourceful Neil decided that the label from a bottle of Newcastle Brown Ale would do the job, and this was duly inserted into the plastic holder on the front windscreen as a temporary measure.

The Hartlepool gig went well and they retired to their digs, waking up the next morning to find the van surrounded by police, who hauled the lads off to the local nick for questioning. The reason for the large police presence was the gas masks the band had bought from a second- hand store and left lying in the van in full view. The coppers were convinced they had stumbled upon some sort of terrorist cell.

Neil, as the band leader and the person named on the documents, copped for the counterfeit tax disc. His court case was heard in Hartlepool after Mythology had broken up, and he had to thumb a lift from Carlisle, and back, to make his appearance.

May 1968 was a memorable month for the band. They met a Leeds University student making a home visit to Carlisle, and bought a small amount of cannabis from him. The student was later arrested in a local pub, and he helped with the enquiries of a certain Sergeant George Carlton. This giant of a police officer was a well-known 'character' in and around the city centre, respected and feared. He was an old-school copper, he was streetwise, he knew what was going on in his patch, and what he said went. He would talk to people and befriend them, he would know who to ask for information, and he kept a close eye on the Gretna Tavern and other city meeting places and hang-outs.

Sgt Carlton had formerly served with the Scots Guards, and he had an unmistakable military presence. He was rarely seen without his peaked cap and stick tucked under his arm. He was known to be strict but fair, and would often offer a 'clip round the ear' as an alternative to a night in the cells. Mythology received a visit from him at their Compton House flat, and they ended up in court charged with drug possession. They were splashed all over the local papers, and the story was reported in some of the nationals too.

The defendants were fully identified to readers as Anthony Frank Iommi (20), musician, 67 Park Lane, Aston, Birmingham; William Thomas Ward (20), musician, 15 Witton Lodge Road, Erdington, Birmingham; Neil Martin Marshall (24), musician, 36a Malleyclose Drive, Carlisle; and Christopher Robin Smith (19), musician, 11 Woodland Farm Road, Erdington, Birmingham. The four pleaded guilty to possession of cannabis resin in Carlisle on 27 May 1968 and were each fined £15. Neil Marshall was placed on probation for two years and Iommi, Ward and Smith were each given a two-year conditional discharge. The police were quoted as saying that, 'All four had been most helpful and co-operative, and did not conceal or deny the offence. They had been arrested as a result of a routine check following the charging of another person, a warrant had been obtained and a search made of a room at Compton House, Compton Street, Carlisle, where all four were residing at the time.'

Sgt Carlton was not heavy-handed when he arrested Mythology. He was quite cool about it, and he was very supportive of Neil and the guys afterwards, helping them through the aftermath of the court case. Amber, their landlady's daughter, confirms that he was 'marvellous', while adding that the band were 'devastated' by the raid. Cannabis possession was seen as a serious offence back then, and Mythology suffered the consequences. Their work began to dry up as cancellations came in thick and fast. This left them with very little money, and reluctantly, after playing their last gig at the Queen's Hotel in Silloth on Saturday 13 July 1968, they disbanded.

Keith Jefferson recorded the gig using a reel-to-reel tape machine. The only surviving record of any of the band's performances, it contains nine tracks including such enduring blues favourites as 'Steppin' Out', 'Dust My Blues', 'Morning Dew', and 'Spoonful'.

Tony Iommi and Bill Ward returned to Birmingham while Chris Smith apparently stayed on to marry a local girl and settle down. Neil Marshall went on to join a band called Smokey Blue and still lives in Carlisle.

✝ ✝ ✝

Back in Birmingham, a band called Rare Breed were doing brisk business on the live circuit. Geoff 'Luke' Lucas, their road manager at the time, remembers that their set was based on flower-power songs like 'My White Bicycle' by Tomorrow, as well as covers of cool American songs such as The Doors' 'Light My Fire'. Rare Breed, led by lead guitarist Roger Hope, featured Geezer Butler playing rhythm guitar. The rest of the line-up comprised Mick Hill (bass), Tony Markham (drums) and John Butcher (vocals).

Butcher received a better offer and quit, leaving Rare Breed in search of a replacement. Before long, they noticed an advertisement that had been placed with Pete Oliver at the Ringway Music Store, a favourite hang-out for budding musicians in the Bull Ring Centre. It read 'Ozzy Zig *needs* a gig', and stated that the singer owned his own PA system. Ozzy Osbourne got the gig with Rare Breed but never even got so far as performing with them. The group fell apart only days later.

However, Ozzy's ad remained on display in Ringway Music, where it caught the eye of Tony Iommi. He contacted Bill Ward, and together they made their way to the singer's address at 14 Lodge Road, Aston, with some trepidation. Tony had known an 'Ozzy' from his time at Birchfield Road Secondary School in Perry Barr, Birmingham, and he and Bill were hoping it was not the same person. During their school-days, Tony had been in the year above Ozzy, who had been, at times, the butt of Tony's jibes and practical jokes. Despite the fact that all four members of Black Sabbath grew up in a working-class environment, Tony and Ozzy had been at the opposite extremes of it.

Tony, tall and good-looking even as a schoolboy, was from a better-off family who had been in a position to start rebuilding their lives when the war and, later, rationing, ended. They ran a general store in Park Lane, which was a bit like Ronnie Barker's Arkwrights, although it was not 'open all hours'. Tony Iommi Senior also worked in a local dairy.

Ozzy's parents were not so fortunate. Lillian, working at the Lucas factory, and Ozzy's dad Jack, in engineering, had a big family to feed. They lived in a small two-up, two-down with Ozzy, his three sisters, Jean, Gillian and Iris, and his two brothers, Tony and Paul. Within their limited budget, Lillian and Jack didn't have the money to dress Ozzy in smart clothes, and he stood out a little from his schoolmates. Playground politics being what they always have been, and kids being kids, the big guys ganged up on the smaller ones, and they picked on Ozzy and his appearance. He took a lot of stick in his schooldays, but he managed to clown his way out of the worst of it. Tony has since stated that he 'hated' Ozzy at school, and used to beat him up. Albert Chapman, a classmate of Tony's, says Ozzy was not singled out for any special treatment. He was picked on as part of the 'normal' school routine where the older kids bullied the younger ones. He used to get his 'marbles' kicked, but then so did the other boys. According to Albert, Ozzy was 'a bit of a pest'.

When Ozzy opened the front door of his home to Tony Iommi and Bill Ward, Tony's heart sank. It was indeed the same person. But after an initial awkwardness, things quickly became cordial. Ozzy introduced Bill and Tony to Geezer Butler, who lived with his family at 88 Victoria Road and who was keen to find a new band after the demise of Rare Breed.

The bad blood was behind them – at least for a few years – and the four lads who would take on the world and win had come together. But they weren't called Black Sabbath. Not yet.

2

THE ORIGINAL TAP

He never mentioned any bullying at school, never mind complained about it. Ozzy would always go out of his way to make people laugh, try his best to make them like him, while he got on with the important business of making music.

Tony Iommi may have felt remorse over the bad time he had given Ozzy, but they were out of school now, they were in the adult world, and they were trying to put a band together.

Ozzy, of course, was on vocals, and he had the hugely attractive advantage of his own PA system, a 50-watt Triumph amp with a microphone and two column speakers. Tony and Bill stuck to their previous roles as lead guitarist and drummer respectively, while Geezer switched from rhythm guitar to bass, converting his six-string Fender to a four-string bass simply by changing the strings.

The band gelled immediately, and when Ozzy and Geezer suggested hiring Rare Breed's former right-hand-man Geoff 'Luke' Lucas as their road manager, there was unanimous agreement.

The handsome and grammar school-educated Luke, a real ladies' man, towered above the others at six feet five. He was one of the easy-going, old-school roadies who could turn his hand to anything. He was hard working, abundantly energetic, methodical and extremely thorough in everything he did, for which he was often teased. He was a real asset.

Luke's initial friendship was with Geezer:

Geezer was a lovely bloke who liked a laugh and was quite laid-back most of the time. His sense of humour was individual and sometimes weird, and it was obvious he was a fan of Frank Zappa.

Back in the days of Rare Breed, we often used to talk about 'going pro'. It was all he wanted, and his flamboyance and attitude onstage made him ideal rock star material. He would always be the most exciting member of the band to watch live. He was definitely a 'poser', in the nicest possible way, and could carry it off perfectly.

He was better educated than the other three, and I always imagined he would be the most sensible with money once it started to roll in, since he had worked in accounts. At the same time, he liked the luxuries that money could buy – he passed his driving test on a Thursday and was driving a Rolls Royce two days later.

But that was still in the future for Geezer. For the moment, he could only dream of wealth and fame as he sat squashed up with the others in a tiny van, travelling to whatever gigs they could get.

The road manager back then had a lot more to do than the modern day tour manager. Luke did all the driving and running about, he made sure the van was properly serviced, and he ensured that the equipment was in working order. He made their travel arrangements, set the gear up onstage and acted as a minder too, protecting the band from over-zealous fans. He rolled the joints, took the flak and willingly acted as a general dogsbody. For better or for worse, he was in charge of four young men crammed into a Transit van, surrounded by equipment and the aroma of smelly socks, stale booze, tobacco and testosterone. Luke's job was purely a labour of love, and he did it without help or support from anyone.

He quickly became familiar with the band members' personal quirks.

Tony was quite vain. He always took pride in the way he looked. He was very much a ladies' man. Naturally a big person, he liked to watch his weight, and he's the only one I remember going on diets from time to time.

Later, when he began to make money, Tony would reveal himself to be a generous character if the mood took him. At first, he was the only member of the band who could drive and, like Geezer, he loved nice cars. He would end up being able to change them as often as he wanted and to have a Rolls and two Lamborghinis sitting in his driveway at any given time.

Bill Ward was always incredibly down-to-earth, relaxed and generous to a fault. He was at his happiest sitting in the local pub with a pint and twenty Woodbines, and he always would be.

And as for Ozzy – to meet him was one thing; to get to know him was 'an experience and a half'.

† † †

Ozzy, Tony, Geezer and Bill decided to go for a big, brassy, blues sound with flavours of the American deep south, and so they took on slide-guitar player Jimmy Phillips and a saxophonist called Alan 'Aker' Clark. After only a few days' rehearsal, they went out to earn some money.

Mythology fans in Carlisle did not have long to wait to see Tony Iommi and Bill Ward back in the city, thanks to the help of their booker friend Monica Linton at CES. She arranged for the new six-piece to appear on Saturday 24 August 1968 at the County Ballroom, where they were billed as the Polka Tulk Blues Band. Unbelievably, it had taken them hours of deliberation to arrive at such an awful name, and there were those who preferred Luke's tongue-in-cheek suggestion of Blues Band Margarine – a pun on that era's most popular brand of marge, Blue Band.

This appearance was the first of just two the six-piece ever made, the other at Banklands Youth Club in Workington. They hadn't rehearsed that much, so the performances were probably more jam sessions than anything else, which was quite acceptable in those days. They almost certainly built the set from Tony's repertoire of blues songs, dating back to Mythology.

On their return to Birmingham, Tony Iommi – the unofficial leader of the band – decided to get rid of Jimmy Phillips and Aker Clark, declaring that Jimmy wasn't taking things seriously enough and that the sax player, as a soloist, did not fit in with the overall sound. Tony reasoned that if you were going to have brass in the group, you really had to do it properly, with a three-piece section at least. With Jimmy and Aker gone, the remaining band members were probably grateful for the extra space in the Transit.

Ozzy, Tony, Geezer and Bill were now working as a four-piece, calling themselves the Earth Blues Band, which was quickly shortened to Earth. Their days in regular employment were well behind them, and they were now pinning all their hopes on a workable income from music. They began rehearsals in the Burlington Suite in the Newtown Community Centre, Newtown Row, Aston. One cold and damp morning, Ozzy turned up barefoot for the rehearsal because he had no shoes to wear. He'd walked over a mile from his home, but he was used to it, and his feet were as hard as nails.

Ozzy would often do things for effect. It wouldn't bother him to walk a mile shoeless as long as when he got to his destination, someone would make a fuss over his plight. He wasn't disappointed. After the gales of laughter had died down, the other guys started feeling sorry for him and had a whip-round, raising nineteen shillings and eleven pence (ninety-nine pence in today's money). Ozzy sped off to the nearest shoe store and bought himself the cheapest footwear he could find, emerging with a pair of sandals, or 'Jesus boots' as they were known then.

Earth worked up a set of cover material, predominantly twelve-bar blues songs recorded by the likes of John Mayall, Cream and Elmore James, and returned to Carlisle for their debut gig. They knew they would go down well there, and they were certain of work through the continuing support of booker Monica Linton. They made their first appearance as Earth in late September 1968 at the Gretna Tavern, owned by Carlisle entrepreneur Tom Foster.

Returning to the Midlands, they worked around their home territory until the end of the year, when Tony Iommi made an astonishing announcement. He was leaving Earth to join the established progressive band Jethro Tull, who were within a few months of breaking into the mainstream with a string of hit singles and albums sparked by a whimsical song called 'Living In The Past'.

Earth had played a gig in Stafford opening for Tull, whose flute-playing singer and frontman Ian Anderson had watched their set, impressed, from the back of the hall. When Tull guitarist Mick Abraham left suddenly, Anderson remembered Tony Iommi and invited him to join the band.

Tony was overjoyed; he reckoned he had made the grade. The rest of Earth were genuinely pleased for him and wished him well. But it was a short-lived affair. Tony didn't take to the strict regime that Anderson imposed on the band members, and he found the singer stand-offish.

Jethro Tull were due to appear at The Rolling Stones' legendary 'Rock'n'Roll Circus' extravaganza, which was being filmed on 10 December at the Intertel studio in Stonebridge Park, Wembley, in front of an invited audience of Stones fan club members. Tony spent four days in London, rehearsing intensively with the band. And then he handed in his notice.

However, he had second thoughts on his way back to Birmingham. He asked Luke to return to London with him as his full-time guitar roadie, and Luke agreed. Arriving for the 'Rock'n'Roll Circus', Tony told Anderson that he had changed his mind and wanted to be reinstated in the Tull line-up. But he was too late. Anderson had already recruited Martin Barre, and he informed Tony that his services would not be required after the TV recording.

As a fitting end to the whole fiasco, the 'Rock'n'Roll Circus' was shelved, only being released to the public in October 1996 when it was launched at the 34th New York Film Festival.

The Stones had been unhappy with the show, reportedly complaining that they had been upstaged by The Who and some of the other supporting acts, including the famous 'supergroup', The Dirty Mac, comprising John Lennon, Eric Clapton, Hendrix's drummer Mitch Mitchell and Keith Richards, unusually playing bass guitar.

The Stones also contended that they weren't satisfied with their own performance – even though they'd played way into the early hours, repeating songs many times over in their efforts to get everything right. They intended to organize another shoot, but never got it together.

The show did, finally, turn out to be a real spectacular, with the studio dressed to look like a big top, complete with half a tent, sawdust and circus performers entertaining the audience between bands.

Tony fell back to Earth afterwards – much to the relief of Ozzy, Geezer, Bill and the fans who welcomed them to Carlisle's County Ballroom on Saturday 21 December. They went on to a series of gigs in Birmingham, before returning to Cumbria for a run of school hall dates. It was not unusual back then for gigs to be promoted on school premises, and when Monica Linton was organizing an itinerary for Earth, she would set up as many gigs in a row as possible, just to make the petrol money worth their while.

The band endured one particularly rough night in the Scottish Borders. Pulling up outside the Buccleuch Hall, Langholm, Luke was surprised to see that the car park was full of tractors. This was Hicksville, the kind of place where men were men and the sheep were terrified. It was like turning up at a local Young Farmers Club for a barn dance, or, if it was really hip, a 'beat night'.

Lots of bands played there, out in the middle of nowhere, where the punters came from local farms and dressed, accordingly, in country threads. There were about a hundred people in the two-hundred capacity venue, and as the band walked in and began setting up their gear, it was like a spaceship had landed. The audience watched every move the aliens made with intense fascination.

Just before they went onstage, Ozzy was approached by one local, who said, pleasantly, 'If you don't play The Rolling Stones, I'm gonna beat the shit out of you.' Ozzy relayed this message to the promoter, who said, 'Don't you worry about it, I'll sort that lot out.' He then left, instructing the band to meet him later at the fish and chip shop he owned in the town to pick up their money and a free supper.

The band struck up and their spectators stood motionless, scratching their heads. However, the cavalry arrived in the form of a bunch of enthusiastic fans from Carlisle, who formed a semi-circle in front of the stage and visibly enjoyed the usual set. There were no Rolling Stones covers. And although you could have cut the atmosphere with a knife, and a couple of skirmishes broke out between the fans and the farmers, nothing serious happened in the venue.

Earth left the hall unscathed and set off for the chippie, looking forward to their few quid and a fish supper. They found the promoter in an awful state, having been badly beaten up by a bunch of guys outside the gig, growling that they didn't like the music.

† † †

It should have been a brilliant buzz, a night to remember, the crowning glory of their career so far. But for Earth, their first appearance at London's prestigious Marquee Club on 3 January 1969 was a crushing disappointment. Most bands of the same vintage will recall their pride and exhilaration at that crucial milestone, but Earth had their Marquee debut ruined.

The Marquee had built up its reputation as a jazz venue in Oxford Street before moving to Wardour Street in 1964, where it became the country's foremost showcase for exciting, alternative talent. The incumbent manager, John Gee, was not at all impressed with Earth's scruffy appearance and ear-splitting volume. Maybe he wasn't too keen on Brummies. But he was particularly incensed by something Ozzy was wearing. In a bizarre foretaste of things to come, he had hung the cross-shaped top of a kitchen tap around his neck on a piece of string. Far from being any kind of religious statement, it was more than likely that Ozzy had found it in a motorway service station and decided that it would look cool alongside the black brooch he also wore on the string.

The crucifix that would become Black Sabbath's trademark was born from this. Ozzy's dad Jack later made an aluminium cross for him, and when he showed it off at rehearsal one day, the rest of the band wanted one too. Jack made about a hundred of them altogether, some with a rhinestone glued into the centre, and Ozzy would throw them out into the audiences.

John Gee was outraged by Earth's performance and promptly banned them from future appearances at the Marquee. Such was his disgust that at the end of the night he turned off the lights in the venue as Luke was loading the gear out, leaving him to fumble around in the dark with a torch. Luke believes to this day that John Gee may have had a fear of taps, he went on about it that much. It was quite literally Ozzy's Spinal Tap moment.

They could, of course, have told Gee to stuff it, but it would have been an empty protest – he wouldn't have cared, and neither would anyone else. Despite the insulting attitude of their host at the Marquee, Earth were anxious to be able to play there again. They were not a name band, and they had no record deal or management. They were beggars, not choosers; they could not afford to lose such an important opportunity.

Help arrived in the shape of Ten Years After, a band who were very much on the rise and had a certain amount of American success to their name. Luke recalls that a huge poster of them was on display in the foyer of the Marquee, where they were treated like gods. They sold out the venue every time they played there, and they were good friends with John Gee.

Alvin Lee, Ten Years After's dazzling guitarist, had struck up a friendship with Tony Iommi at the Jethro Tull 'Rock'n'Roll Circus' gig, and so he and drummer Ric Lee (no relation) badgered John Gee to grant Earth a reprieve. Reluctantly, Gee agreed, on condition that Ozzy got rid of 'that tap' and the whole band agreed to smarten themselves up.

Like it or not, they had to comply. The Marquee was a key venue, and it would certainly prove to be a vital stepping stone over the coming months, helping Earth become one of the 'in' bands.

During this same period they acquired proper representation, signing with Jim Simpson at Big Bear Management in Birmingham.

Simpson also managed Bakerloo Blues Line, the blues-jazz orientated Tea and Symphony, and Locomotive, for whom he played trumpet. Big Bear needed an outlet for their bands to perform and Simpson opened a blues night at the Crown Hotel in Station Road, Birmingham. He called it Henry's Blues House. One of the first bands to play there was the newly formed Led Zeppelin.

Jim Simpson was a decent and honest man, and probably not ruthless enough for the rock'n'roll industry. As a musician himself, only a few years older than Earth, he got on really well with Ozzy, Tony, Geezer and Bill, although it was generally felt that he was more interested in Locomotive, his own band, and Bakerloo Blues Line. Earth and Tea and Symphony came third and fourth in his affections. Later, the band would outgrow Big Bear. While Jim remained in Birmingham, they needed a manager who could dash to business meetings in London at a moment's notice and keep his finger on the pulse of the industry.

But in these early days, Jim Simpson kept the band in work. One of his first projects involving Earth was the 'Big Bear Ffolly', a UK package tour of the four bands on his books. Kicking off in Birmingham's Opposite Lock Club at the end of January 1969, the tour also featured Earth's return to the Marquee on 6 February.

It was all valuable experience for the musicians, and it enabled them to build followings in areas they might not normally have covered. Each group performed individually, and at the end of the show joined forces for a jam session.

The Earth was definitely moving – in the early spring, they set off on a short tour of Europe, their first trip overseas. The itinerary took in Scandinavia and Germany, where they were booked into Hamburg's Star Club, legendary for its association with The Beatles, for ten nights.

Amber, the Carlisle landlady's daughter, says this was the last time she saw the band, setting off from Compton House. Asked where they were heading, they said, 'Hamburg in Germany'. She replied, 'You'll be lucky to get over Shap Fell in that van.' The next time she heard news of them, they were playing the Hollywood Bowl.

Their last return to Compton House was also a rare one. It had been a home from home for Mythology, up to their split. Earth, on the other hand, had taken to staying with Keith Jefferson when they were touring in Cumbria. It was a friendly part of the world – fans and friends would become voluntary roadies, helping to hump gear in and out of the gigs, and Keith was no exception. He had invited the guys to stay at his flat in Warwick Square, off Warwick Road, when they were in the area, thus keeping their expenses to a minimum.

Keith, as a DJ, had a vast collection of records, and it was at his place that Ozzy, Tony, Geezer and Bill heard, for the first time, the debut album by Led Zeppelin. Impressed by the innovative vocals, guitar work and arrangements, but not to be outdone, they famously remarked that theirs would be even heavier.

† † †

Ozzy was the last pick-up en route to the ferry port at Harwich, Essex. Like the rest of the band, he was still living with his parents and Luke vividly remembers him rushing out of the house wearing his dad's old peaked cap, like Andy Capp. He was clutching a carrier bag containing one pair of socks, one pair of underpants and a shirt. In the other hand he had a pair of jeans on a coat hanger that he had borrowed from his girlfriend, a young lady he'd met at a gig in Henry's Blues House. Sadly, her name has vanished into the mists of time, but everyone around Earth in those days remembers her name for Ozzy – Oswald. Oswald was certainly travelling light on his first trip to Europe. 'We didn't stop laughing until we got to Harwich,' recalls Luke.

The journey to Denmark, by ferry and Transit van, was less amusing. It seemed never ending to the band as they travelled from Harwich to Esbjerg in Denmark and finally on to Copenhagen.

Arriving in Denmark, they were greeted by heavy snow. The roads were open but driving was difficult, and the old Transit van eventually broke down in the middle of nowhere. It was absolutely freezing. Luke got out to investigate the problem. Ozzy followed, and a strong gust of wind blew his dad's cap off his head and into a field. Luke still enjoys the memory of Ozzy chasing after the cap, shrieking that his dad would kill him if he went back home without it.

He returned about thirty minutes later, cap on head, and announced that he had found a place where he was able to get assistance, and a tow truck was on its way. Ozzy was the hero of the hour.

The promoter in Copenhagen sent a representative out to travel in the van with Earth, to show them round and collect the money from the gigs. They were on a very tight budget, and one day they decided to look up an old friend who was living there. He made them welcome, gave them a cup of tea each and set out a plate of biscuits. The moment his back was turned, they went for the biscuits like a pack of wolves, and cleared the plate in seconds. None of them had eaten for twenty-four hours, but they still felt guilty because they hadn't left a crumb for their friend.

And so to Germany, where they toured air bases and played their first residency at the Star Club in Hamburg. There, they were presented with an exhausting schedule of five forty-minute sets a night. As a result, they spent a lot of their spare time asleep and had no great X-rated adventures on that trip to tell the folks back home.

But it was still a very exciting time for them. They were out there with their eyes wide open, taking in all the sights, customs and cultural differences that the continentals had to offer. The gigs themselves were a great success. Like many bands that were coming out of Britain at the time, Earth were thought to be at the cutting edge of the music scene.

Returning to England, they went straight back on the road. They were hard workers. One night towards the end of April 1969, they played the ultra-trendy Speakeasy club in London, and the next day thought nothing of jumping into the van and travelling hundreds of miles north for a gig at the Banklands Youth Club in Workington. It was one of their favourite haunts, they always went down a storm, and they had forged a bond with their fans in Cumbria that exists to this day. They would go out of their way to play for them, and also to accommodate Monica Linton at CES. She had been a real lifeline for the boys when they were short of gigs. Tony knew that if he phoned Monica, she would invariably find the band three or four bookings, and he has never forgotten the help she gave them in those lean spells.

✝ ✝ ✝

One morning, Keith left the band sleeping on in his flat while he went to work as an engineer on the M6 Carlisle bypass. He returned to be confronted by his formidable landlady, brandishing a notice to quit. She had come round to the premises earlier, perhaps to do some cleaning or to check that everything was in order, and had found a group of 'hairy bohemians' milling about by the communal bathroom. She was having none of it. She had already seen off Earth, who had shot off back to Birmingham. Now she was seeing off Keith.

Shortly after this, Earth asked Keith if he would like to join the band as a roadie, since Luke was struggling with an ever-increasing amount of equipment. Keith jumped at the offer. Having nowhere to live, he quit his job and set off for Birmingham in his ex-GPO Morris 1000 van, with his last month's wages in his pocket. He said it was like 'running away from home to join the circus', and he was right.

3

JIMMY UNDERPASS AND
THE SIX-WAYS COMBO

Keith went on to share a ground-floor flat with Luke in Handsworth, Birmingham, but first he moved into the back room of the shop that Tony Iommi's mum, Sylvie, ran in Park Lane, Aston.

Sylvie was a lovely woman, with an olive complexion and dark hair. She was very supportive of the band and the crew – without her, there would have been no Black Sabbath. It was Sylvie who acted as guarantor when the band needed a decent van for touring. She treated all of the lads as her own, fed them and looked after them. She even slipped Bill and Ozzy the odd packet of No 6 cigarettes, and Bill could always depend on her for his bus fare home.

Jim Simpson, their manager, was sometimes as broke as the band. Luke remembers going to his house for petrol money to get to the next gig. He ended up hiding in the kitchen with Jim while the milkman banged at the front door, looking for two weeks' money.

In the early summer of 1969, with Earth formalizing plans to record their first album, Jim wrote this promotional piece for his protégés:

Earth are exciting, blues-based, hard rock. Write a lot of their own material, which is melodic but heavy. They have tremendous rapport, which makes the union of four good musicians into a great band. Singer Ozzy has a big tortured voice. Geezer Butler looks like Zappa, plays fierce, ever grooving bass – has incredible rapport with Bill Ward, who is a musical rarity – a drummer who writes songs, digs big bands and swings like mad. Guitarist Tony Iommi, who doubles on flute, played with Jethro Tull – including the Rolling Stones TV spectacular – before deciding that Earth was the band for him. Very fast and melodic. Earth are currently recording an LP produced by Gus Dudgeon, who does Bonzo Dog, Locomotive etc. Regularly played the Marquee – had extremely successful tours of Sweden, Denmark, and Belgium.

Distributed as a flyer, Jim's work paid dividends as bookings for the band came in from far and wide. Soon, they were on the road with a vengeance, slogging up and down the endless miles of British motorway.

Keith recalls:

To relieve the boredom, the band – like many others at the time – would indulge in the popular pastime of mooning at passing cars. This would amuse the occupants of our van but it would shock the families and elderly people in the vehicles overtaking us. It was almost always Ozzy and Bill baring their arses to the UK, usually under the influence of alcohol. Tony and Geezer would cheer them on, while not taking part themselves.

The boys got on really well together. They were like a band of brothers, possibly because they had no financial pressure, and their workload kept them busy but it wasn't too heavy. They spent long periods on the road in a small Transit van with two roadies, so they became very close.

I found Tony to be very polite, a real gentleman to everyone he met, although being the figurehead and focal point of the band in the late sixties, he knew the musical direction he wanted. He was no pushover, and he usually had the final say.

Geezer was also very focused, and like Tony, he had some great ideas for the band's early original material. He wrote most of the classic lyrics. He seemed a happy sort of guy, he would almost always have a smile on his face.

Ozzy was the clown of the band, always messing about, doing

daft things to amuse and impress the others, but behind the front he seemed a little insecure, probably because of his humble background.

Bill appeared to be a deep thinker, but he was also a bit of a joker. He always got on well with everyone, and for me, he was the nicest bloke in the band.

It was not long before Earth were heading back to the Star Club in Hamburg, this time for a week-long residency. They piled on to the Dover to Dunkirk ferry on 9 August 1969, and it was during this voyage that they made the momentous decision to change their name to Black Sabbath.

They had recently discovered the existence of another band called Earth, who were playing pop and Tamla Motown covers, after a mix-up at a hall in Manchester. The hall manager, expecting the other Earth, had taken one look at Ozzy and co as they straggled towards the dressing room and demanded, 'What sort of music do you guys play?'

'Rock and blues at high volume,' they told him.

Clearly imagining full-scale riots in his venue if he allowed them to go ahead with the show, he advised the band that, 'You will not go down at all well here,' handed them twenty pounds for their petrol costs and wished them luck for the future. In effect, he paid them to go away.

Sitting around in the ferry en route to Hamburg, the band mulled over ideas for a new name. Geezer had already written the song 'Black Sabbath', whose title was inspired by a Boris Karloff movie. It had become a stage favourite, and Black Sabbath suddenly seemed like a great name for the group. However, they didn't make the change immediately.

Disembarking in Dunkirk, the band drove through the night to get to Hamburg the next day, a Sunday. Staying in the annex of the city's Hotel Pacific, they were allocated two rooms with three beds in each. Tony, Bill and Geezer were together in one room, while Ozzy, Luke and Keith shared the other.

Coming offstage at the Star Club in the early hours of the morning, they would then head for the takeaway restaurant just along the street for a plate of 'pommes frites'. By this time, the transvestites who had been working the street would be in there having supper and beginning to show undeniable signs of masculinity with their five-o'clock shadows and husky voices becoming more obvious by the minute.

For the band and crew, this was one of their two meals of the day, and only after wiping their plates clean would they finally go back to the hotel and crash out. They usually wouldn't be seen again until about two in the afternoon, when they were back in the café for their other daily feast: a sago or rice pudding with a spoonful of jam in the middle. They couldn't afford luxuries like proper eating while they were away, although they didn't quite starve. Geezer, who was in charge of the finances, obviously drew on all of his experience in the accounts office to stretch the limited budget as effectively as possible. Still, the guys looked forward to a good, square meal with their parents at the end of every trip.

The Star Club was in the Reeperbahn, the famous red-light district in the St Pauli district of Hamburg, but Earth were just about as restrained on this visit as they had been on the first, focusing almost entirely on playing, eating (a little) and sleeping. They were still naïve kids, really; down-to-earth and happy just to look around and take things in.

Ozzy distinguished himself during one performance when he daubed himself with purple paint, not from head to toe as legend would have it, but on his hands and his face, with a snake painted on his chest.

On the final night of their Star Club residency, Earth gave a rendition of the John Lennon/Plastic Ono Band anthem 'Give Peace a Chance' with two other bands, Tremors and Junior's Eyes, who were starting the next week's residency at the venue. Earth stayed on in Hamburg for an extra night to celebrate a successful trip, but it was a fairly low-key event – a night off and a few beers.

Returning to England, they instructed Jim Simpson that they had changed their name to Black Sabbath. Jim was not impressed; he felt that they should reconsider and, in all seriousness, proposed the name

'Fred Karno's Army'. Ozzy, amused, shot back with an equally ridiculous suggestion, 'Jimmy Underpass and the Six-Ways Combo'. He would often bring up Jimmy Underpass in later years when joking about other bands' names.

✝ ✝ ✝

It was time for a single. Returning from Germany, they ate heartily for the first time in a week and, fortified, went straight into two days' rehearsals for the recording session. The song proposed was 'The Rebel', and the band were joined on organ and piano by Norman Haines, from Jim Simpson's band Locomotive. Haines had composed most of Locomotive's great tracks, including their one and only hit, 1968's 'Rudi's in Love'.

On arrival in London, the group – in their last days as Earth – checked into the Grantly Hotel at 50 Shepherds Bush Green, and went directly to Trident Studios in St Anne's Court, Soho, where they recorded 'The Rebel' on an eight-track machine.

Overseeing the session on 22 August 1969 was producer Gus Dudgeon, who had previously produced Locomotive and had at one time been a member of Tea and Symphony. Eventually, he would go on to great things, producing albums for David Bowie, Elton John and many other members of the rock elite.

This was Earth's first studio experience. They felt they were really making progress as a working rock band and, naturally, the set-up and recording techniques intrigued them. But they weren't too impressed with Gus, who repeatedly drew comparisons to Locomotive and how they would have done things in the studio.

Engineer Roger Bain was then invited to take over. It was his first attempt at production, and he did a sterling job. 'The Rebel', an uncharacteristically light and commercial track, and 'A Song For Jim', the projected B-side which no one can remember much about, were the property of Jim Simpson and were never finally released to the public. However, the band were so comfortable with Roger that they retained his services for their first three albums – a period considered by many to be their most creative.

That period arguably began at Banklands Youth Club, Workington, on Tuesday 26 August 1969, when Earth announced to the audience that they were about to change their name to Black Sabbath.

They played under the new name for the first time on 30 August – Keith's birthday – at Malvern Winter Gardens in Worcestershire. Luke had changed the name on the bass drum skin, using black electrician's tape. And as if to stamp the name of Black Sabbath across the country, the band followed on with a period of relentless gigging.

By now, they were playing mostly their own material on stage. The set list for their recent second residency at the Star Club had included such classic Sabbath favourites as 'Black Sabbath', 'The Wizard', 'N.I.B.', 'Warning', 'War Pigs', 'Rat Salad' and 'Fairies Wear Boots'.

They'd been writing their own songs for ages, which was why they would be able to record their first album so quickly, but they'd had to introduce the original material gradually onstage. At the club gigs they'd been playing, they had been obliged to concentrate on blues-rock covers because people wanted to hear songs they could relate to.

Tony Iommi later told journalist Richard Green:

We couldn't keep playing twelve-bars. We just got fed up with Earth music. It was jazz-blues stuff. It was good for practice but nothing else. A lot of other groups were playing the same thing. When we changed, the whole thing just snowballed. We wanted something of our own that we'd like and people would like. We wanted something loud that people would listen to.

The first time any of them remember playing a Sabbath song onstage was at the Pokey Hole, a club in Litchfield, Staffordshire. There, they premiered 'Black Sabbath', written during their rehearsals at the Newtown Community Centre in Aston. They went down an absolute storm that night, and from that point on, encouraged, they would throw in another one or two of the songs they'd written, adding more and more as the months went by. From the outset, Geezer's lyrics dabbled in underworld imagery, with 'Black Sabbath' talking about Satan and the flames of hell.

At the same time, Sabbath were turning into one of the heaviest bands in the country, if not THE heaviest. Again, the process had been gradual. But by the time that Earth finally became Black Sabbath, people were just in awe of them. Audiences would be rooted to the spot at the front of the stage, gaping, transfixed by what was going on in front of them, shocked and thrilled by the sheer power of it all.

The wall of sound was staggering, often deafening. People physically vibrated. Sabbath always had more amplifiers and speaker cabinets than most other bands, and would force them to their full capacity. The juggernaut of a rhythm section was topped with Ozzy's inimitable vocals, screaming out chilling lyrics mostly written by Geezer Butler and, in Tony Iommi, the people had a true guitar hero. He could be playing a light, acoustic melody one minute and thundering out a heavy, menacing chord the next. He was continually experimenting with exciting, haunting, memorable riffs, and he played solos that would go on for fifteen or twenty minutes. Often, Geezer would follow Tony's riffs note for note, lending weight to the song structure, while Bill Ward was behind some extremely complicated drum patterns and powerful solos. The fans would find themselves transported by the music, gloriously spaced out.

Sabbath had their own distinct identity running through the stuff that they played, which came through naturally and suited the way they looked – hairy, scowling, gloomy and straight-faced, the opposite of pop groups who smiled cheerily in their promotional photos. Sabbath looked like they had a message for their audience, and everything was coming together perfectly. It just evolved. Sabbath were pioneers, and that was the secret to their success.

Their most important gig around this time was at the Lafayette Club, Wolverhampton, on 4 September 1969. They played here for expenses only for the benefit of BBC Radio 1 DJ John Peel, who had a residency at the club. He could offer them a slot on his revered, progressive radio

show *Top Gear*, which in those days was broadcast on Saturday afternoons. *Top Gear* did not simply reflect what was cool and happening,
it also dictated it. Sometimes wilfully obscure, John Peel was nevertheless one of the leading influences on the alternative music scene at
the turn of the seventies, and beyond.

Turning up in the audience that night to lend support to Black
Sabbath was Robert Plant, Led Zeppelin's sensational vocalist. As half
of Zeppelin's members hailed from in and around the Birmingham
area, the two bands were on friendly terms from the beginning. Bill
Ward would later become great mates with Zeppelin's drummer John
Bonham, while Geezer Butler would find himself drinking with Robert
Plant at the same country pub when they both became a bit richer.

Back in the early days, Led Zeppelin were musically more complex
than Sabbath. Like other bands such as Deep Purple, they were loud,
but they were also melodious and they liked to have sophisticated
arrangements. Sabbath also had a lot of light and shade, and tempo
changes, but they specialized in crunching riffs, with Geezer's bass often
following the lead guitar note for note to double the impact. The sound
of the Sabbath was huge.

In the same week, Black Sabbath played a less successful gig at
the Top Rank in Hanley, Stoke-on-Trent, where they were met by a
hostile crowd of skinheads. Bombarded by jeers and chants during
'Wizard', the band instantaneously swung into a rendition of the 1967
Eddie Floyd soul classic 'Knock on Wood', and then walked offstage in
disgust.

The M1 was becoming very familiar. Travelling back down to London
on 19 September, the band and crew headed first for a meeting with
Roger Bain and their publishers, Essex Music, to run through some different ideas for a single. Essex Music was responsible for the 'writing'
side of the band's operation, dealing with everything from credits to
sleeve notes.

Sabbath's first attempt, 'The Rebel', had been shelved, since the band and the management alike thought the song too 'pop' to make a striking debut. Returning to Trident Studios to try again, they recorded several numbers which would be considered not only for the single but for their first album.

They went on to play a couple of key auditions at the end of September, both on the same day but a hundred miles apart. The group were, as usual, happy to put in long hours in the van to keep to a hectic schedule as new opportunities kept opening up. To their excitement, the industry was finally taking notice, and the prospect of a record deal was on the horizon.

Sabbath spent an afternoon at the Pied Bull in Islington, London, performing for Lou Reisner of CBS-Mercury records. He didn't hang around for long, but he seemed pleased at what he'd heard, bought everyone a drink and then left. A few hours later, Black Sabbath were taking the stage at Henry's Blues House in Birmingham, playing for an executive from Philips Records.

The next morning found them pointing the Transit north to Scotland where they would carry out another two engagements in one day, this time in Edinburgh at the Oasis and Cavendish clubs. No one can say that Black Sabbath didn't pay their dues. And before you could say 'pommes frites' or 'sago pudding', they were on their way back to Hamburg's Star Club for their third and final residency at the historic venue.

Keith Jefferson recently retraced their footsteps on his way through Hamburg to Kiel, where he had arranged to see his old friend Mike Harrison – ex-VIPs and Spooky Tooth – playing with the Hamburg Blues Band:

> I made a nostalgic return visit to the Star Club to see what remained of that great venue. To my surprise, a new building had taken its place and to the rear, in a sort of paved shopping area, stood a black marble monolith.
>
> Inscribed in gold below the famous Star Club logo were the

names of the all-time top acts from the USA and Europe who had played the club from 1962 to 1969. It included The VIPs, which gave me a great feeling of pride for Carlisle and Cumbria, but I could not understand the omission of Black Sabbath, who'd appeared there on three occasions in 1969 before the Star Club finally closed its doors on New Year's Eve that same year.

It was around the time of their third and final appearance at the Star Club that Jim Simpson finalized a recording deal with Philips Records – a deal which also involved a promotional trip to the States.

Not for the first time, the band had to start thinking about a single and, again, they turned for help to their old Locomotive friend, Norman Haines. They turned up at Henry's Blues House to watch his new band Sacrifice go through their paces and booked a rehearsal room at the Birmingham Arts Lab, where they tried out one of Norman's songs, 'When I Came Down', as a possible single.

After a UK tour, finishing in mid-October, the band went into Trident studios with Rodger Bain (who had added a 'd' to his Roger). They recorded their first album, *Black Sabbath*, in a matter of days.

Luke still cringes when he remembers how, arriving at the studio, he started to set up the PA system – to the amazement of the engineer. He did not realize that you don't need a PA when you are recording. Everyone had a good laugh at his expense, and he felt like 'a right plonker'.

At Trident, they recorded the classic songs that are still loved more than thirty years later. Of their own compositions, 'Black Sabbath', 'The Wizard', 'N.I.B.', 'Behind the Wall of Sleep' and the tiny, acoustic 'Sleeping Village' have influenced generations of bands across the world. The album also included cover versions of 'Warning' and 'Evil Woman'.

The album certainly had its own style. When it was released early the next year, the band would finally make their presence felt. *Black Sabbath's* combination of heavy music and macabre lyrics would scare the shit out of unwary listeners – nothing like this had ever been heard before.

Meanwhile, Sabbath's Radio 1 debut was on John Peel's *Top Gear* on 29 November. He played four tracks: 'Black Sabbath', 'N.I.B.', 'Behind The Wall of Sleep' and a number called 'Devil's Island', renamed 'Sleeping Village' for the album. The session had been recorded a couple of weeks earlier at the BBC's Maida Vale Studios in London. Peel, a champion of alternative music, was initially a great supporter of Sabbath.

By the end of 1969, Keith Jefferson had given up his job in the Sabbath crew, after just a few months. Returning to his home city of Carlisle, he set up one of the first mobile discos in the north of England. At the time of Keith's departure, Sabbath were right on the verge of their major breakthrough, but still they were slogging their way round Britain and Europe like there was no tomorrow. The year's end found them in Switzerland, playing in venues like Zurich's Hirschen Bar, where they were expected to perform six forty-five minute sets a night. That's a lot of rock by anyone's standards.

Arriving home on Christmas Day, they allowed themselves one night off to celebrate the festive season before clambering back into the van to work the rest of the holiday period. They didn't know it then but, for once, they could count on a really happy new year.

4

BLACK MAGIC? NOWT TO DO WITH ME, MATE!

At last, they came to a decision about their first single. 'Evil Woman', a cover of a minor American hit by a Minnesota band called Crow, was released by Fontana, a Philips Records subsidiary, in January 1970. It was re-released a couple of months later by Vertigo, a new, progressive label set up by Philips.

It bombed both times, but Sabbath weren't too worried. In those days, there was a rule of thumb that progressive, underground bands should steer clear of the singles market to avoid any accusations of selling out to the pop sector, or only being in it for the money.

Led Zeppelin had set this particular trend, and they rigorously practised what they preached, along with other like-minded bands and musicians such as Irish guitar hero Rory Gallagher. Other artists were more flexible, with Cream and Jethro Tull among those enjoying regular hit singles.

Led Zeppelin were streets ahead of Sabbath in many ways. As Stephen Davis describes in *Hammer of the Gods*, they had toured America five times before the end of May 1970, and they could easily sell out major London venues like the Royal Albert Hall for a week on the trot, while Sabbath were still content to gig around the smaller halls and clubs of the UK and Europe.

Zeppelin's first two albums had achieved sales in excess of six million copies worldwide, and they had been awarded gold and platinum discs in recognition of a million record sales in Sweden, a feat which had previously only been achieved by The Beatles.

The mighty Zeppelin were formed in 1968 by guitarist Jimmy Page and band manager Peter Grant, both working with The Yardbirds. Jimmy had joined The Yardbirds as a bass guitarist in June 1966 because he wanted to go out on the road, and he played his first gig with them at the Marquee. Prior to this, he had been a successful session musician and had made a lot of money even then.

The Yardbirds were managed by Simon Napier-Bell, who eventually moved on to pastures new. He was succeeded by Mickey Most and his partner at the time, Peter Grant. Mickey Most looked after mainstream artists such as Donovan, Lulu and Herman's Hermits, while Grant took up the gauntlet with The Yardbirds, steering their blues-based and musicianly career with great success.

The new band Led Zeppelin would quickly rise to superstardom despite their refusal to release singles and to co-operate with any PR and promotional stunts. Peter Grant made Led Zeppelin a lot of cash with a no-nonsense management style, hammering out deals that would benefit the band financially and creatively to an unheard-of degree. By overturning the terms and conditions traditionally insisted upon by record companies, he opened the doors for other bands to negotiate decent contracts. With the rise of Zeppelin, Jimmy Page acquired the nickname of Led Wallet, an affectionate reference to the amount of money he had amassed. Page was a wealthy young man in the early seventies.

Such riches had yet to come for Sabbath, who were still living hand-to-mouth. But their change in fortune began with the release by Vertigo on Friday 13 February 1970 of their debut album, *Black Sabbath*.

In addition to the heavy sound, the riffs and the dynamic light and shade of the arrangements, the album has mystical and doom-laden overtones, a quality reinforced by the sleeve photograph. Taken at Mapledurham in Oxfordshire, near Reading, it features a young lady wearing a black cloak in a field beside a lake, with a water mill in the background. Few people ever notice that she's holding a black cat.

A girl claiming to be the model in the photograph turned up at a Sabbath gig in Holland one night and spoke to Richard 'Spock' Wall

Mythology 'Mark III',
taken in Dumfries,
June 1968. *Left to right:*
Bill Ward, Chris Smith
(seated), Neil Marshall
and Tony Iommi.

Courtesy of Neil Marshall

Mythology support the Move
at the 101 Club, Carlisle,
30 April 1968.

The band's first ever billing,
as the Polka Tulk Blues Band,
21 August 1968.

Probably the only surviving
Big Bear promotional poster for
Earth, September 1968.

Earth pose for a photo in
Warwick Square, Carlisle,
before returning home to
Birmingham after a string
of gigs in Cumberland.
15 March 1969.

Earth crammed onstage at Wigton Market Hall, Cumbria, 28 March 1969. This was their last gig before departing on their European tour.

Opposite. Hamburg harbourside, 1969.
Earth take time out on a windy day in Hamburg. Ozzy is wearing
his Jesus Boots and sporting a Henry's Blues House t-shirt.

Above. Earth onstage with the manager of the Star Club.
Left to right: Geezer Butler, Tony Iommi, Kuno Dreysse,
Ozzy Osbourne and Bill Ward.

On stage at the Star Club. The band basically followed this line-up pattern all their
career, with Geezer stage right, Bill hidden behind his kit, Ozzy and Tony stage left.
Ozzy daubed himself with purple paint (including a snake across his chest)
to try and get a reaction from the crowd.

Earth pictured outside Keith Jefferson's flat in Warwick Square, Carlisle.
Ozzy is sporting his infamous tap necklace.

Andromeda and Black Sabbath
in the **COSMO**
WEDNESDAY, MARCH 18th :: 8 p.m. - 12 midnight
Tickets 8/- from E. T. Roberts, Lowther Street, Carlisle.
Proceeds to Oxfam.

DRILL HALL, DUMFRIES
SATURDAY, 27th SEPTEMBER
BLACK SABBATH
(The Blues Group, formerly EARTH)
plus TIMOTHY PINK
8.30 p.m. · 11-30 p.m.
Admission 6/-.

BLACK
SATURDAY
OCT. 17th

SABBATH
+ PRINCIPAL EDWARD'S
MAGIC THEATRE FARRM
WHERE ?
QUEEN MARY COLLEGE of course!
Tel. 980 1240   Tubes: Mile End, Stepney Green
"RAVE ON, RUPERT PEOPLE !!!"

BILL GRAHAM PRESENTS IN NEW YORK

ROD STEWART
& SMALL FACES

BLACK SABBATH

IF

PIG LIGHT SHOW

November 10, 1970

FRANK ZAPPA
and the
MOTHERS OF INVENTION

SHA - NA - NA

JF MURPHY &
FREE FLOWING SALT

November 13-14, 1970

FILLMORE EAST

Black Sabbath hit the American music scene running. Playing Bill Graham's Fillmore East in New York, and then on to Fillmore West in San Francisco where they impressed the Warner Bros representatives in the audience.

who had just started working for Sabbath as their tour manager at the time of the album release. Spock didn't know whether or not to believe the 'model', since there were all sorts of strange people rolling up at the gigs. One woman arrived at the dressing-room door with a blanket. She had embroidered the words Black Sabbath on it, and was asking if any of the band would like to buy it.

The inside artwork of the album features writing on an inverted cross that set the scene for everything people came to imagine and believe about Black Sabbath. It talks about the falling rain, blackened trees, rabbits born dead in traps and other such strange portents.

It all sounded very mysterious, and combined with the general darkness of the music, the band's black dress and Geezer's lyrical journeys into the underworld, it created an impression of Sabbath that was as compellingly macabre as it was mistaken and it took the fashion for black-magic imagery to new extremes. Up and down the country, thrill-seeking teenagers had been getting out the 'weegee' (Ouija) board, and trying to contact 'the other side'.

Sabbath complained that they had not seen the sleeve artwork and the inverted cross until it was too late to do anything about them. Yet, these things compounded the Satanic image of the band in the public imagination.

Little wonder, then, that the band were seen as Satanic devil worshippers, fully signed-up members of the occult. Despite their later protestations that many of their fans were taking things too seriously, they certainly went along with this devilish association to start with. It suited their image perfectly, but it was something they were to regret as time went on. They would try their best to distance themselves from the whole thing when the repercussions of the Charles Manson 'family' murders in America in 1969 began to affect their own career.

Coinciding with this, strange things started happening closer to home. On one occasion, Sabbath declined an offer by a Satanic organization to play at Stonehenge in Wiltshire, and were then informed they were being cursed. Alex Sanders, the 'Chief Witch' in England at the time, warned the band that these people were serious, advised them to wear crosses around their necks and reassured them that he would put a protective spell around them.

The band were amused by all this, and not that easily frightened. They had their feet too firmly on the ground for all that malarkey. As writer Keith Altham would later remark, 'They struck me as four typical northern lads without pretension or affectation . . . more Brum than Beelzebub.'

Intriguingly, Sanders was making an album himself at this same time. Titled *A Witch Is Born*, it was all about the initiation ceremony of a new witch into the coven, and the sleeve was emblazoned with a stern warning: 'For Adults Only'. The record was rapidly withdrawn by A&M when the company executives discovered the true and supposedly macabre content of the album. It's now an ultra-rare collector's piece.

✝ ✝ ✝

Some of the reviews for *Black Sabbath* were discouraging. One critic, with a remarkable lack of imagination and foresight, moaned that the band were dull and uninspiring, although other music publications were more impressed. 'They are . . . very much in the progressive bag and good with it,' enthused one reviewer. *Record Retailer* thought they were 'vibrant and exciting', while *Music Now* told its readers: 'We strongly advise those of nervous disposition NOT, repeat NOT, to listen alone.'

During this period, an amusing story was doing the rounds. Sabbath had been invited to appear on a German television show, and the promoter had sent their plane tickets to Jim Simpson. There were five return tickets for the band and their manager, and a single ticket for the sacrifice victim – the one that they would bring along to dispose of during the set.

It's such a lovely anecdote, it's a shame that it was quite untrue, having been made up in Simpson's office for release to the music media. It was all part of the mystique that was being built up around the band, whose closest brush with real black magic would have been Geezer Butler reading Dennis Wheatley horror stories in bed.

But nobody wanted to believe that, and from then on the band would spend fruitless hours defending themselves in the press against charges of Satanism. A *New Musical Express* headline in the 4 April 1970 issue screamed: 'Black Sabbath Have Nothing To Do With Spooks! says lead guitar Tony.' In that article, Iommi stated: 'Everybody thinks we're a black magic group, but we just picked the name because we like it. I agree some of the numbers on the LP are about supernatural things, but that's as far as it goes . . . We're worried about this black magic bit in America. People might take it seriously.'

'Our music did seem to be more evil than a lot of other groups,' Bill Ward told *Disc and Music Echo* the next month. 'But this black magic thing has got out of hand. We are mildly interested in it and people gave us crosses to wear, but that is as far as it goes. It seems to have exploded and now there are millions of black magic bands. But we didn't set out to be one. We don't do black magic, but we play some doomy numbers.

'Our songs are more likely to be about dreams and things like that. We do a couple of numbers about black magic but they are really warning about the dangers of it – they are anti-black magic songs.'

Jim Simpson summed things up pretty succinctly in the same article: 'We are not the black magic group – we are the ones who sell records.'

The album was a top ten hit in the UK, rising to its peak position of number eight in March 1970. If this came as a shock to certain members of the music establishment, it also surprised the members of Black Sabbath, whose hard work was now paying off. They had been gigging one night stands relentlessly throughout 1969, they'd played virtually all of the blues houses on the continent, and their growing legion of fans rushed out to buy the album. Five thousand copies reportedly crossed the counter on its first day of release, with especially large sales recorded in Cumbria – the backbone of Sabbath's fan base at that time. Several months later, the album would reach number twenty-three in America on its release there by Warners.

Things started happening quickly for Sabbath. They began playing bigger gigs, and they were getting airplay on the radio. At the same time, they were being ignored, as ever, by British television – a situation which continued acting to their advantage, since it kept the band 'underground' and enhanced their strange, 'forbidden' mystique.

The same was true for other 'progressive' bands like Led Zeppelin and Cream. The people who ran the BBC back then were a conservative lot, often university graduates more in tune with the technical bands of the day like Yes and Pink Floyd, superb musicians who probably did appeal to a much wider audience. Sabbath were too controversial, too heavy, maybe even too working class to be accepted by the television authorities. There doesn't seem to be any record of them ever appearing, for instance, on BBC2's *Old Grey Whistle Test*, which was the only 'alternative' music show on television and was hosted by 'Whispering' Bob Harris.

Over on the Continent it was a different story. With their first album riding high in the charts in Germany, Belgium, France, Holland, Switzerland and Sweden, Sabbath made regular TV appearances and filmed a documentary in Germany, to be screened in Holland. The mainland European countries have always been more tolerant and more liberal in their approach to music. There, Sabbath were finally getting the recognition they deserved, with standing ovations wherever they played.

Although they now had a hit album to their name and could command more money and larger bookings, the band were still happy to honour a string of smaller gigs which had been arranged before they found success.

They made a memorable return to the Marquee in March 1970, when the club was enjoying its first week with a licence to serve alcohol. It had been dry since its inception in 1958. John Gee was no doubt rubbing his hands when he saw the till roll after Sabbath's appearance.

Sabbath were hailed as conquering heroes on their return to Henry's Blues House in Birmingham, playing a Tuesday-night residency for several weeks and breaking the attendance record previously held by Jethro Tull.

They had another Birmingham residency around the same time, for four Wednesdays at Mothers Club in Erdington. Phil Myatt and John

Taylor, the owners, had wanted to build up the mid-week attendance figures at the club, and had agreed to pay Sabbath the usual modest sum. But before the residency began, *Black Sabbath* had charted in the UK, and the venue was crammed. This was a great coup for Phil and John, who were able to stage a big-name band and get away with paying them just £25 a show. The fans were also delighted, since they were seeing Sabbath for a mere ten shillings as originally advertised.

Mothers was a regular circuit gig for bands of the day. Pink Floyd played there on Mothers Day, 8 March 1970. It was that night that John Peel, who was DJing there, jokingly asked the band which one was Pink.

Despite the fact that Mothers had a maximum capacity of around eight hundred, at one time it boasted a membership of some 36,000. In the early seventies, lots of people were so stoned that they joined the club many times over, forgetting that they had already paid out their two shillings and sixpence membership fee on any number of other occasions.

Mothers had previously been known as The Carlton Ballroom, and the West Midlands brewing company Mitchell and Butler, who supplied the beer, had sponsored a local group of musicians to be the resident band. They went under the name of MB5 (Mitchell and Butler 5). The band decided to keep this MB tag when they later changed their name to The Moody Blues.

For some time, Sabbath continued their slog up and down the motorways of Great Britain in their trusty dark-blue Transit van. It carried six passengers at a pinch, three in the front and three in the back. None of the lads' wives or girlfriends were travelling with them in those days because there was no room, although occasionally they would squeeze in the odd groupie.

The motorway system was less extensive back then, and it took an age to get anywhere. The driving could be very tedious. The band would pass the time talking about the issues of the day and about their gigs, dissecting every note they played and every move they made onstage.

They never got tired of laughing at any unfortunate caught farting, and they were still keen 'mooners'. Ozzy once bared his arse to a car full of nuns as they drove along the motorway.

Geezer Butler looked after the gig money, and would share it out four ways. In the early days, it would not be a great deal, perhaps five or ten pounds each. Ozzy spent his cash as soon as he got it, usually on cigarettes and a meal at the services. Luke recalls that money 'burnt a hole in his pocket', and that Ozzy was always broke and borrowing off the others by the time they came to do the next gig. This would shortly change.

At the Lyceum Ballroom in London, Sabbath blew the audience away. The band were also impressed by their support act, Flare, who used an electric piano onstage. This was regarded as a real novelty, 'an instrument of the future', as someone remarked at the time. Sabbath discussed the idea of getting a Hammond organ with a Leslie cabinet, like the one that Emerson, Lake and Palmer's Keith Emerson used onstage. Luke was privately horrified by the suggestion. 'Not a fucking Hammond organ!'he muttered to himself. 'Do they not think I've enough gear to carry on and off the stage?' Thankfully for him, the organ remained an idea and not a reality.

✝ ✝ ✝

Festivals, these days a permanent and important part of British rock culture, were in their infancy but growing in popularity in 1970. Sabbath made their first big festival appearance in late spring at the second Essen festival in Germany, performing alongside Renaissance, the Keef Hartley Band, Hardin and York, The Groundhogs, Marsha Hunt and American artists Taj Mahal, Flock, Ten Wheel Drive and Rhinoceros. The three-day 'Song Days Festival' was held in Grughalle, a large indoor arena in the city centre, with German police standing by with water cannons to quell any wild crowd behaviour, disturbances or riots.

Back in the UK, Sabbath played at two festivals on the May bank holiday weekend. The first, at Plumpton racecourse in Sussex, also featured Ginger Baker's Airforce, Ritchie Havens and Chicken Shack. Black Sabbath played on the first evening, a Saturday.

Spock remembers that there wasn't much in the way of backstage hospitality, unlike today's generous provision for the VIP performers. At Plumpton, if you wanted food, you had to go into town to buy it, or in among the audience to grab a hot dog or whatever primitive snacks were on offer. People who attended these early festivals used to bring their own food and drink (and drugs) since the concessions stands were quite expensive. Many's the time the vans were literally rolled over by unhappy festival-goers because of the exorbitant prices they charged.

The backstage experience was also a lot less exciting and less well organized than it would become in later years. Everybody just did their own thing. You arrived, set the gear up onstage just before your turn, did the gig, dismantled the gear and got out. It was all pretty hectic. None of the bands hung out together, partying. The only people who really went for it were the audiences.

After their Plumpton performance, Sabbath played later that same night at Ewell technical college, in a typical example of their hard-work ethic. Leaving the college, they drove through the night for their festival engagement the next day, at Hollywood, Stoke-on-Trent.

Travelling north up the M1, they were involved in a minor collision with another van. The occupants of this vehicle jumped out furiously to inspect the damage – only to discover they'd been hit by Black Sabbath. As fate would have it, they were on their way to Stoke to see the band at the next day's festival, and they vowed to keep the dent in their van as a souvenir of the day their heroes crashed into them.

The Hollywood Festival staged a spectacular array of musical talent. Sabbath, along with Colosseum and Quintessence, appeared in the afternoon in the supporting line-up for The Grateful Dead, who were playing their debut UK gig. The evening bill featured Traffic and Free.

The day before, fans had witnessed an extraordinary performance by Screaming Lord Sutch, but the surprise hit of that day was the good-time pop band Mungo Jerry, who appeared early on the sunny afternoon. Their hit song 'In The Summertime' struck a warm chord with the audience, which included this book's co-author Graham Wright. Sabbath would meet up with Lord Sutch in August that year when they played on the same bill, along with The Kinks, at the Blizen Blues and Jazz Festival in Belgium. Ever the showman, Sutch started a fire at the front of the stage, leading into a cover of Jerry Lee Lewis' 'Great Balls Of Fire'. He practically gave the promoters heart failure, and fire marshals were quickly on the scene. He had accomplished the stunt by siphoning petrol out of Sabbath's Transit van.

Another weekend, another festival. Friday 29 May found Black Sabbath playing the eight-day Music Festival Extravaganza '70 at London's Olympia. A bizarre music and fashion mix billed as the 'swingingest' thing of the year, and the best thing since the relief of Mafeking, it confronted audiences with beauty demonstrations, flared velvet pants in abundance, and a grand diversity of musical talent, including Bo Diddley, Matthew's Southern Comfort, T. Rex, Procol Harum and Wild Angels.

Festivals in the early seventies were a celebration of both music and lifestyle, and drugs were very much a part of the whole experience. The members of Black Sabbath, like everyone else, used alcohol, uppers, downers and hash – the drugs of choice at the time – but never to the point where they would screw up their responsibilities to the band. They were totally committed to it.

All four had also experimented with LSD, although Ozzy and Geezer were more into it than Tony and Bill, who liked his drink. Cocaine was not on the scene – yet. That would figure later in the band's career.

5

PARANOID INTO AMERICA

As well as Black Sabbath, there was a band on the scene called Black Widow, who were much more serious than Sabbath about using and promoting occult imagery.

They had secured the services of Maxine, wife of England's chief witch Alex Sanders, to appear in their stage show as Lady Astaroth, a tormented girl from the eighteenth century who was driven insane and who threw herself to her death. Maxine would end up naked at the end of the show, simulating sex with the band's lead vocalist.

At one London Lyceum gig, the band were forced to promise that Maxine would not strip completely naked. She did, and there was uproar. The organizers tried to stop the show, and they searched everyone leaving for cameras. But someone smuggled out a film and a picture of the chief witch's wife in the nude appeared in the Sunday newspapers.

By June 1970, Black Sabbath were still in the charts with their debut album, they were selling truckloads of records, and they were earning £350 a gig. Black Widow were selling next to nothing, but they were pulling in £500 a show. And so when Sabbath were approached by Black Widow's manager, Patrick Meehan, they had every reason to listen to what he had to say. He told them he could increase their earnings, maximize their opportunities in America and push their career in new and exciting directions. Clearly, it was an offer they couldn't refuse.

Patrick was a real man-about-town, from a well-to-do background. After thinking it over for some time, the band agreed he was just the person they needed to guide them onwards and upwards. Jim Simpson had helped the band to their current level of success, and they appreciated everything he'd done, but they felt that he was perhaps too 'nice'. On top of that, Jim was still based in Birmingham, isolated from the cut and thrust of the industry, and it seemed unlikely they would be able to make much more progress together. Sabbath went ahead and signed up to Patrick Meehan's management.

Legend has it that they notified Simpson by letter, only hours after borrowing a hundred pounds from him to get to a date in Liverpool.

Ozzy was later quoted by author Mick Wall in his 1985 book *Ozzy Osbourne: Diary Of A Madman* as saying:

So there we were, playing huge gigs, two albums in the charts and a Top Three single, and we were still broke! Fucking unbelievable . . .

Don't get me wrong – Jim Simpson is as honest as the day is long, but record companies take fucking ages to cough up the royalties, and most of the festivals were played for free anyway . . .

The minute somebody . . . came along who could offer us the things we thought we were owed from all the successes, we were theirs for the taking.

They had already booked their first American tour for July 1970, but they quickly cancelled it, partly because of the management changeover, but also because they feared they would suffer the backlash of a nation still reeling from the shock of the Charles Manson atrocities in Beverly Hills almost a year earlier. Members of Manson's cult 'family' had murdered pregnant actress Sharon Tate, wife of film director Roman Polanski, along with four other people who were in and around the house. His disciples also slaughtered husband and wife Leno and Rosemary LaBianca later that same night.

The murders were said to be the handiwork of a Satanic sect, and there were also claims of evil forces at work at The Rolling Stones' Altamont festival appearance in California in December 1969, when a member of the Hell's Angels security force stabbed a fan to death. The hippy dream of peace and love was going off the rails, and since Sabbath had saddled themselves with dark and demonic associations, they decided to avoid the States until the hysteria had died down.

Ozzy was, of course, no devil worshipper, but he did eventually get his hands on an acetate recording of an album by Charles Manson's band, produced by Dennis Wilson of The Beach Boys. Dave Tangye, co-author of this book, would later listen to it with Ozzy at his cottage, where the singer deemed the material 'too far out' even by his own outrageous standards. The tracks were all very weird, and none had any discernible tunes, which is probably why the album never made it past the acetate stage.

Other negative vibrations were troubling the United States at the time of Sabbath's aborted visit. Americans may still have been glowing with pride at having put a man on the moon in 1969, but the chilly blasts of the Cold War were blowing bitterly, Vietnam was continuing to fuel the paranoia of the younger generation, and there was an unabating redneck threat to unconventional individuals daring to show their faces in the midwest and southern states during that era, as depicted by movies like *Easy Rider*.

And so with America crossed off the calendar for the time being, Sabbath found themselves back in the van, criss-crossing the UK. On 26 June, they set out for a one-off gig in West Berlin at the invitation of the American Forces Network in Germany. With Ozzy, Tony and Bill having convictions and court appearances for their various misdemeanours, it was a major headache for the management to sort out the travel arrangements in the first place. It was agreed that the band should fly to West Berlin, to steer clear of any further problems that could potentially arise if they took the land route through the east/west corridor, along the Berlin wall. At that time visas were required to travel in East Germany, and it would be several years before the Berlin Wall came down.

In the end, it was the road crew – Luke and Spock – who had to deal with all the hassle as they transported the band's equipment through the checkpoints on the west and east of Berlin. They drove from

Hanover to Berlin, crossing the west/east border at the Helmstadt checkpoint and entering the city at the Dreilinden checkpoint situated on the south-west section of the wall. As they travelled along the East German autobahn, 'The Corridor' as it was known, they saw that they were not allowed to exit the motorway, although they were permitted to stop at some very basic service areas that sold hot and cold food and were staffed by elderly German *frauen* wearing headscarves and grim scowls. Everything about East Germany seemed grey and at least fifty years behind the rest of Europe.

But it was not the East German border guards who caused the trouble for 'long-haired freaks' Luke and Spock. It was the West German soldiers who ordered them to unload all of the equipment from the Transit in a vain search for drugs, contraband and even weapons. They went over the van with a fine-tooth comb, holding mirrors underneath the wheels and the seats. They even pulled the backs off the speaker cabinets. It was with a sense of great relief that Luke and Spock finally arrived at the university campus venue in West Berlin, although, to their horror, they would be subjected to the same hostilities on the way back.

The gig had sold out well in advance, with American troops and local residents clamouring for tickets. The six hundred capacity lecture theatre where Sabbath played had a semi-circular seating arrangement, descending in tiers to the stage, which was at floor level. When the doors opened, a huge crowd of people who had missed out on tickets just stormed in. They surged down the steep gangways, gathering speed as they went, and in so doing, wrecked the expensive camera equipment that the American Forces Network had set up in the aisle to record the show.

Faced with the prospect of a full-scale riot, the promoter told the ticket holders and gatecrashers alike that if everyone sat down in an orderly fashion, the concert would go ahead. There were bodies everywhere, including on the stage. People surrounded the drum kit, they were crammed in between Geezer and Tony and their speaker stacks, and they blocked Ozzy's access to the microphone at regular intervals. If it was claustrophobic for the band, some members of the audience fared worse – the volume brought tears to the eyes of those determined fans squashed right in front of the speakers.

Black Sabbath returned to such a hectic schedule in the UK that Spock and Luke – driving all night, setting up gear the next day and taking it down again, ad infinitum – rarely knew what town they were in, never mind which venue. They were running on a sort of exhausted autopilot.

Yet some gigs from this period stand out in their memories. One was at Klooks, a brand new rock night at London's Lyceum, on Friday 17 July. Klooks Kleek had been a small but bustling music venture in the Railway Hotel, West Hampstead, next door to Decca Records' offices. All of the up-and-coming acts of the late sixties had played there before the concept of 'Klooks' was transferred to the Lyceum, a much bigger hall, and promoted as 'a festival every Friday'.

Moving to Dunstable Civic Hall the next night, Sabbath started worrying about the rising cost of admission to their gigs. Fans were now being asked to pay a pound for an advance ticket, which they, and other bands, were not too happy about. They had seen prices soaring in the past few months and feared this might antagonize their fans. But concert-goers, looking back, will undoubtedly feel that their pound notes were well spent, at least in Dunstable. On the three consecutive weekends from 18 July, they had the opportunity to see Black Sabbath, The Who and Free – all bands who would go on to become rock legends.

✝ ✝ ✝

With the summer festivals and gigs tailing off and with *Black Sabbath* nearing the end of an amazing forty-two week run in the UK chart, the band were preparing to release its follow-up.

They had crammed the rehearsals and recordings into short periods of spare time earlier in the year. Recording was a rapid process for Sabbath in these early days – their attitude was, 'Get in there, get it done and get it out.' They were never in the studio for long enough to get any kind of routine going. The real work was done beforehand in rehearsals, where the band developed the ideas for tracks that they would later record. This was much cheaper than going into a recording studio straight away.

To prepare material for the *Paranoid* album, Sabbath hired a rehearsal studio at Rockfield, a famous residential recording facility in the beautiful countryside near the market town of Monmouth, Wales. The band and crew all slept in the same room in the farmhouse where the musicians were accommodated and every morning owner Kingsley Ward would go out and milk the cows and bring in fresh milk for breakfast. The rehearsal room was in a separate building, an old barn with great acoustics. Sabbath played at such volume that they rattled the Welsh slates off the roof and they smashed to smithereens on the ground.

Set up with their backline equipment, PA, drums, guitars and their own Revox tape machine, the band would jam for an hour or two, just to see what came up. Tony would often hit upon brilliant riffs, while the rhythm section – Bill on drums and Geezer on bass – would create a suitable, musical launchpad for these riffs, and Ozzy would usually sing along on top, inventing tunes and using whatever words came into his head. The band would later listen to tapes of each session to see if they liked anything enough to turn it into a song, at which point it would be handed over to Geezer to supply the lyrics. Producer Rodger Bain was also around for much of the time, keeping an eye on the songwriting progress.

Luke remembers:

In the early days, Ozzy went along with the decisions and didn't offer many opinions of his own. He definitely wouldn't tangle with Tony, which was probably a good thing, it kept Ozzy in line.

Not that Tony was a bully. He was a decent and tolerant bloke, but he was without doubt the leader of the band. I always thought he was an under-rated guitarist, and he was an accomplished musician, playing flute, keyboards et cetera.

Having said that, Ozzy had considerable talents as a front-man. He was the perfect singer for a heavy metal group in the seventies. And he had a natural flair for PR. He's not the most educated person, and this showed in the interviews he gave. But he was the only member of the band who really wanted to do them, and his personality and humour connected with the journalists and readers. People were drawn to Ozzy. They liked him.

Ozzy would probably agree with this assessment. He once told the *New Musical Express*:

> I go on stage purely to entertain, not for them to go home and work my show out, y'know? If you can stamp your foot to it and nod your head, it's good as far as I'm concerned. It's good old rock'n'roll, and God bless it, man, because that's what it's all about for me.

† † †

Rockfield grew from a rehearsal facility called Future Sound Studio, which had been created by brothers Kingsley and Charles Ward early in the sixties in the grounds of their home. They lived in the old farmhouse, which had a courtyard and a variety of outbuildings.

The Wards had founded one of Wales' first rock bands, emerging around 1960 under a variety of names including the Charles Kingsley Combo. They secured a record deal in America – a rare feat back then – and changed their name to The Thunderbolts. They never really sold many records, but had quite a cult following for a while.

After setting up Future Sound, the brothers signed a deal with EMI to produce music for the record company. The recording side of things started in the attic of the farmhouse, shortly afterwards moving into the bigger Courtyard Studio. The main recording studio would be built later.

Renamed Rockfield, the complex was first made famous by Dave Edmunds for the sound he achieved on his late-1970 hit single, 'I Hear

You Knocking'. Edmunds had previously been involved in a managerial capacity, helping to run the rehearsal studio in the old barn. Before long, bands were travelling from far and wide to rehearse and record at Rockfield, an idyllic place and a peaceful, relaxing escape from the pace and pressures of London. Ozzy especially liked it. It remains a favourite location for bands, along with Monnow Valley Studios, originally also owned by the Wards, which is located a little further along Rockfield Road.

With the rehearsals and then the recordings complete, Sabbath were ready to issue their second album under the title *War Pigs*, which was also its opening track. But they were under pressure from the record company to change the title because of what was going down in Vietnam at the time.

Yet when Sabbath went on to play 'War Pigs' live in the mid-seventies, they projected scenes from World War Two and images of Adolf Hitler and his gang on to a screen behind them onstage. 'War Pigs', generally believed to be a protest against the Vietnam War, was probably about World War Two all along.

Sabbath had no wish to find themselves in the middle of a political controversy, and they certainly did not want to make waves in America, where they were set to test the waters with a tour in October, so they went along with the new album title of *Paranoid*. Again, it was named after one of the tracks. The band had written 'Paranoid' in about twenty minutes at the end of the main recording sessions, to fill up a four-minute gap in the master tape.

Spock and Luke remember having to drive up to Birmingham to collect some spare amps. Immediately returning to London with the amps, they went back to the studio, where they were called into the mixing room. The band asked them what they thought of their new track.

'Paranoid' hadn't existed when Luke and Spock set off for Birmingham. Now, it was in the can. It had taken roughly five hours to write, record and produce. And it was a true metal classic. Vertigo loved its unforgettable riff, its immense power and its succinct catchiness, and released it as a single. The band, however, were not so enthusiastic, given the dismal performance of their first attempt, 'Evil Woman', and the prevailing feeling against singles, spearheaded by Led Zeppelin. They certainly never dreamed that 'Paranoid' would roar up the singles chart to number four when it was released in August 1970.

Now Sabbath were worried that they would be accused of selling out, and their fears worsened when young, excitable pop kids started turning up to the live shows wanting to hear the single. The band were interested in playing to serious fans who would listen to the entire set, they did not want hordes of teenyboppers squealing at their gigs, and they made this point in various interviews at the time, with Ozzy threatening to stop releasing singles altogether.

However, they soon realized that they were seen to be offending youngsters who might actually be, or might become, genuine fans, and they began to take a more diplomatic tone. Tony Iommi spoke to *Record Mirror* about the controversy: 'What we actually said was that there was a small percentage who came along to make a row, scream and generally spoil it for the others. It is true that we are attracting some younger people into the gigs but most of them are a new generation who are prepared to listen and just dig the music. No one really minds if they jump about a bit as long as it is not all over us or the equipment.'

Ozzy told music writer Nick Logan: 'It was just that we were pulling in people who were not interested in the music but just wanted to hear the single and look at my face or Tony's and see what clothes we were wearing. It was just a minority of the audiences but they made me feel uncomfortable, and it was a shame for the other ninety per cent of the people who would be into the music. Their evenings would be completely spoilt by these screamers.'

In the event, the teenyboppers disappeared almost as suddenly as they had come.

Paranoid the album was released in Britain in September 1970, and rock journalists generally predicted that it would do just about as well as *Black Sabbath*. They were astonished, and the band were euphoric, when it rocketed up the chart to topple Simon and Garfunkel, whose *Bridge Over Troubled Water* had been sitting in the prized number one spot for months.

The band were in Belgium when it happened, although they didn't find out immediately. Nobody could get in touch with them. They didn't always have access to a phone in the budget accommodation they normally used, and Luke remembers driving Ozzy to a public phone at a railway station in Brussels so that he could call home to find out what was happening. Hearing the bombshell news, Ozzy rang round his family and best friends to share his excitement. Luke was with the band when they drove around Brussels, shouting loudly out of the van window that their album was number one. Five months later, *Paranoid* would smash into the US chart at number twelve.

✝ ✝ ✝

Bidding farewell to the UK with a gig at the Newcastle Mayfair, Black Sabbath finally set off in search of the American Dream. They couldn't hang on for ever, and they would have to brave whatever prejudices might await them. Patrick Meehan and his team had spent weeks arranging a tour, liaising with American promoters, sorting out visas and booking hotels. There was only one more thing for the band to do before they left.

They and the crew were summoned to the management office to pick up their flight tickets and be granted an audience with Meehan's dad, Patrick Snr, who owned the company, Worldwide Artists. He told the guys, in a fatherly pep talk, that he expected them to behave on the plane and in America – they were ambassadors for England.

They touched down at JFK airport on Wednesday 28 October 1970. Welcome to the Big Apple! It was the first time that any of the four had set foot on American soil, and they didn't care that it was a low-budget tour, since they were playing some of the most prestigious small gigs on the east and west coasts.

Sabbath took only one of their two full-time roadies to America, and that was Spock Wall. Luke remained in Birmingham, devastated to be told he had to stay behind, but the decision had not been taken lightly. Despite the unexpectedly huge success of *Paranoid*, Sabbath had yet to reap the financial rewards and they had to keep their costs to a minimum. They chose Spock because he was a guitar technician and knew a little about amplifiers.

The band checked into the Loew's Midtown Hotel on 8th Avenue, New York City. The most dedicated local groupies had already confirmed that they had landed, and were ringing their rooms to find out if the guys were ready to party. Perhaps surprisingly, they were not. They were on a mission, an important one. They meant business on this trip, and they kept that in mind throughout the tour.

Spock did not have the luxury of retiring to a hotel room to put his feet up, switch on the television, order a drink and receive phone calls from eager young ladies. After picking up the equipment at JFK, he had to transport it immediately to the neighbouring state of New Jersey, where the group would play their first gig at Glassborough State College on Friday 30 October.

The band had brought all their backline equipment, no less than twelve four-by-twelve Laney speaker cabinets, six 100-watt Laney top-set bass and lead amplifiers, Bill Ward's drum kit and Ozzy's PA system. This consisted of a 100-watt Laney amp with six 100-watt slave amps and six column speakers with horns. Sabbath used a lot of power even in those days but, surprisingly, they didn't have any onstage monitors.

Their first night was a great success, attended by around 1,500 fans who had obviously bought the first Sabbath album and were shouting for 'The Wizard'. However, the gig was not without problems. The American voltage system was different to that demanded by Sabbath's gear, and they simply didn't have enough power to drive the amps. One of the promoters suggested they should contact a guy called Whitey Davis, who owned a hire shop in the city. He proved invaluable, lending gear, advising on sound systems and generally helping with the show.

Spock was rushed off his feet. After this first gig, the band had to leave on a red-eye flight for an outdoor gig in Florida the next afternoon, supporting Canned Heat at the University of Miami, Coral Gables. Spock had to move quickly to get the gear off the college campus and back to the airport to be freight transferred to Miami.

For their part, the band were walking around in a daze. Things had speeded up and everything had such a different vibe about it in the States. But it took them less than a week to get over the culture shock. They would go on to spend a lot of time in America – for better and for worse.

6

JUST OFF TO AUSTRALIA, BACK IN A MINUTE . . .

Spock was really up against it, almost single-handedly humping the gear in and out of venues. He needed someone who could find their way round Sabbath's equipment. Much to his relief, it was agreed that Luke should come over to join him.

Luke flew out to America on his own, pretty broke. No one in the London management office had thought fit to give him any money for expenses. It was his first time on an aeroplane, and when the attendants came round with the in-flight meal, he refused it because he thought he would have to pay. He caught up with Sabbath on 2 November at a venue called The Club in Rochester, upstate New York.

Things ran more smoothly after Luke's arrival, although the band spent more time than they wanted to in Rochester when they were stranded there by severe and unexpected snow storms. Frustrated and infuriated, they had to call off a gig in Plainfield, Vermont.

After a string of gigs in Pennsylvania, Oregon and Ohio, they returned to New York City for a crucial engagement at Bill Graham's famous venue the Fillmore East on Second Avenue on 10 November. For Sabbath, supporting Rod Stewart and the Faces, it was a litmus test. New York audiences were notoriously hard to please, and all the media people who really mattered were regulars at the Fillmore. They could make or break a band's career.

On the day, Sabbath arrived at the gig for an afternoon soundcheck. Rod and his band were already there, going through their paces. As headliners, they were entitled to unlimited time for their soundcheck, but they took so long about it that they left virtually no time for Sabbath's turn. Sabbath were totally pissed off by this, given the importance of the occasion. Since the Fillmore was the most prestigious gig on the east coast, it was vital that they got everything right. When Sabbath went on to headline around the world they were a support band's dream because, after the first couple of gigs, they didn't do any soundchecks – the crew did them!

Back at the hotel before the Fillmore show, Sabbath found themselves in the elevator with Rod and the Faces, and the two bands exchanged forced pleasantries. As the lift doors shut behind the headliners, the Sabbath entourage burst out laughing, having noticed just how short in stature Rod's band were. Harking back to the name of Stewart's previous group, Sabbath joked that they really were the 'small Faces'.

This defused their animosity, and when Sabbath went onstage, they played superbly, the sound was excellent, and the whole show rocked. The crowd loved this new, heavy sound, and called the band back for three encores. Black Sabbath had well and truly arrived.

It's unlikely that the Faces watched their performance. It wasn't usual for headliners to watch the support act unless they had a special interest. But Rod would certainly have been aware of Sabbath's triumph that night, and in many ways, the Faces had not measured up to it. A typically direct Ozzy announced: 'We obliterated them!' *Billboard*'s Fred Kirby concurred, reporting, 'Black Sabbath went over better in a heavy programme which included "Black Sabbath" from their first Warner Bros. album. John Osbourne's emphatic vocals were a key as the repetitive, heavy-handed performance proved no handicap for the enthusiastic audience.'

The next concert took the band to the west coast and another famous venue, the Whiskey A Go Go on Sunset Boulevard, Los Angeles, where they were playing two and three shows a day over five days. There were queues for tickets.

The Whiskey was the scene of Sabbath's first experience with cocaine. Luke remembers being in the dressing room after one of the gigs, when a guy who was dealing coke walked in and offered his wares to the band. While they were talking to him, another fellow appeared in the room and literally chased out the dealer, explaining that he sold crap coke. If the band wanted to indulge, then *he* had the best that was to be had in LA. He was so forceful and persuasive that they all agreed to try it out, and the man turned out to be as good as his word about the quality of his cocaine. He became their regular supplier in LA – and indeed, he went on to tour with Sabbath for a while, ostensibly to look after the luggage and lend a hand to Luke.

The entourage stayed at the legendary Hyatt House hotel on Sunset Strip for the first time. Affectionately nicknamed the Riot House, it more than lived up to its name. It was the haunt of most of the musicians and their crews who were gigging in the Los Angeles area. The hotel had a twenty-four-hour coffee shop and twenty-four-hour groupies. Some of the girls even had keys to the rooms, and it would be nothing to go back to your billet to find a couple of LA beauties waiting and ready to 'party'. Others would hunt in packs, patrolling the corridors and knocking on doors until they tracked down their quarry.

The Riot House became famous in the early seventies courtesy of bands like Deep Purple and The Who, who found it a great place to 'let off steam'. It would not have been out of the ordinary to see Who drummer Keith Moon prowling the hotel corridors early in the morning dressed in the uniform of a German SS officer, complete with a short moustache and an imitation machine gun, chasing a bevy of young girls. And it was at the Riot House that the popular sport of throwing TV sets out of bedroom windows was first perfected. While other hotel managers would immediately ban any groups found behaving wildly and disturbing the peace, the Hyatt management revelled in the media attention that such antics received. Behind the reception desk in the foyer was a sign that read, 'Be nice to your next guests – they may have just sold a million records.'

Sabbath, like all the English bands arriving at the hotel for the first time, were fast-tracked into the groupie scene by these sometimes girls. Even though the band drew a largely male audience and attracted less female interest than many of the 'prettier' bands of the day, they took advantage of the opportunites on offer, with Tony usually appealing to the most beautiful and sophisticated ladies.

The band eventually got bored with the routine availability of sex and with the demanding attitude of the American groupies, and became a little more selective. Ozzy declared that he had started to crave some time to himself to do normal things, like sleep and eat. Graham remembers:

> He would often complain that other bands' roadies attracted better-looking girls than he did, and referred to his groupies as 'two-baggers' – meaning that they were often so ugly, they needed two bags over their head, just in case one fell off.
>
> Ozzy took one groupie to his room in a hotel somewhere in America and before long, called for some of the crew to come in and see his latest party piece. He asked this girl to spread her legs, which she did. He took a felt pen and drew two eyes and a nose right above her pubic hairs. Grabbing hold of her, he then performed a 'ventriloquist' act, singing Al Jolson's 'Mammy' and marvelling at the fact that his 'dummy' looked just like Bill with his beard.

Other landmark gigs during Sabbath's first American tour included four nights at Bill Graham's Fillmore West in Market Street, San Francisco, sister club to the Fillmore East. There, they played with The James Gang featuring guitarist Joe Walsh, who would later achieve fame with The Eagles. The Fillmore was overrun by Warner Brothers executives, who had recently signed Sabbath to the label for their American releases. During their time in San Francisco, the guys stayed at Fisherman's Wharf and grossed out in a multitude of seafood restaurants. In another first, they held a signing session at Tower Records.

They were overwhelmed by their success in America, which surpassed their wildest dreams.

'The only bad thing was the food,' Ozzy told *Melody Maker*'s Chris

Charlesworth. 'You needed a stomach pump after every meal, and everything was three times more expensive than in England.'

After those dates, Ozzy told writer Nick Logan: 'We need a rest badly. We're all very tired. We've never done travelling like we had in the US before.'

✝ ✝ ✝

Flying home for a good dinner in December 1970, they could clearly see a bright future ahead. But there was work to do before Christmas, including another London session for John Peel's *Top Gear*, and a short European tour.

Most memorable was an outdoor gig in Germany, which seemed doomed from the beginning. There were equipment difficulties, the amps were buzzing strangely and Tony Iommi was having more trouble than usual keeping his guitar in tune. His problems arise from the fact that he uses such light strings because he wears prostheses on the ends of his fingers, as a result of the factory accident which chopped off his fingertips. The lighter strings are more manageable, and need less pressure exerted on them to hold down a chord.

In the very early days, Tony used to make his own prostheses from the hard, plastic tops of washing up liquid bottles. He would mould them with a soldering iron and make them fit the ends of his fingers. Luke remembers: 'He overcame the accident to his fingers through sheer dedication. It was fascinating to watch him making his "thimbles" with Fairy Liquid bottles, leather, glue and a soldering iron."

Despite the problems on the night, Sabbath went down really well in Germany and were called back for an encore. They duly obliged, and then they left the site. They were totally shagged out, mostly because of the long-distance travelling they were doing in the van. The backstage area was like a swamp due to heavy rainfall, and after all the hassles they had encountered with their sound they simply wanted to get out of there.

But the crowd wanted more from Sabbath, and when it became clear that they weren't going to get it, the whole place erupted into violence, while the crew worked frantically to clear the gear offstage as quickly as they could. Ozzy told *Melody Maker*: 'In Germany, the fans seem to get impatient. They start stamping if you are trying to tune up, and we were really shattered most of the time . . . It is just a handful of people who start the trouble, and everyone follows. They think the group are just music machines, turned on to make music who should go on forever if necessary.'

There was always some kind of trouble with German bookings. Army bases were the worst – too much testosterone about. At one particular gig, Ozzy jumped offstage and started to fight with this guy who'd been giving someone in the front row a bad time. Tony put his guitar down and joined in. The crew and the hall security intervened and stopped the scrap, although the crowd loved it.

Sabbath continued their mini-tour of Europe with a storming performance at the Paris Olympia, which was filmed by a French television company. The soundtrack later materialized in the shape of an album, *Live In Paris 1970*. Dave Tangye still has fifteen minutes of it on video.

Immediately after the Christmas and New Year break, Sabbath went down to London to make a start on their third album, *Master of Reality*. They were not intimidated by the success of *Paranoid*, and were not feeling any great pressure to follow it. It was simply business as usual for the band. They got on with the music in their own way, and left everything else to the management and record label.

They were booked into Island Studios in Notting Hill Gate, London, where they managed to lay down three backing tracks for the album before setting out on their first ever headlining tour of the UK.

The tour was supposed to start on 5 January 1971 at London's Royal Albert Hall. Unfortunately, the venue decided to ban Black Sabbath, fearing they would attract hostile audiences who would cause untold damage to the splendid building's fixtures and fittings. Sabbath joined an illustrious list of bands, including Emerson, Lake and Palmer and, later, Mott The Hoople who were excluded from playing there. It was a popular saying among the groups of the day that if you weren't banned from playing the Albert Hall, you weren't happening at all.

The tour had sold out well in advance. Sabbath were supported by a band called Curved Air, fronted by the very charismatic female singer Sonja Christina. Promoting their newly released album, *Air Conditioning*, they raised their profile on the Sabbath tour and provided a contrast to the headliners' crushing heavy metal with their light, orchestral arrangements. Also on the bill was ex-Procol Harum drummer Bobby Harrison with his own band, Freedom.

At this time, Sabbath were coming under fire from some quarters, mostly the press, for their sheer volume. Tony Iommi defended their policy to writer Keith Altham: 'We play loud because we like to build up an atmosphere in the hall – something which is physical and can totally involve and absorb the audience. The only people who complain about our being loud appear to be the writers, but we never get any complaints from our audience. The people who really matter to us are our audiences . . . when we do a concert, we like to pull out all the stops and hit them hard.'

With Spock and Luke driving the van, Black Sabbath had hired two Zephyr Zodiac cars with chauffeurs for the tour. Tony and Geezer travelled in one, with Ozzy and Bill in the other. A happy by-product of this arrangement was that one of the chauffeurs began a romantic involvement with Sonja Christina.

On one occasion, driving along the M1, Sabbath's two cars drew alongside each other. Geezer looked out through the window at Ozzy and pulled a face. Ozzy responded by dropping not only his pants but a 'Richard the third', which he flung at the window of Geezer's car. Perhaps unsurprisingly, Geezer threw up.

The tour generally went really well for Sabbath, although there were nights when they had to concede that Curved Air stole their limelight. After eleven dates at venues they had never played before, Sabbath finished the tour at Leeds University on 23 January. Six days later, they were in Sydney, Australia.

They flew thousands of miles just to play at the three-day Myponga pop festival in Adelaide. It was an exhausting journey, recorded by Spock on a piece of hotel notepaper which he kept as a souvenir.

He wrote:

Left UK starting at 5.30 Wed evening, flew to Frankfurt, Rome, Bahrain, New Delhi, Singapore, Perth, Sydney, which took thirty-six hours. On arrival in Sydney, 9.30 Fri morning, discovered we were booked on the 3pm flight to Melbourne thru to Adelaide.

After a TV reception in a hotel, went back to airport for another six hours' flying. Arrived at hotel in Adelaide after more TV and press on the way from the airport, 10pm Friday.

Saturday was spent meeting people in charge, doing TV interviews and sorting out drums etc. Sunday went to the [festival site] in afternoon to get ready for the evening. The lads played at ten o'clock that night. All things considered, it went fairly well.

Ozzy told one journalist, 'It looked like the audience had been to see the movie *Woodstock* several times, just to get the gist of how to behave at a festival.' People were stripping off their clothes all over the place, climbing the sound system towers and flashing peace signs to one another. The heat was scorching.

The band had a few days off in Adelaide after their festival appearance, and they did a bit of sightseeing. Visiting a local zoo, Ozzy spotted a giant soldier ants nest, but there wasn't an ant to be seen. Ozzy proceeded to jump up and down on the nest, proclaiming that he had paid good money to get in there, and he wanted to see a show from the ants. Everyone fled as the giant ants spewed out like lava from a volcano. The band decided to play golf one day, but were chased from the course because of the damage they were inflicting to the green in their attempts to hit the ball. There were huge divots everywhere.

They were staying at a plush hotel, which was built around a swimming pool. On one occasion, Ozzy was sunning himself by the pool when someone shouted his name from their overlooking balcony, trying to get his attention. The other guests in and around the pool were a bit annoyed at this, wondering why someone was shouting 'Aussie!'

Even a trip to the beach became controversial when Sabbath were involved. They had hired cars during their stay; soon, they would discover that cars don't mix with sand. They had to get a tow-truck to pull them off the beach, with the vehicles stuck in deep, up to the back axles.

Spock's 'tour diary' gives a shorthand account of the band's days off:

> Got up Monday with the intention of having three days' relaxation. First we went to the national park, after which we went to the beach and spent most of the evening digging the cars out of the sand. Tuesday, we went to Marineland. After, we played golf and then returned to the hotel for a lobster dinner. Went to the pictures and watched *M.A.S.H.*, then finished off the night getting drunk.
>
> Wednesday, another game of golf and paddle in the sea. After lunch, shopping, then went to a club to see an Australian group and got drunk again.
>
> Thursday, said goodbye to everyone. Got to Perth 11am. From there, we flew to Singapore, Bangkok, Bahrain, Istanbul, Frankfurt and Amsterdam.

It was on this first stop in Amsterdam, on notepaper supplied by the Esso Motor Hotel, that Spock made his notes. They conclude: 'We are meant to be in Rotterdam tomorrow night and Amsterdam on Sunday night.' Presumably they got there.

† † †

Sabbath were still 'the four musketeers', ordinary lads from Aston who were all for one and one for all, and the band was their number one priority. Without stopping to catch a breath, and despite their jetlag, they flew from Amsterdam to England and travelled straight to the studios in London to resume work on their new album. Then they went back to America for another tour, which started in New Jersey's Asbury Park on 17 February 1971.

With the exception of a couple of return gigs at the Fillmore East on 19 and 20 February, the band were playing much bigger venues this time around. Their *Paranoid* album had just gone on general release in America, and they had been promoted to arenas holding up to 20,000 people. Some of these were headline gigs with groups including Fleetwood Mac and Yes, who were on the rise in America, supporting Sabbath. On other occasions, they supported bands such as Mountain. The guys found it incredibly uplifting to see all those faces in the crowd, sensing that they were about to crack the US market in a big way. They were flying high.

Appearing in Seattle on 22 February, Sabbath stayed at the city's Edgewater Inn, a one-time sleepover for The Beatles. It was also the scene of the infamous story involving Led Zeppelin, a groupie and a freshly caught red snapper . . .

Ozzy's room overlooked the waterfront, and he decided to do a spot of fishing from his balcony. Guests could obtain a rod and line from the hotel reception desk in order to fish the waters of Elliott Bay. Ozzy got right into it, catching a couple of mud sharks which he placed in the bath to show off to anyone visiting his room.

He then hit upon the idea of holding a television set out above the water, with the contrast set to give the maximum white light from the screen. Fish are attracted to bright light and will investigate anything that shines. Luckily for the fish, he lost his grip on the TV, and it reached the end of its working life at the bottom of the drink.

The Edgewater Inn is situated on a wharf, cut off from the downtown area by a rail track. Sabbath had the misfortune to be setting off for their Seattle gig at exactly the time that a massive, slow-moving freight train was beginning its trundling, thirty minute journey past the rail crossing. They only just made their onstage deadline.

Travelling on to a gig in Memphis, Tennessee on 1 March, Sabbath had a scare onstage when, half-way through their set, a man hauled himself up on to the stage and made a dash towards Tony Iommi. As he lunged forward, one of the crew members, David Hemmings, saw that he was holding a large knife. In a flash, David flew at him and disarmed him by twisting his arm up his back. Members of the venue's security staff forcefully bundled him offstage and held him until the police arrived to take him off to the cells.

Shaken, Sabbath finished the set and returned to their two-storey motel. As they arrived, they were greeted by a group of people in black cloaks. Given what had happened at the gig, the band were quite disturbed by this reception committee. When Luke reached his room, he was shocked to find the door daubed with blood in the shape of an inverted cross, about four inches square.

The entourage complained to the receptionist, who called the local police. Eventually, the officers called by to disperse the weirdos, promising to make regular checks during the night to ensure the band's stay was safe. So much for Sabbath as veterans of the black arts . . .

The group left America with a hit album. Returning to the UK at the end of March, they went back to the London studios yet again to complete the *Master of Reality* album, which was scheduled for release in August.

Tony Iommi has subsequently stated that things had become a little strained by now, with the other band members increasingly depending upon him for ideas, dashing off to the nearest pub while he laboured in the studio. But nobody around Sabbath at this time was aware of any major stresses affecting the band's togetherness. Following their usual pattern, they were in and out of the studio before they even had time to think about what was going on.

They continued to tour themselves into the ground, playing ten dates in Europe in April and returning for a show at the Royal Albert Hall, from which they had previously been banned. This sudden, unaccountable change of heart by the Albert Hall management took everyone by surprise, and no one knew why it had happened. It was probably a financial rethink, since the management would have known that Sabbath could sell out the venue, no problem. On the night, the band played a sensational gig and ran over their time by about fifteen minutes.

A couple of weeks later, the band received a bill from the Royal Albert Hall – not for damage to the ornate hall as originally feared, but for staff overtime for Sabbath's extra quarter of an hour.

Ironically, they had only exceeded their time limit because they had been detained by executives from their record company before they played, presenting them with gold discs for sales of their first two albums, *Black Sabbath* and *Paranoid*, and advance sales of *Master of Reality* before it had even hit the shops.

Having finished that album, Sabbath were keen to start yet another. They packed their bags and retreated to Rockfield, where they spent six weeks rehearsing for what would become *Vol. 4*.

Their first three albums had been utterly and uniquely heavy, raw and doomy and filled with lyrics from the dark corners of Geezer's spooky imagination. Now, they were working on a new approach. It was early days, but they would eventually arrive at a stronger sense of melody, a lightness of touch to set off their more typically thunderous moments, and a definite move away from their notoriously macabre lyrics.

But while all this was going on, *Master of Reality* was taking the charts by storm. Released in August 1971, it rose to number five in Britain and number eight in America. To capitalize on its success, Sabbath ventured across the Atlantic for the third time in the autumn for a concerted attack on the west coast. Playing a one-off gig at the Whiskey in LA, they couldn't have looked anything less like a metal outfit in the top hats and tails that they hired on Sunset Strip from a shop owned by veteran actor John Wayne. Luke was the best-dressed roadie ever, rushing onstage half-way through the set in his top hat to nail down Bill's drum kit.

After that appearance, the band retired to the beach to chill out for a couple of days as guests of Warner Brothers. Tony Iommi was so inspired by the scenery that he wrote 'Laguna Sunrise', an instrumental piece that would appear on *Vol. 4*, complete with acoustic guitars and strings.

Sabbath certainly blitzed Los Angeles, with additional appearances at The Forum and the Hollywood Bowl. Ray Davies from The Kinks turned up one night, and shared a couple of aftershow drinks with the band. He also joined Spock, Luke and a couple of members of Black Sabbath on a trip to see Elvis Presley perform at The Forum.

From California, Sabbath ventured south for gigs in Tennessee and Texas, and travelled on to Hawaii in October. One day, while they were sightseeing at a blowhole geyser, thieves broke into their rental car and stole Geezer Butler's movie camera and Luke's cash and cowboy boots. It was a trivial but deflating episode, a nasty little postscript to the band's great achievement.

Sabbath had made enormous strides forward, but they were run-down and wrung-out by the sheer volume of work they had undertaken since the turn of the year.

Bidding farewell to America for the time being, they were relieved to touch down in England after weeks of homesickness and illness. Ozzy went straight to his bed with laryngitis and a temperature of 105 degrees. Tony Iommi was laid out with flu, while Bill and Geezer were absolutely knackered. None of them was in any condition to play the UK tour that had been set up for November, and it was hastily rescheduled for 1972.

Sabbath were in a state of physical collapse. They had been working hard and, with all the drink, drugs and entertainment on offer to a major league band on tour, they had been playing hard too. It was time to stop, but not for long.

7

MULE PACKS IN
STRADELLA DRIVE

Once he had recovered from his fever and throat problems, Ozzy
was able to spend some quality time with his wife and children. He met
the beautiful, dark-haired Thelma at a night spot in Birmingham and
married her in 1971.

The newlyweds had started their life together in a flat above a
launderette in a small shopping precinct in Wheeler's Road, Edgbaston,
with Thelma's son from her first marriage, Elliot. Ozzy legally adopted
him shortly afterwards. The family shared their home with Luke for
a short while, when he was stuck for somewhere to live. This arrangement was helpful to everyone. Thelma was heavily pregnant, and since
Ozzy couldn't drive, Luke did a fair amount of chauffeuring. Ozzy
had just bought himself a new Range Rover with the registration
number DOG 300, and Luke drove him all around town, showing off
the new car.

Ozzy and Thelma had their daughter, Jessica, early in 1972. With
Sabbath laid off until the end of 1971, he took the opportunity to
prepare himself for fatherhood.

The family lived close to the home of former Move singer Carl
Wayne, who had left the band in 1970 to go into cabaret. The Move had
emerged in the late sixties as a psychedelic pop group, enjoying a string
of hits, one of which – 1967's 'Flowers In The Rain' – was the first record
played when Radio 1 was launched. The rest of The Move, including
Jeff Lynne, Bev Bevan and Roy Wood, who had by now formed Electric
Light Orchestra, were leading members of Birmingham's musical elite.

Luke remembers that they, along with their friends, were indifferent towards the more down to earth Black Sabbath.

Indeed, Sabbath had been snubbed by The Move in the early days, when both bands happened to be on the same train travelling from Birmingham to London. Sabbath were roundly ignored by The Move as they queued together at Euston's taxi rank. Etiquette demanded that The Move, as the more successful band, should have broken the ice and made conversation, but they didn't. As time went on, however, and as Sabbath's star began to rise, the musicians all became more friendly.

1972 found the band back at work. Suitably rested after their assortment of illnesses, they regrouped at the Marquee recording studios, behind the Wardour Street club. They had decided that they were going to produce their fourth album themselves, with Patrick Meehan.

The first three records had been successfully produced by Rodger Bain, but the band wanted more control over their own music. Given the time they had spent in recording facilities, and Meehan's experience in producing albums for Black Widow, they were confident enough to go into the studio with just a sound engineer who knew his way around the mixing console.

In three nights at the Marquee Studios, they nailed two tracks, starting with 'Snowblind'. This was intended to be the album title, but the band would once again fall foul of record company censorship, due to the obvious reference to cocaine, or 'snow' as it was fondly known at the time. The second track was a short instrumental called 'FX', which grew out of an unusually practical application of the crosses that Sabbath wore around their necks – Tony tapped his cross on the body of his guitar while employing reverb control and repeat echo to achieve a unique sound.

Sabbath worked flat out during those three days and also managed to get down a couple of backing tracks that they would use later on for other compositions.

Now they had to limber up for the UK tour which they had called off in November. There were nineteen rescheduled dates, beginning on Monday 24 January 1972, with support from Wild Turkey, fronted by former Jethro Tull bassist Glenn Cornick. Tony Iommi had, of course, got to know Glenn during his own brief stint with Tull. Wild Turkey had just released a single, 'Butterfly', a tribute to Jimi Hendrix, from their debut album *Battle Hymn*.

Sabbath's big concern was to see that their fans in Birmingham and Cumbria were properly served. There had been an unprecedented demand for tickets for the tour's opening night at Birmingham Town Hall, and the promoter swiftly arranged for a second show at the venue.

The band were also finally able to play a charity show at Carlisle Market Hall, after haggling over it for months. Carlisle City Council, which ran the hall, had written so many bureaucratic conditions into the band's contract of appearance that talks had broken down more than once. Sabbath urgently wanted to play the gig in recognition of the fans in Cumbria and south-west Scotland, who had supported them from the earliest days and helped them on to the road to success. To their relief, the show finally went ahead on 30 January.

The tour included a return visit to London's Royal Albert Hall on 17 February. Frank Mundy, who was in charge at the venue, had obviously got over his initial worries about the audience and had forgiven Sabbath for running over time on the previous occasion. This time, the management seemed to be very concerned about potential damage to the stone steps at the loading area at the back of the hall where crews brought their sound equipment in. Despite the uneasy relationship between the venue and the group, this was the most prestigious gig on the tour. London concerts were always extremely important to bands, because the media always turned out in full force, as did most of the record company executives.

† † †

Sabbath had clearly not learned their lesson about the perils of incessant touring, or else they had chosen to ignore it. No sooner had they come to the end of the British dates than they set off again for

America, on 1 March, for a gruelling thirty-two concerts in thirty-four days.

The 'Iron Man' tour was a coast-to-coast event, taking in two dates in Quebec, Canada, and the support bands included Wild Turkey and Yes. The combination of Sabbath and Yes was awkward in more ways than one. For a start, the bands just didn't get on. There had been bad vibes between them since a university gig in London when Geezer had tried to start a conversation with Yes bassist Chris Squire and had met with a blank stare. Sabbath became convinced that Yes were looking down their noses at them, and when they were out in America together most members of the Yes entourage kept themselves to themselves. There was no interaction with Ozzy, Tony, Geezer and Bill. The down to earth Sabbath must have found this insulting and hard to understand. They should have all been in it together, enjoying whatever America had to offer.

Sabbath did, however, strike up a great rapport with keyboard player Rick Wakeman, who had recently joined Yes. Rick was open and friendly. He opted to travel not with Yes but with Sabbath when they flew from LA to a gig in the Las Vegas Rotunda and back, on a private plane once used regularly by Elvis Presley. It had been his favourite jet apparently, and the interior was jungle themed, complete with leopard-skin seats. The VIP passengers were served in-flight cocktails and sandwiches made from bread dyed hideous shades of red and green.

Musically it was probably a bad idea to put Sabbath and Yes on the same bill. They were worlds apart. Yes would hit the stage with all their famous glitz and glamour, Rick Wakeman dressed in a shiny, silver cape behind spectacular banks of keyboards. They were a conceptual, 'progressive' band with a jazz-rock approach, full of complicated rhythmic patterns and time changes. Nothing could have been further from the heavy, doomy, driving sound of Sabbath in action. Clearly, they appealed to different audiences and there were nights when Yes stole the show.

This tour turned out to be a hard slog for Sabbath. Later it would take its toll as, once again, the various members caved in under the enormous strain of working too hard, travelling too far too quickly and partying just a bit too enthusiastically.

It culminated at the three day Mar Y Sol festival in Puerto Rico on 1, 2 and 3 April. It seemed like a rock fan's paradise with a line-up including Sabbath, Emerson, Lake and Palmer, the Allman Brothers, Rod Stewart and the Faces, Dr John, John McLaughlin's Mahavishnu Orchestra, Fleetwood Mac, Billy Joel, Roberta Flack and Alice Cooper – but it ended in utter disaster.

More than 35,000 fans bought tickets – only half the number hoped for. The disappointing sales were an early pointer to the eventual fate of the festival. The promoter, Alex Cooley, was operating out of Atlanta and he had organized the festival with Eastern Airlines. Tickets were $149 each. This price included admission to the festival, camping on 429 acres of beach and the return air fare from mainland America. Planes had been laid on to take the fans to the Luis Munoz Marin Airport, which was near the festival site.

Sabbath had flown over from Miami. The crew arrived at the site, as usual, before the band did. However, as it drew closer to the time for Sabbath to leave for the gig, it became clear that they would never make it, at least on land. The road leading to the festival ground was gridlocked.

Spock used a pay phone to call Patrick Meehan, who was with the band at the Redondo Beach Hotel, to warn him of the traffic problems. Meehan told him to expect the band as and when they could get there. Their only chance would have been to hire a helicopter, but none was available. Meehan then decided that the band should admit defeat. They had nothing to lose as they had been paid in advance, unlike many of the other acts on the bill.

Sabbath had one immediate problem. They only had a day room at the hotel, somewhere to freshen up before they set off for the festival. Patrick decided that they should go to the bar and stay there until an earlier flight could be arranged to get them off the island. But he couldn't inform the crew, who were still at the site waiting for the band, and he had no way to contact anyone there.

Luke, who was by now acting as the group's personal assistant, decided to take a shower before abandoning the suite, and Ozzy decided to throw him a cherry bomb while he was in there. Cherry bombs were fireworks, so named because they looked like large cherries, about 30 mm round with a fuse sticking out of the top. They made a very loud bang and created a lot of coloured smoke. Kids would sometimes bring them to the gigs and let them off. The equivalent of a quarter stick of dynamite, they left everything in the vicinity a cherry red colour. By the time Ozzy had finished, the hotel suite looked like a scene from *Apocalypse Now.*

Luckily, Sabbath didn't have to stay around the hotel long enough to explain the bomb site they'd created. All that was left of them was a vapour trail by the time their trashed room had been discovered. By then, the festival had broken down irretrievably, with many of the other bands who had also been unable to reach the site demanding payment.

Spock and the road crew, meanwhile, were still in the dark. Finally, they decided to drive back in the truck, complete with equipment, to the Redondo Beach Hotel, to find out what was going on. But there was no sign of Black Sabbath, Luke or Meehan.

The crew, unlike the band, had beds booked for the night, and so they decided to check in while they thought about what to do next. The duty manager politely offered to show them to their rooms. Stopping the lift on the second floor, he directed them to the suite that the band had left in explosive disarray, explaining that they were welcome to stay there 'if you don't mind the mess'.

Opening the door, they immediately realized what had happened. Knowing that the manager's icy civility would soon give way to a fury they'd rather not get involved in, they did the only sensible thing and made for the airport, where they jumped on the first flight back to Miami.

Back at the festival site, the whole scene was descending into chaos, and the fans' disappointment mutated into anger and frustration as they headed en masse to the airport, where they found themselves stranded. Their return tickets were for chartered flights only, so they couldn't just get on a plane and go.

The army were called in to deal with the emergency, setting up tents on the perimeter of the airport for the fed-up hordes while they waited for flights home.

This had been Sabbath's fifth tour of America. Ozzy had suffered throughout from throat infections, and he was warned by the doctors who were looking after him at the time that he must cut down on his cocaine use. Ozzy had his own remedies. He kept throat sprays in the form of liquid honey at the side of the stage and, during performances, he would rush over at regular intervals to 'oil' his throat.

† † †

The band were exhausted, again. They vowed that come 1973, they would cut back on touring and spend more time in the studio. Flying home from this latest American outing, they wanted to rest, but carried on with a short tour of Europe, and were back in an aeroplane heading for California in May 1972. This time, they were going to record.

They had rented a mansion at 2023 Stradella Drive in the exclusive Bel-Air district of Los Angeles. It was massive, complete with a huge swimming pool, gardens and a private cinema, which Sabbath used for rehearsals. The property belonged to the wealthy Du Pont family, who were industrial pharmaceutical and chemical manufacturers. The band stayed there for the duration of their work at LA's Record Plant studios. They intended to finish the *Vol. 4* album they had started in London earlier in the year.

The road crew joked that they had drawn the short straw, being billeted at the Hyatt House Hotel on Sunset Strip. Poor guys – it was dreadful for them, what with all the groupies and late-night orgies and drug-fuelled parties that were standard entertainment at the Riot

House back then. Security at the hotel was fairly lax, so anything went, and the wilder the better.

It was on this Californian visit that Bill fell madly in love with a woman who was living at Huntingdon Beach. He met Mysti – real name Melinda Strait – at a gig in Hollywood and soon introduced her to the rest of the band. He called home to tell his wife, Theresa, that he had met someone else.

'She took it very hard,' says Luke. 'She was a lovely lady, very friendly. Like Geezer and his wife Georgina, she and Bill were childhood sweethearts. After she passed her driving test, she virtually became Bill's road manager and they shared everything.

'But Mysti was the woman Bill wanted. He was later prepared to put up with hassles from the authorities over her visa and permission to stay in the UK.'

Closeted away in their Bel-Air mansion, Sabbath spent a lot of time rehearsing, talking about the album, doing drugs and generally enjoying life in the Californian sun. The swimming pool opened up a world of possibility for Ozzy. On one occasion, he poured four boxes of washing powder into it, creating a massive bubble bath and a cloud of foam over the greater Los Angeles area. The next day, as Bill Ward dozed by the pool, Ozzy spray-painted his feet blue.

The mansion was staffed with gardeners and a maid. There was a call button on the wall in the sitting room, and one day Bill, feeling peckish, decided to ring for the maid to see if she would rustle him up a sandwich. Ten minutes later, two police officers arrived at the front door of the mansion, wanting to know what the emergency was. Bill had pressed the panic button by mistake.

Down at the Record Plant, the guys got to work on the album. They were really happy with the small studio they had rented there. Even Bill Ward, who was very particular about his drum sound and usually took forever to get it right, was satisfied. The band were taking a new approach in the studio. They were not in any huge rush to record and release the album, as had been the case with their first three. They were more interested in creating art, something they could be proud of. They threw all of their energies into it, and, to this day, it's considered one of their finest albums. The Record Plant was full of state-of-the-art equipment, which was very different to the studios they had been used to back in dear old England. And they had plenty of time on their hands to experiment with all the new gadgets and gizmos it had to offer.

Plus, the money was rolling in like the waves on Blackpool seafront. Sabbath were enjoying their new-found wealth, and their attitudes were undoubtedly changing. Around this time, they were getting pretty spaced out. Ozzy once remarked, with his usual eye for a colourful image, 'They were bringing the Colombian marching powder to us on mule packs.' In early-seventies America, cocaine was fast becoming the recreational drug of choice in the music business, and it was especially plentiful in California. There was a kind of cool elitism about it, since it was not yet readily available in Europe and the UK.

Their only real problems in the studio involved a track called 'Under the Sun'. Bill Ward totally lost the plot over this track. He was indulging in a cocktail of coke and alcohol during his time at the Record Plant, and he nearly drove himself to a nervous breakdown. He just couldn't get the drum pattern and the tempo right, and he was so paranoid he convinced himself he was about to be kicked out of the band.

The rest of the guys were amused by Bill's predicament, but when they realized he was having real problems with the track, they rallied round. They tried everything to help him get it right, even asking the sound engineer to leave, but Bill just worked himself deeper and deeper into the mire. Eventually, after what seemed like an eternity, he mastered it. Bill was always a drinker, but very rarely appeared drunk. Retrospectively, that might have been a danger sign. Now, his self-control was clearly slipping.

In June 1972, the band gave up their lives of luxury in the Du Pont mansion and returned to England. They went into Island Studios to put the finishing touches to *Vol. 4*. Bill finally finished off 'Under the Sun', which the band wearily rechristened 'Everywhere Under the Sun', referring to the trouble it had caused the drummer.

Just a month later, they returned to America for the sixth time. They had chartered a private jet to save time and spare them the monotony of hanging around America's municipal airports for scheduled flights, but this was the tour that would see their health problems getting serious.

8

KILLING YOURSELF TO LIVE

Ozzy's voice went on the second night. He saw a doctor immediately and was given medication. After only a couple of days' rest he went back onstage, which was a big mistake – it put the tour back ten days. The band were on tenterhooks every night after that, wondering whether or not Ozzy's voice was going to hold out.

They travelled to places they had never been before – the American deep south, and the Mormon capital Salt Lake City, Utah, a 'dry' town and a place that Sabbath agreed was a 'heavy trip' for a rock band with their reputation and capacity for alcohol and drugs.

In those days festivals were a bit hit or miss. Some promoters showed a greater flair for organization than others, and with a festival at Bull Island in Chandler, Illinois, Sabbath ran into another flop. Indiana's Soda Pop Festival ran out of fizz when the promoters overlooked the small detail of transport for the bands booked to play. They also failed to provide a way for the road crews to get the equipment to the festival site, and the sanitation was primitive to say the least. Afterwards, Sabbath enjoyed an unexpected day off at a hotel in Evansville, Illinois, alongside Joe Cocker and other artists who had been on the bill.

Flying on to their next gig in Jackson, Mississippi, Sabbath offered their support band Fleetwood Mac a lift on a private jet that they had hired. The Fleetwoods all accepted, including guitar legend Peter Green who had come out of retirement to rejoin the band for this one-off American tour.

Predictably, the 700 mile flight turned into a party. However, the guests were not impressed when Ozzy persuaded the pilot to let him take the controls of the aircraft and tried to turn it over in a 360 degree roll. The pilot quickly regained control of the aircraft, but there was champagne everywhere. Tony Iommi was particularly annoyed with Ozzy, since his drink had spilt over the crotch of his trousers and left an embarrassing stain.

By the time Sabbath showed up for their penultimate concert at the Hollywood Bowl on 15 September, they were absolutely drained. No sooner had they finished their set and walked offstage than Tony Iommi collapsed. Doctors called to the venue diagnosed extreme exhaustion, and the band cancelled their final gig in Sacramento. They were ordered home to rest and recuperate.

Returning to the UK, Bill Ward succumbed to severe hepatitis and was rushed into hospital. However he had contracted the illness in the first place, the amount of alcohol he was used to drinking would certainly have aggravated his condition. Bill was facing serious medical worries, and the band were forced to consider a worst-case scenario: who would replace him if his health did not improve?

And Bill was not the only one to face a spell in hospital. Geezer Butler, who had been suffering with a kidney complaint, had to be taken in for observation. Despite his liking for drink, the bassist insisted on a healthy diet. He was a strict vegetarian, but he hadn't been able to eat well on the recent tour. On the road in America, you couldn't always get a nut cutlet when you wanted one. The limited options were rarely to his taste, and he would go for long periods without eating much, which would have contributed to his health problems.

Black Sabbath were clearly falling apart. Their lifestyle had finally caught up with them and knocked them off their feet. Geezer wrote a set of lyrics about the whole unhappy situation, and they became 'Killing Yourself To Live', a track from the band's next album, *Sabbath Bloody Sabbath*.

'We were in a terrible slump,' Geezer has since recalled. 'We were all exhausted from touring. We weren't getting on very well.'

'It was just the travelling and the food – nervous exhaustion, really,' Tony told *New Musical Express*. 'We'd been working solidly for about three years . . . and we hadn't had a real break.'

Behind the scenes, an element of uneasiness was developing between Ozzy and Tony. Perhaps it dated all the way back to their schooldays; perhaps not. In Sabbath, there had always been a certain rivalry between the two as they vied for attention. On the one hand, there was the charismatic singer and on the other, the talented musician and writer.

Their live set-up was very unusual. Ozzy would be at the far left of the stage, never in the centre – the rock singer's usual position. Tony would stand behind Oz and when he took a solo, would stride out into the centre spot to claim his rightful place as the leader of the band.

Ozzy responded by clowning around relentlessly. He would change the words, so that 'Iron Man' would become 'Ironing Man', and he was always turning his back to the audience and pulling silly faces at the rest of the band. He had a remarkable ability to look straight ahead with one eye while moving the other from left to right, and it cracked Bill up every time. He used to signal to the crew that he needed his oxygen bottle, not because he had winded himself by his powerful drumming but because he couldn't breathe for laughing at Ozzy.

Tony was, of course, the main man when it came to writing the songs, but as the years went by, the press were queuing up to talk to Ozzy. For his part, Oz loved the adulation of the audiences and he enjoyed giving interviews, usually with Bill in tow. It must have got under Tony's skin that while he was doing most of the work, Ozzy was copping all the credit. It all conspired to create a certain tension with the band at a time when they were least able to laugh it off.

They had money pouring in and records selling by the truckload, but the price of that was a never-ending schedule of appearances and one night after another in Holiday Inns that all looked the same. Sabbath would gaze out of the windows at downtown America and wonder where they were this time.

They were musicians, not machines. There had to be a cut-off point somewhere, and this was it. They took a long break.

The lay off gave them the chance to take stock of their career. It was time for a change. They decided that they were going to enjoy life at a steadier pace instead of busting their balls touring, and when they went back to America it would be for weeks, not months, at a time.

Now they could spend some proper time with their families. All four had been house hunting, and they were moving out to larger homes in the country.

Geezer bought a place in Cleobury Mortimer, near Kidderminster, Worcestershire, and quickly made his presence felt in the village pub. During one visit, his snakeskin jacket and cowboy boots caught the eye of an elderly local, who asked him if he was in some sort of band. The old boy then informed Geezer that another of the customers was also in a group: 'They call him Ted Zeppelin.'

Ted Zeppelin turned out to be Robert Plant. And as neighbours and regulars in the same pub, Geezer and Robert became friends. Geezer later told writer Ray Telford: 'Living in Birmingham was beginning to drive me mad. I found kids climbing in the windows and hanging around the door all day and that's the last thing you want when you come back from a tour.'

Tony found a property in Acton Trussell, Staffordshire. Shortly after he moved in, builders began to develop some of the land behind his house – but rather than throw a rock-star tantrum over the 'blight' on the landscape, he bought one of the new houses for his parents.

Ozzy treated his parents to a new home, in Northfield, Birmingham, and he moved his own family into a farmhouse in Ranton, Staffordshire. It soon earned the nickname of Atrocity Cottage, as Ozzy now had the space and the money to indulge his increasingly outrageous personality.

Bill rented a place called Fields Farm in Bishampton, near Evesham in Worcestershire, prior to settling down in his own Summerville House, outside Malvern.

It was during this period of tranquillity, in September 1972, that *Vol. 4* was released. It was everything the band had hoped for. Introducing a previously unheard variety to their music, it contrasted classic heavyweight Sabbath tracks such as 'Snowblind' and 'Tomorrow's Dream' with the short and experimental 'FX', Tony's instrumental 'Laguna Sunrise' and the restrained and tuneful 'Changes', arguably the world's first power ballad.

It raced up the UK chart to number eight. And on its subsequent release in America, where it reached number thirteen, Sabbath became the first band ever to have three massive billboard advertisements at one time on LA's Sunset Strip – a real vote of confidence from Warner Bros, who had paid for the hoarding space.

'We wish to thank the great COKE-Cola Company of Los Angeles,' state Sabbath on the album sleeve, in a tongue-in-cheek reference to the record company's rejection of the band's favoured title *Snowblind*. They never seemed particularly put out by this interference, understanding that the record company couldn't be seen to condone the use of drugs in any way.

Sabbath's primary aim was the same as their label's: to get the album out and sell as many copies as possible. However, in a final piece of mischief, Ozzy managed to sneak a whispered reference to cocaine on to the recording. With that, the dedication to the great COKE-Cola Company and a publishing company called Rollerjoint, they had put their message across quite clearly, and there was no point worrying about the album title.

+ + +

Black Sabbath were rejuvenated, ready to face the world again. Bill and Geezer were in better health than they had been for a long time, and the atmosphere around the band seemed unified and healthy. As they headed down to Heathrow Airport on New Year's Day 1973, they were thinking of their Antipodean tour as more of a holiday than a work commitment.

They stayed at the airport's Skyline Hotel that night in readiness for their early morning Pan Am departure on what was known as the 'mail plane'. It left at 8.00am, stopping at all points south to collect

Ozzy and Tony on stage at Alexandra Palace 1973.
Sabbath were playing to a full house and
received great reviews.

Necromandus'
rhythm section
at Clearwell Castle.
Left to right: Frank Hall,
Dennis McCarten
and Baz Dunnery.
Missing from the
picture is vocalist
Bill Branch.

morgan

stereo master

mono master

Client: WORLDWIDE ARTISTS
Artist: BLACK SABBATH
Producer:

Studio: II
Date: 28/9/73
Tape No: 7014

	Title		Ti
1	SABBATH BLOODY SABBATH		
2	NATIONAL ACROBAT		
3	FLUFF		
4	SABBRA CADABRA		
5	KILLING YOURSELF TO LIVE		
6	WHO ARE YOU		
7	LOOKING FOR TODAY		
8	SPIRAL ARCHITECT		

Engineer: MIKE BUTCHER / GEORGE

Speed: 7½ IPS
Replay E.Q. NAB

Morgan Recording Studios Limited,
169–171 High Road, Willesden, London N.W.10.

Telephone: 01–459 7244
Cables: Morganmus Lond. N

Sabbath Bloody Sabbath in the can at Morgan Studios, Willesden, London.

Opposite. The itinerary and running order (*top*) and promo poster
for the prestigious California Jam. Emerson, Lake & Palmer were
drafted in at the last minute to boost ticket sales.

Black Sabbath

CALIFORNIA JAM SHOW SCHEDULE
ONTARIO MOTOR SPEEDWAY
APRIL 6, 1974.

BEGINNING TIMES	ENDING TIMES	DURATION	ARTIST
10:00 AM	10:45 AM	45 minutes	RARE EARTH Performance
10:45 AM	11:15 AM	30 minutes	SET CHANGE
11:15 AM	12:00 Noon	45 minutes	EARTH, WIND & FIRE Perf.
12:00 Noon	12:30 PM	30 minutes	SET CHANGE
12:30 PM	1:15 PM	45 minutes	EAGLES Performance
1:15 PM	1:45 PM	30 minutes	SET CHANGE
1:45 PM	2:45 PM	60 minutes	SEALS & CROFTS Perf.
2:45 PM	3:15 PM	30 minutes	SET CHANGE
3:15 PM	4:00 PM	45 minutes	BLACK OAK ARKANSAS Perf.
4:00 PM	4:30 PM	30 minutes	SET CHANGE
4:30 PM	5:30 PM	60 minutes	BLACK SABBATH Performanc
5:30 PM	6:00 PM	30 minutes	SET CHANGE
6:00 PM	7:30 PM	90 minutes	DEEP PURPLE Performance
7:30 PM	8:00 PM	30 minutes	SET CHANGE
8:00 PM	9:30 PM	90 minutes	EMERSON, LAKE & PALMER

ENDING TIMES AND MAXIMUM PERFORMANCE TIMES ARE FIRM -

NO EXCEPTIONS!!!!

abc ENTERTAINMENT, INC.
PRESENTS

DEEP PURPLE

EMERSON, LAKE & PALMER

BLACK SABBATH · SEALS & CROFTS

BLACK OAK ARKANSAS · EAGLES

RARE EARTH · EARTH, WIND & FIRE

SATURDAY APRIL 6th
10 A.M. - 10 P.M.
ONTARIO MOTOR SPEEDWAY

CALIFORNIA JAM

BRISBANE 1974

Bill wears his 'new shorts'.

Ozzy bares all.

Ozzy practices
his peace sign!

Spock and Geezer . . .

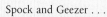

. . . and Tony:
a soundcheck
before the show.

Ozzy in full fringearama,
backstage in Australia.

© Les Martin

Tony's sleeves got
longer and longer.
Colston Hall,
Bristol, 1975.

© David Tangye

Bill on one of
his rare flights,
in Alabama.

Backstage in Philly. Bill, Mysti
and Gerald Woodroffe (keyboards).

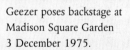

Geezer poses backstage at
Madison Square Garden
3 December 1975.

Ozzy is ready to leave while
Bill is still recuperating after the
Madison Square Garden gig.
Albert Chapman is on the left.

© David Tangye

Full-page advert in *Billboard*, 20 December 1975.

and deliver postal cargo en route to Hong Kong, where it was due to land the next day. In one particularly obscure stopover, the aircraft was surrounded by soldiers armed with machine guns, apparently to stop passengers disembarking. It worked, no one wanted to.

After such a long journey, the last thing they needed was to be refused entry into Australia. However, the band had not had the necessary vaccinations, and they were shepherded away to a clinic in the airport complex to receive their compulsory jabs. Arms throbbing, they made a last-minute dash through the airport for the Qantas flight that took them to their final destination of Auckland, on the North Island of New Zealand.

In total, Sabbath had spent fifty-five hours and forty-five minutes in transit, not bad for a band who had so recently decided to cut back on travelling. Luckily, they had a few days to unwind and recover from the side effects of their jabs before their appearance at The Great Ngaruawahia Music Festival of Peace on Sunday 7 January.

Black Sabbath were a big draw in New Zealand, and were called upon to attend a few official press meetings and introductions to the local representatives of Phonogram, Vertigo's parent company. They were presented with gold discs for sales of *Paranoid*, bringing their tally to sixteen gold awards worldwide, and they were informed that the first pressing of *Vol. 4* had sold out in New Zealand only a week after its release.

The Festival of Peace, New Zealand's first three day outdoor festival, was held at Charlie Coleman's farm on Huntley West Road from 6 to 8 January 1973. It was a multi-cultural event spanning everything from traditional Maori music, skiffle and jug bands to four hours of rock nightly. Fairport Convention, the folk-rock outfit fronted by female singer Sandy Denny, were the only other English band on the bill. The majority were from New Zealand and one local outfit, Ticket, went on to support Sabbath in Australia.

In contrast to some of the festivals Sabbath had seen, the Festival of Peace was meticulously planned and organized. Robert Raymond, director of Music Festivals Ltd, and his co-promoter Barry Coburn had gone to great lengths to get every little detail just right. Coburn had spent five months away from New Zealand attending festivals in America and Britain to see what lessons could be learned from them, noting how crowds behaved and how large numbers of people could best be catered for over three days.

The pair also scoured the North Island for months to find the perfect location for the event. Ngaruawahia, on the banks of the Waikato river, about seventy miles from Auckland, was ideally situated. The Maori name Ngaruawahia means 'break open the food pits', and this area of Waikato was home to the tribe of the same name. The festival symbol was a barefoot Maori boy holding a guitar, with the official sign of 'International Ecology' set behind him.

The festival site was accessible to the crews and service providers by one road, crossing a bridge, which was closed off to all other traffic. Provision was made for car parking to accommodate 5,000 vehicles in the town of Ngaruawahia, across the river. Special trains and buses had been laid on from Auckland and Wellington, and the public reached the site via an 800 yard footpath.

The area is surrounded by deep, impenetrable forest bush on one side, and the river on the other, with the site in 250 acres of private farmland set in a natural amphitheatre, rising to a height of 250 feet above the stage area.

The organizers had estimated an audience of 25,000, each paying only eight dollars admission. When the numbers fell short by some 7,000 they lost a packet, but it was still a brilliant event. There was even an inter-denominational religious service on the Sunday morning – which Sabbath regretfully declined to attend.

The stage was the biggest ever built in New Zealand. Made from two units joined together, it was 100 feet long, 40 feet wide and 12 feet high. The sound system weighed seven tons and was housed in 40 foot towers, one on either side of the stage. A 16-track recording facility was employed to tape the whole show for the possible release of a compilation double album. There were also plans to televise the event.

The festival started with a male singer from Wellington, New

Zealand, who stripped off naked on the stage, explaining that it was too hot. The local magistrates thought that he was too hot, later convicting the entertainer of 'obscenely exposing his person in public' and ordering him to pay a heavy fine. It was the height of summer in New Zealand, and many members of the audience followed the singer's example, flinging their clothes off to skinny dip in the Waikato river.

Arriving at the festival on the Sunday afternoon, Ozzy borrowed a Honda motorcycle from one of the backstage helpers and went for a spin around the site to see what was going on. He came back with a pillion passenger – a naked girl who jumped off the bike and streaked around the backstage area.

Sabbath blew the audience clean away with a massive wall of sound like the sonic boom from a jet fighter – louder and more menacing than New Zealand could have imagined. High on the hill overlooking the stage, the organizers had erected a huge, wooden cross which burst into flames at the moment the band struck up. It was a simple but massively impressive effect, with the crowd erupting into a frenzy straight away.

After Ngaruawahia, Sabbath had a three day break. They retreated to the island of Fiji for rest and relaxation while the crew sorted out the equipment and made their way to the next gig in Sydney, Australia. Arriving in Fiji, the band were met by a limousine that took them along a dirt track to the Beachside Hotel, which someone in New Zealand had recommended. Climbing into bed on the first night, Tony found a scorpion on his pillow. Understandably freaked out, he insisted on sharing a twin room with Luke for the rest of their stay.

Black Sabbath arrived in Sydney on 10 January and were surprised to be met at the airport by hundreds of squealing girls. Later, they discovered that the crowds had in fact been waiting for The Osmonds. Despite this small disappointment, they were welcomed to Australia with great enthusiasm, attending a press conference at the airport and a record company reception at the Town House Hotel, where they received more gold discs.

Bill Ward went off to a television studio for an interview about the

Australian tour. Leaving his dressing room, he got lost on his way to the presenter's desk and ended up outside in the parking lot. Bill had to ask the commissionaire for directions, eventually arriving a few minutes late. And no, he wasn't drunk. Bill would make sure he was fairly sober for his TV appearances, and you wouldn't be able to tell that he'd had a drink.

It was raining when they moved on to Melbourne on Saturday 13 January. This was unseasonal, quite unexpected, and it caused delays to Sabbath's outdoor concert at the Kooyong Tennis Pavilion. Luke and Spock were worried about the rain getting into the amplifiers. They finally managed to get hold of some tarpaulin sheets that smelled of sheep's piss and draped them over the back-line equipment.

Now the band had to wait for the downpour to subside. Someone coaxed Luke onstage to tell a few jokes to entertain the audience in the meantime. He'd never done anything like this before, but he gamely ran through his repertoire: 'Have you heard the one about . . .?' Sabbath were probably lucky to have an audience left when they finally hit the stage.

Finishing the last few Australian dates, the Sabs carried on to an eleven-date tour of Europe, which was recorded by The Rolling Stones' mobile studio. It looked strangely like the sort of mobile grocery store that was a common sight in rural parts of England. The unit was painted in camouflage colours, undoubtedly to hide from the flak of irate guitarists like Tony Iommi.

Tony was, on one occasion, working on some overdubs when he overheard the engineer make an off-hand comment: 'How long's it going to take him to get it right?' Tony immediately marched out to challenge his detractor, and a heated exchange took place. The engineer emerged the worse from this encounter, and was probably a lot more careful with his comments in future.

The live album never happened.

Their first UK tour of 1973 opened on 9 March at Glasgow Greens Playhouse – later known as the Apollo, but since demolished. It was a rough place to play in the seventies. The stage was about twelve feet high, which was just as well, as it served to keep the audience at bay. By the end of the gig, the first half dozen rows of seating were totally flattened.

Sabbath were supported by former Yes keyboard player Tony Kaye with his own band, Badger, and in the opening slot, a Cumbrian group called Necromandus who had signed a management deal with Tony Iommi and were in the process of recording an album. Halfway into the tour Badger threw in the towel, admitting that they were being blown offstage every night by Necromandus.

The tour continued, and when Sabbath arrived in Liverpool for a gig at the Stadium, they had several hundred pounds' worth of equipment stolen out of their truck. Les Martin, Geezer Butler's roadie, had his suitcase taken in the same raid. No one envied the thieves, who would have been the proud new owners of a collection of smelly socks, stained Y-fronts, second-hand copies of *Hustler* magazine and a couple of tuna salad sandwiches, which Les always kept for emergencies. There was no further incident as the tour travelled south towards the London Rainbow, which sold out in four hours.

† † †

The band had originally planned to rehearse and record *Sabbath Bloody Sabbath* in Los Angeles.

They did try. They flew out to California at the end of April 1973 and settled back into the luxury of the Du Pont mansion. Everything was hunky dory until they went to the Record Plant to start recording and were unable to use the small studio that suited their sound so perfectly. Stevie Wonder, no less, was working on an album and had filled the room with his own organs and synthesizers.

Tony Iommi has also said he was suffering from writer's block at this time, which could not have helped. A disgruntled Sabbath flew home, and resumed rehearsals for the album in what they hoped would be an inspirational setting.

Clearwell Castle, situated in picturesque Gloucestershire countryside close to the border of England and Wales, is a neo-gothic structure built as a stately home for the Wyndham family in 1727, on the site of a Tudor manor house. The owners in the 1970s were called Yates, proprietors of the Yates Wine Lodge company. They were living on the premises and renovating them.

The castle was perfect for Sabbath, not only for the obvious reasons but also because it was close to their own homes. They arrived to discover a moat, a portcullis, a dungeon and every other eighteenth century mod con that they could wish for, including, reputedly, a ghost stalking the corridors in the dead of night.

Bill Ward was determined to show that he was not afraid of any ghost, and elected to sleep in the room where it was said to have materialized. However, despite his bravado, he kept his sheath knife stuck in the wood panel next to his bed . . . Luke remembers Ozzy and Tony claiming to have seen an apparition, although he still isn't sure whether or not to believe them. Geezer also confided in Luke that he had felt someone sitting on his bed.

The ghost was a favourite topic of conversation, and Tony particularly took great pleasure in staging elaborate wind-ups. He was generally a shy type of bloke, but at the same time he was a great practical joker. Luke's room had a huge, stone hearth with a decorative feature in the fireplace. It was a square-rigged model sailing ship standing two feet high and three feet long.

One night, Luke was catching up with some paperwork in his room when he heard a scratching sound at the door. He turned round and saw, to his shock, that the ship was moving across the hearth as though it was in full sail. Freaking out completely, he flew out of the room to tell the rest of the crew.

A long time afterwards, he found out that Tony had set up the whole effect. He had tied a piece of cotton to the ship, threaded it under the door to the corridor, and tugged it gently to make it move.

On another occasion, Tony and a friend of his called Graham Wilche found a dressmaker's dummy in a cupboard. They kitted it out in some old clothes, took it up to a third floor bedroom overlooking the court-yard, and waited for Bill and Geezer to come back from a shopping trip. Bill and Geezer drove in, parked the car and were just beginning to walk across the courtyard when a 'body' crashed to the ground and lay spread-eagled in front of them.

The castle was a huge and magnificent place, complete with four-poster beds for everyone. There was a real sense of history in every room. Suits of armour peered down from ledges, and shields and broadswords adorned the walls in the great hall.

It was in Clearwell Castle that Dave Tangye, co-author of this book, first experienced the hilarious charm – and the dangerous habits – of Ozzy Osbourne.

Dave was working at the time for Tony Iommi's protégés, Necro-mandus. Fresh from a gig in Tenby, South Wales, the band and their crew travelled to Clearwell at the invitation of Spock Wall to borrow some Laney four-by-twelve speaker cabinets and any other equipment that Sabbath might not immediately need.

'I had met Sabbath during their March UK tour, when Necro-mandus supported them,' recalls Dave. 'They were a great bunch of guys with no airs and graces about them. Tony once came round to the squalor that we, Necromandus, were living in at Station Road in King's Heath, Birmingham. He arrived in his Rolls Royce and we had to borrow a shilling off him for the gas to make him a cup of tea.'

Then there was the trip to Clearwell Castle:

We pulled up in our Transit van and were immediately greeted by Spock, Luke and Les Martin. They showed us round the castle and we then went into the rehearsal studio to see the band, who were in session at the time.

They broke off from what they were doing, and we had a laugh and a joke about all the things that were happening to us on the road.

After the pleasantries, Ozzy took us to the village pub, the Wyndham Arms, where we got well and truly oiled. We managed to give the local darts team a good thrashing, which didn't go down too well. We could hear them muttering, 'Long-haired hippies!' We left the pub with a supply of cider.

Back at the castle, we went into the sitting room area to carry on drinking. There was an inglenook-style fireplace with a fire built, ready to be lit. Ozzy got it blazing, he liked banking fires up to the hilt, and we set about the flagons of cider like they were going out of fashion.

One of the Necromandus lads needed a leak, which is simple enough if you know where to find the bathroom. In castles, it's not that easy, especially when you've had a skinful of cider. He got as far as the scullery area and realized he would have to make do with the sink. At the very moment he started, the lady of the castle walked in and caught him in the act. He immediately reassured her, 'It's OK, love, I'm not pissing on the dishes, I've moved them to one side.' She smiled weakly and left the room.

Back in the rehearsal room, everyone was crashing out. We were woken from a stupor at about three in the morning and could smell burning. The carpet around Ozzy was alight, and his flares were on fire. I rushed over to where he lay and shook him. We picked up pint glasses and threw the leftover cider over his jeans, which extinguished the flames. The rest of the guys put out the carpet blaze, which had been caused by an ember leaping out of the fire. What a mess there was to clean up. Luckily, we were thinking straight enough to turn the carpet around and hide the burnt bit under a Welsh dresser.

It was, literally, a baptism by fire. But Dave would later become used to the chaos around Ozzy when he went to live in the Osbourne household as Ozzy's personal assistant.

9

THERE'S NO BUSINESS LIKE SNOW BUSINESS!

It was London's biggest indoor rock extravaganza and it took place over ten nights, from 27 July to 5 August 1973, at Alexandra Palace.

Black Sabbath headlined one of the shows, supported by blues-rock trio The Groundhogs. The attractions on other nights were Argent, Nazareth, Beck, Bogert & Appice, Ritchie Havens, Wizzard, Incredible String Band, Steeleye Span, Ten Years After, Wishbone Ash and Uriah Heep. They were some of the biggest draws on the touring circuit, and the promoters hoped that, together, they would launch the event as an annual fixture.

It's impossible to know what went wrong – perhaps the north London location in Wood Green was a little inconvenient – but the people simply did not turn out for what should have been one of the biggest events not just of the year but of the decade. Someone later remarked that there were more drug counsellors than punters at the Palace. Sabbath did the best business of all the acts with a full house of nine thousand, they played a rousing set and, unusually, they received great reviews.

✝ ✝ ✝

Rumours abounded in the studio at the time that they paid Rick Wakeman for *Sabbath Bloody Sabbath* not in cash but in beer – two pints of John Courage Directors best bitter. He came along to London's Morgan Studios in September 1973 to guest on the recording sessions, contributing keyboards to the rock'n'rolling 'Sabbra Cadabra'.

If *Vol. 4* had been the first of the new style Sabbath albums, with its different musical directions, the transformation continued on *Sabbath Bloody Sabbath*, which the band produced themselves. They even invited an orchestra to play on the track 'Spiral Architect', but couldn't cram all of the musicians and their instruments into Morgan Studios. They ended up at the nearby Pye Studio along the road, with Ozzy trying to explain what he wanted them to play like some sort of mad conductor. He had no written music to give the orchestra, he just hummed the part and they picked it up.

Other tracks were less experimental. Hardline fans were still provided for – the monstrous, sinister weight of the title track is archetypal Sabbath, and 'Killing Yourself to Live', with its memorable Iommi guitar solo, doesn't stray too far from the original blueprint.

Tony had long been accepted as the guiding musical force within the band, the superior authority. While Geezer supplied most of the lyrics and Ozzy invented tunes to top everything off, it was almost always Iommi's riffs, arising from jams or from personal practice, that gave rise to the songs in the first place. He would spend hours in the studio on his own, working on arrangements and production. He has since declared that his total commitment to Black Sabbath ruined his personal life – for long periods, he didn't have one.

Released in December, *Sabbath Bloody Sabbath* streaked up the British album chart to number four, and later climbed to number eleven in America. It attracted some excellent reviews, with *Melody Maker* instructing its readers: 'If you don't understand it, don't knock it!'

After a four-date UK tour in December, the band put their feet up for Christmas, their diaries clear until mid-January. They had vowed to take things easier in 1973 and did manage to reduce the pressure in their lives. Geezer Butler later said, 'It was a really good year . . . I'll always look back on that album and remember it with a good feeling.'

Bill was sufficiently happy to tell *Disc* that December: 'We're never going to split. We couldn't be more together now, because we love each other and because we dig each other's music.'

And so it was in this frame of mind that Black Sabbath went back to work to promote the album. It was time to think of their growing audiences in America. They started off gently a couple of weeks into the new year of 1974, with an eight-date tour of Europe. There was a huge fuss going on at the time about an oil crisis, and petrol rationing had been introduced. A lot of British bands were refusing to go to Europe because of the situation, but not Sabbath. Disregarding dire warnings of driving restrictions and other limiting measures, the band went ahead to discover that there was very little problem across the Channel; the crisis was affecting motorists in the UK more than in any other part of Europe, and even then there were ways and means of getting round it.

On their return, they lashed out at their more cautious colleagues. Ozzy was quoted in the *NME* dated 2 February 1974 as saying: 'I can only think that those managers and agents who have cancelled European tours simply can't have investigated the situation thoroughly. Or maybe there's some other reason – perhaps they just needed the publicity. We were touring around Sweden, Denmark, Holland, Germany and Switzerland, and we had no problems at all with petrol or diesel. In fact, the Europeans laughed at talk of shortages. It is true to say that we had more hitches at home than on the continent. As for electricity, there just isn't an energy crisis.'

Europe was a warm-up. Sabbath were about to return to America, where tickets were rapidly selling out for their shows at 10,000 capacity arenas. They had not played live in the States for more than a year, and they were ready for it. The band had taken things at a leisurely pace during 1973, there had been no arduous touring, and they had made time to enjoy the trappings of their new-found wealth.

Their absence from the live scene may have given rise, in part, to the rumours circulating around America that they were about to split up. Admittedly, it was a difficult time for Sabbath, who were experiencing communication problems and differences of opinion over various business issues with their management. They would later go their separate ways. Graham recalls: 'I remember driving Bill down to London to meet the rest of the band in Meehan's office. It was very flash – all leather and polished wood. Ozzy was particularly pissed off and carved crosses into the wood panelling.' At the same time, the band were also facing legal action from their previous manager, Jim Simpson, which would later end up in the High Court.

But far from splitting up, the band were thrilled to be back on American soil for twenty-two dates beginning in the chocolate town of Hershey, Pennsylvania. This was a 'Lear Jet' tour, with the band hiring private planes, at great expense, to travel the States conveniently and comfortably.

Tour support was Bedlam, a British band which included the late, great showman drummer Cozy Powell and also featured ex-Procol Harum guitarist Dave Ball, his brother Dennis on bass and Frank Aiello providing vocals.

Sabbath flew back to the UK in March 1974, and even though the gigs had been a huge success, the atmosphere around the band had become slightly strained. The management problems were gnawing at their usual good humour, and a feeling of, 'What are we doing this for?' was beginning to creep in. They also needed a break from each other. They had gone through a lot of changes personally during the past four years and achieved a great deal, but they had worked hard for it.

Looking back on this period, Tony Iommi has said that he was coming to resent the band's almost complete musical dependence on him, and he was fed up with the amount of time he was spending in the studio. Bill Ward recalled that, 'I was really diminished by my narcotics use.' And Ozzy has revealed that he actually thought for the first time about leaving the group, while confessing: 'I wasn't prepared to own up to the rest of the band. I didn't want to give up the success and recognition.'

None of the band confided their woes to anyone else, and as the weeks passed, their mood would lighten and they would be back on top of their game with a vengeance.

For now, though, they had some time off before a brief return to America for a prestigious appearance at the California Jam festival.

Spock Wall decided to stay in America, seeing no point in sending all the equipment home just to bring it back out three weeks later for the California Jam. Waving goodbye to Sabbath for the time being, he set about loading their gear into the Semi truck, along with a sound system belonging to the equipment hire company Tycobrahe. First, Spock had to go to Detroit, where the truck and the sound system were to be picked up by Deep Purple.

Arriving in the 'motor city', Spock and an LA driver called Ryan rented a 22 foot bobtail truck from the Ryder company and filled it up with Sabbath's gear. They were bound for LA, and since they had plenty of time to get there, they intended to see some of America on the way.

They set off across the snow-covered east side of America, and bowled along Interstate 80 towards the west coast and the sunshine. Taking a slight detour via Aspen, Colorado, where they intended to rest up for a while, they discovered that a band called Sweathog were playing locally. Sweathog had supported Sabbath quite a few times and Spock was quite friendly with them. Needless to say a party ensued, so there wasn't much sleep on that stopover.

The next day, Spock and Ryan were back on the road, driving over the Rocky Mountains. Everything seemed fine as they breezed along the flat desert plains of Utah, heading for Las Vegas. But the mountains must have put a lethal strain on the truck; it soon became apparent that there wasn't much more than the breeze moving the truck along.

The rental depot in Salt Lake City promised to send a replacement truck immediately. Three and a half hours later it rolled up, and the guys began to unload the cargo, but they soon realized that the replacement was two feet shorter than the original. After much pushing, shoving and swearing, Spock and Ryan had to give up. The cargo was not all going to fit into this new truck. They would have to leave behind five huge boxes of plastic snowflakes, and make arrangements to collect them later.

At that time, Black Sabbath used big snow machines for one of their spectacular stage effects. The machines worked with a corkscrew action, and were usually suspended from the lighting truss over the stage, loaded up with the snowflakes Spock was transporting. When Sabbath launched into 'Snowblind', the machines would start a snow shower while Ozzy raced around the stage with one finger on his nostril, miming to the audiences that he would like to get a nose full of the stuff.

Anyway, Spock and Ryan thought no more about it. They resumed their journey and made it safely to Las Vegas, Nevada, checking in at the Circus Circus casino hotel.

They quickly discovered that if you played the dollar slot machines for a while, you would be served complimentary drinks by the roving waiters and waitresses. They strung their time out, playing the one-armed bandits and pretending to be 'high rollers' as they ordered one free drink after another. They didn't hit the jackpot, but they left the casino well refreshed.

Finally arriving in California, Spock and Ryan drove to the Portofino Inn at Redondo Beach. The crew had taken to staying there when they were in LA because it was near the sound and lighting companies, Tycobrahe and Obie's.

It was lunchtime. Spock and Ryan parked the truck, checked in and went to their rooms. Unbeknown to them, the Portofino car park had been under surveillance for a number of days by certain members of the band's lighting crew. The crew had flown back to LA from the final tour date in Long Island, New York, arriving long before Spock and Ryan.

Spock had just stretched out on the bed for a doze, waking with a start when a frantic banging began on his door. To his surprise, one of the guys from Obie's Lighting was standing there. Without so much as a hello, he demanded the keys to the back of the truck as he had 'left something there by mistake' in Long Island.

Spock was not in the mood for conversation, so he handed over the padlock keys and went back to his nap. About an hour later, the phone rang.

'Where is it?' yelled the voice at the other end.

'Eh?'

'The plastic snow. Where has it gone?'

Spock got up and went to see what the commotion was all about. It looked like a garage sale in the parking lot. Sabbath's gear had been dumped all over the ground, and the two guys from Obie's were sitting on the back of the empty truck, looking downcast.

Spock told them about the breakdown and found out that they had hidden twelve bottles of grain alcohol in the boxes of snowflakes – and Spock and Ryan had been the unsuspecting coast-to-coast couriers.

Also known as White Lightning or moonshine, grain alcohol is distilled from corn or rice, similar in its outrageous strength to the Irish drink poteen, which is made from potatoes. The lighting crew had picked up the bottles in Pennsylvania, one of the very few states where it could be bought legally; in most parts of America there's a stiff penalty for anyone caught in possession.

The Obie's boys had paid twenty dollars a bottle, which was a lot of money back then, so they wanted to recover the contraband. It also gave them a kind of macho kudos in rock'n'roll drinking circles. They contacted the rental firm in Salt Lake City, only to be told that the company had found and destroyed 'the Devil's brew'. The snowflakes, however, were ready for collection at any time. In a mischievous moment, Spock considered telling them the significance of the 'snow', but decided against it.

† † †

Black Sabbath should have been packing their bags and getting ready to come back for the California Jam at the Ontario Speedway Circuit on Saturday 6 April. It was the biggest festival in America in 1974, with 270,000 people set to attend.

But it looked as though they might be about to blow it out. The band were still working through their own personal dissatisfactions, and since, crucially, they had little communication with their management, there was no key person on the ground in England to boost their morale, to mobilize them, or to deal with the arrangements for the trip.

In the end, it all fell to Spock, who realized that he had to take charge. By now, he'd moved into a rented apartment at LA's Hermosa Beach, but it had no phone line. Almost unbelievably, he dealt with the whole international crisis from a payphone on the corner of the street, outside Critters Bar.

After a series of transatlantic calls to all four band members back in England, Spock managed to convince them that they had to play the festival. It was a massive show backed with extensive radio advertising, all of it mentioning Sabbath. To cancel their appearance would cause untold damage to their credibility and reputation as a premier rock band in the USA. There was also the tiny detail that the promoters would sue them to kingdom come if they didn't turn up.

It was a last-minute dash, but they made it, squeezing in a four hour rehearsal the day before the festival in an old, disused theatre in a seedy district of downtown LA. They took a helicopter to the site, and walked into a backstage fraught with arguments and temper tantrums.

Sabbath and Deep Purple had originally been booked as the head-lining bands, but Emerson, Lake and Palmer – a huge attraction in America just then – were drafted in at the eleventh hour to boost ticket sales.

Deep Purple and ELP were laying down the law about the running order. Deep Purple had agreed to go on before them, but with condi-tions. Their intransigence was causing all sorts of hassle. Sitting it out in their dressing-room trailers and running miles behind schedule, they were insisting to Donnie Branker, festival co-ordinator, that they would not set foot on the stage until after dark.

Sabbath just wanted to get on and play; they had no intention of getting tangled up in the bullshit and the battling egos. They were happy to perform their sixty minute set in broad daylight. It was a beau-tiful afternoon, the crowds were eager and alert, and Sabbath – suddenly invigorated after their weeks of confusion – were ready to rock like the demons they sang about. They went down an absolute storm, and they can still look back on the California Jam as one of the highlights of their career.

Things were not going so well for Deep Purple. When they did eventually play, guitar wizard Ritchie Blackmore smashed his headstock over one of the cameras which were filming the event at the side of the stage.

Emerson, Lake and Palmer had rigged up a quadraphonic sound system, which they had banned the other acts from using. Naturally, they wanted the best sound for themselves, but their grand ambitions flopped when it failed to operate properly.

Media coverage of the festival was colossal and it did wonders for Sabbath's profile in America. Greatly encouraged, they enthusiastically went into rehearsals for the 'Sabbath Bloody Sabbath' UK tour when they arrived back in England.

† † †

Black Oak Arkansas were the support band, booked by legendary London promoter Harvey Goldsmith. Black Oak were from America's deep south and the May/June tour was their first visit to Britain.

Black Oak were a spectacular band in action. Jim Dandy was a supreme showman with long, blond hair and a deep southern drawl, and he played a mean, suggestive washboard. Unusually for a heavy metal hero, he appealed to both sexes in the audience. The boys admired him and the girls adored him. Black Oak's drummer, Tommy Aldridge, was also hot. His drum solo was the best in the business, and the most visual – he climaxed by wrecking his kit in a frenzy while keeping a perfect beat on what was left of it. In later years Ozzy, as a solo artist, wanted Aldridge in his band, and did eventually succeed in claiming him.

The Black Oak tour was also memorable for a gig at the Free Trade Hall in Manchester – especially for Malcolm Horton, an artist friend of Bill Ward's. The fake snow had created another problem. This time, the crew discovered that there was no room on the lighting truss for the snow machines. Malcolm, an accommodating chap, had volunteered to climb some 35 feet up a metal ladder to the roof space backstage to throw the plastic snowflakes by hand when the band went into 'Snowblind'.

All had gone well in rehearsal. Malcolm had gauged exactly how long the snow would take to reach the stage, and he had located the best spot for its release. Unfortunately, he had not taken into account the time it took for him to get up the ladder and into position.

Come showtime Malcolm was a bit spaced out, having enjoyed a couple of spliffs, and he left it a bit late to start his ascent to the roof. He was only about three-quarters of the way up the ladder when he heard the opening strains of 'Snowblind'. Undaunted, he rushed up there and hurriedly began to open his bags of snow.

In his haste, he dropped one of the big, half-opened bags and as he watched in horror, it landed like a ton of bricks on Ozzy's head with a perfect starburst. The crowd went wild. When the show was over, Malcolm sidled into the dressing room expecting a bollocking. 'That was fucking great, Malc!' whooped Ozzy. 'Can you do that again at the next gig?'

'No problem,'replied Malcolm, blushing slightly. 'No problem.'

✝ ✝ ✝

Graham Wright, co-author of this book, spent three years at Middlesbrough Art College, then went off travelling around Europe and lived in Amsterdam for a while. Returning to England, he did a few odd jobs before a friend asked if he'd fancy helping out a band called Osibisa on their European tour. And so, quite by accident, Graham found himself working as a drum roadie for the band, who used a battery of Afro-Caribbean percussion.

He continued his career as a drum technician with glam rockers

Silverhead, a band called Glencoe who would go on to find fame with Ian Dury as The Blockheads, a Liverpool musician called Jackie Lomax who had played with The Beatles, and Tony Kaye's band Badger. By the summer of 1974, Graham was already a tour veteran of Europe and America, and was sharing a flat in Notting Hill with friends from his native north-east.

Sabbath were on the road in the UK with their 'Sabbath Bloody Sabbath' tour when Graham heard through the grapevine that they were looking for a drum tech.

Luke had left the band by then, as a casualty of the rift between Sabbath and Patrick Meehan. He had been the reluctant intermediary, caught for some time between the two sides. But Luke felt that Meehan personally disliked him and was looking for ways to get rid of him. He claims that the manager attended a band meeting and persuaded them that Luke had to go because he was 'over-ambitious'.

A roadie friend passed Graham Les Martin's phone number, and he was invited to come and meet Bill Ward on the afternoon of their 21 May London gig at what was then called the Hammersmith Odeon. Graham recalls:

I vividly remember walking into the hall that afternoon and approaching a lad who was sat at the side of the stage on a flight case. I asked him if he knew where Les Martin was and he pointed over to the drum kit were Les was finishing off the set up. I noticed that the drum riser was shaped like a four-poster bed. I knew that drummers had a reputation for being crazy, but a bed? I wondered if Bill spent a lot of time sleeping.

Les was pleased I'd turned up, explaining that he needed help with his increasing workload. He was really Geezer's roadie, but he had been doubling up as drum tech. He then took me to meet Bill Ward, and we wandered over to the lad who was sitting on the flight case. I had taken him for a local stagehand. He certainly didn't look like the rock star I'd imagined. Dressed like any of the rest of us, down-to-earth, affable and obviously working class like myself, I liked him straight away.

After a few minutes of talking to Bill, I knew it would be a pleasure to work for him. He explained that he wanted someone not just for touring but to be on hand full time, someone who would be prepared to move up to Worcestershire.

Graham thought about his life in London, considered the offer for a couple of seconds, and made the decision that would change everything.

10

MAUDE'S MORGUE

Graham met Bill Ward for the second time on 9 June at the Coventry Theatre, the final gig of the 'Sabbath Bloody Sabbath' tour, and was introduced to the rest of the band. He was surprised by how friendly and likeable they all were, and he identified with their easy sense of humour; he could tell straight away that Ozzy was a natural-born comic.

Sabbath were not high on Graham's personal playlist in those days. He was more into American music, especially west coast bands such as the Grateful Dead. However, after starting work with the band, he came to like their music a lot. 'Maybe I got brainwashed sitting behind Bill's drumkit for so long,' he chuckles.

Graham travelled home with Bill after the gig. They finally reached the main road from Worcester to Hereford, and turned off into a country lane leading to Bromyard. A mile on, high up in the beautiful Malvern Hills, stood Summerville House. It was an old, detached, Victorian residence surrounded by open farmland, with several acres given over to crops of raspberries. Bill lived there with his American partner Mysti and their newborn son, Aaron. It was a typical country residence, right down to the Aga in the kitchen. Bill was still drinking, but only cider or beer Graham recalls:

He had kicked the spirits into touch and had decided by the never to touch the 'hard stuff' again. Bill had been drinking heavily around the time he split up with his wife, Theresa, and was worried he was an alcoholic. His solution was to stick to milder drinks, and by the time I came along, he was not a heavy drinker compared to some people I knew back home in Teesside. He wasn't drinking twenty-four hours a day. He was never drunk onstage; he always had water beside him when he was playing. In his private life, he drank partly, I think, to escape from the business pressures surrounding the band at the time. It wasn't long before he introduced me to his local in the nearby village of Cradley. The landlady of this incredibly quiet pub was called Maude – and its nickname was Maude's Morgue.

After a game of darts and a few pints, Bill's tipple being the local cider, we found a few things in common. I told him that I was from Stockton-on-Tees and he turned out to have fond memories of that area – when he was a child, his parents would take him and his brother Jim to Seaton Carew during the summer holidays.

Bill owned five cars. Pride of the fleet was a beautiful, navy blue and silver Rolls Royce, and because he did not have a driving licence a major part of Graham's job would be to drive him around. This was why Bill was so keen for Graham to live nearby. He suggested that Graham move into Fields Farm, the place Bill had been renting in 1973 after splitting with Theresa. When Mysti arrived in England to be with Bill, he bought Summerville House and they moved in there together. It was the fulfil-ment of the English working-class dream: a big house in the country remains a powerful status symbol, the proof that you have really made it, as well as a guarantee of privacy. Bill's artist friend Malcolm Horton (who'd been responsible for the dramatic 'snow-job' at Manchester Free Trade Hall) had taken over the lease at Fields Farm and was living there with a couple of hippie mates. Graham was happy to move in with them:

I returned to London, gathered my then meagre belongings, and set off for my new life in the country. It was a beautiful summer's day in July 1974 when I travelled up to Fields Farm near the village of Bishampton in Worcestershire, a three-storey, Georgian farmhouse set back from the road to the village, surrounded by fields of wheat and barley.

For the first time, I turned into the long drive leading to the farm. There was a small lake next to the farm buildings, and parked beside the lake were a couple of police cars and an ambulance. I was told that the previous evening a lad who was visiting the farm had taken a canoe out on to the lake. Tragically, the canoe capsized and he had drowned. What a welcome.

Bill had also taken to rural life in a big way, once telling interviewer Chris Walters: 'Growing your own food is very satisfying. You wouldn't believe how good vegetables taste when you planted them yourself. I work hard on my land when I'm home . . . it relaxes me.'

Graham spent a few months acting as Bill's chauffeur and personal assistant. His first actual job for Sabbath was to set up their equipment in a sports centre at Cannon Hill Park, Birmingham. They had decided to rehearse for a possible two week Australian tour, which didn't greatly appeal to them.

The sports hall was a most unlikely place to find Black Sabbath. It was a small building sandwiched between a bowling green and some potting sheds. Surprisingly, there were no complaints from the senior citizens playing bowls nearby. They must have turned down their hearing aids.

On the night of 3 November, the phone rang in Graham's house, and it was Bill: 'Graham, we have to go to Australia in two days' time.'

Arriving at Summerville House, he found Bill standing in his kitchen holding a bunch of contracts.

'I have signed these now,' said Bill. 'I want you to drive to Geezer's, Ozzy's and Tony's, get them to sign them, and have them in London by 8.30am!'

Graham managed to complete the paperwork, and forty-eight hours later, they were on their way to Australia: 'It was my first flight with Sabbath, and I was sitting with Les Martin, Spock and the rest of the crew in business class. The band and their minder, Albert Chapman, were in the first class compartment in the hump of the jumbo. The cabin crew soon allowed us to join them for a drink.'

The centre of attention throughout the twenty-four-hour flight was not Ozzy but Albert Chapman, an old schoolfriend of Tony Iommi's.

He kept up a stand up comic routine and a never-ending string of jokes that had everyone in stitches. He was, and is, a giant of a man with a personality to match his size.

Albert currently owns a club and restaurant called the Elbow Room in Aston, Birmingham. At the time of the trip to Australia, he had been running the door at Birmingham's city-centre Rum Runner nightclub. He'd been a very handy boxer in his youth, so he was ideally qualified to handle the band's security and, eventually, to go into tour management. During his career in the ring, Albert had made friends with many people in the boxing fraternity, including some of the sixties' most notorious villains. He knew the Kray twins, who had been promising boxers as young men, and he was particularly close to their older brother Charlie.

Graham remembers the trip well:

Albert kept us, and the flight crew, entertained for hours. The flight was that long we had the chance to get drunk, sober up and get drunk again, several times. We touched down in Perth to let some passengers off, and the flight attendants walked up and down the aisles spraying insecticide over all the passengers. Les noticed that the cheeky buggers seemed to be paying particular attention to us.

As we took off for the final leg of the flight to Sydney, the jumbo started to bank heavily to one side. Someone yelled, 'What the hell's happening?' as we looked out of the windows, down on to a golf course. The captain asked his passengers to wave; we were passing over a tournament sponsored by Qantas, our airline. In seconds, we were roaring back up to the right altitude.

In Sydney, the entourage were booked into the Kingsgate Hyatt Hotel in the city's Kings Cross area. It was ideally placed for nightlife, and the band and crew went out to explore the bars and clubs of the district called Woolloomooloo. Graham has colourful memories of that first excursion:

At the end of the night, we found ourselves in a club that was decorated in zebra patterns. When we thought we saw Tarzan and Jane swinging from the rafters, we decided that it was definitely time to go back to the hotel.

We staggered into the lobby and over to the elevator doors. As I pressed the button for the lift, Ozzy said, 'I need a piss and I need it now!' I looked up and saw that the lift was still on the twenty-fourth floor. Ozzy had unzipped his fly and was directing a flowing torrent into the potted palm next to the lift doors.

I watched the box that showed the progress of the lift. It was descending in slow motion and stopping at every floor. Ozzy looked at me with his silly grin and asked, 'Have you ever had a piss when you thought it was never going to end? I think this is going to be the longest one I've ever had in my life.'

By now, the plant pot was overflowing at an alarming rate. Again, I checked the lift. It was frozen at the sixth floor, and a river of urine was flooding across the polished marble floor of the lobby. I shouted, 'Ozzy, tie a knot in it!' but to no avail. He kept on going. I was about to make a run for it, as I had noticed the receptionist staring at the floor in horror.

Just then, the lift doors opened and a well-dressed couple strolled out. I grabbed Oz by the scruff of the neck, yanked him past the couple and into the lift, and lunged at the buttons. I will never forget the look of shock on the faces of those two people just before the doors closed, as they looked back to see Ozzy in the corner of the lift, still in full flow. Amazingly, the mess was discreetly cleaned up. We never heard a word about it from the hotel staff.

Ozzy wouldn't be so lucky when he was famously arrested in San Antonio for urinating liberally over the Alamo in Texas in 1982. He obviously needed a piss, and he needed it 'now!'

The tour opened on 5 November with a sold out gig at the Hordern Pavilion, Sydney, a resounding triumph for Sabbath. Les Martin came to find Graham while the support band were onstage, urging: 'You've got to come and see this. There's this schoolboy in uniform with a cap on and a satchel, prancing about the stage playing guitar.' Everyone had a good laugh at AC/DC, not knowing then that within three years, they would be supporting the Sabs on a European tour and heading onwards and upwards towards their own superstardom.

The band moved on to Brisbane, as Graham recalls:

The next day was free. I was looking forward to the day off. Wrong! Bill decided he was sick of flying and wanted to drive 500 miles to Brisbane for the show on 7 November. He was brilliant at throwing you a curved ball, Bill.

There's an expression that's used in the West Midlands, 'going round the Wrekin'. It means taking the long way round something, choosing the difficult way instead of the easy one. Bill was a great exponent of this. But I wasn't that bothered about missing the day off because I was getting the chance to see something of the Australian countryside.

We rented a car, drove out of the urban sprawl of Sydney, and the Australian bush came up on us thick and fast. Bill slouched next to me in the passenger seat, the reassuring odour of a faraway land oozing from him – or maybe it was the cider. The road was only marginally better than a farm track, and Bill was spellbound by the strange vegetation. Suddenly he exclaimed, 'Bloody hell, have you seen the size of their rabbits?' I didn't have the heart to tell him they were wallabies.

It seemed like a year later that we arrived in Brisbane and I shovelled Bill, who was still drunk, into his hotel room. The rest of the lads had been lying around the pool, enjoying the sub-tropical heat. Ozzy sneaked into Bill's room and cut one leg off his jeans, knowing that he had not packed any shorts. Bill later modelled his customized jeans around the pool, and he wore them like that for a few days before the other leg came off.

The gig in Brisbane was outside in some sort of tennis court. I don't remember much about it, since I was in the grip of Outback-lag.

The band flew back to Sydney for another show at the Hordern Pavilion, and were treated by the promoter to a leisurely afternoon boat trip around the harbour, a huge expanse of water. Boarding the launch, they were welcomed aboard by the captain, complete with white naval shirt, shorts, a cravat and a sailor's cap jauntily angled on his head, remembers Graham:

We sailed off, eating, drinking and enjoying the hospitality and the sights. As we approached the mouth of the harbour, the captain said we were going to come closer to the shore because there was a beach we may like to see. We could make out lots of figures waving and shouting at us. The captain was eagerly waving back.

Eventually, we could see that it was a nudist beach. And as we sailed even nearer, we realized that the naked figures were all men, hordes of them, standing on the rocks waving their willies at us. I remember the captain smiling. And I remember somebody shouting at him in a broad Birmingham accent to turn the boat around at full speed. These were not enlightened times; at least not for a bunch of boys from Aston.

After Sydney, it was on to Melbourne. The flights had all been booked, although it came as no surprise to Graham when Spock approached him in the bar the evening before departure to explain that Bill was throwing another curve ball. Once again he had decided not to fly, and he had been booked on to the overnight sleeper train, the Southern Aurora Express. Two tickets had been purchased – one for Bill and one for Spock.

Only two hours before the train departed, Bill announced that he had, after all, plucked up the courage to fly. His ticket was going spare, and Graham took it. He wanted to experience everything he could.

The final gig was in Sydney, and the band and crew, after 'doing' Australia in two weeks, were equally knackered and jet-lagged.

They saw the year out in their country homes. Graham was occasionally called upon to drive Bill to Ozzy's house, and it wouldn't have been Christmas without a session or two in Maude's Morgue. But it was a definite calm before the storm. Black Sabbath were gearing up for action, and it was all going to start happening in the new year of 1975.

11

SABOTAGED

Ozzy's country farmhouse in Ranton, Staffordshire, was the location for the rehearsals for the next Black Sabbath album starting in January 1975. The band set up in a large room that Ozzy had had built on to the back of the house as an extension, with windows overlooking an extensive garden.

It was comfortable, and a stuffed grizzly bear stood guard outside the door. Ozzy intended, one day, to transform the room into a fully functioning recording studio. Now, though, the only equipment was a Revox tape player, a small PA and Ozzy's synthesizer.

Graham spent several weeks on the motorway with Bill Ward and Geezer Butler, driving them to and from the rehearsals. Usually, they travelled in Bill's Rolls Royce. It boasted a state of the art, eight track cassette player, cutting edge technology in those days. 'Our favourite album was Paul McCartney's *Band on the Run*,' recalls Graham. 'We all sang along to it in the Roller and changed the words to "boils on the bum".'

The conversations in the car were always pretty light-hearted. Bill and Geezer did not discuss band politics in Graham's presence, even though they, like Ozzy and Tony, were known to be worried and upset about their continuing business problems – the management dispute, their financial affairs, the continuing legal action and their way ahead. Their bitter disillusionment with what had gone before was spilling out into the songs that were emerging in Ozzy's back room.

Sabbath had recently come to a decision to manage themselves, to be masters of their own destiny. It was said that they came out of their deal with Meehan with their houses, their cars, the band name and much less money than they would have liked. Tony Iommi was quoted as saying the band had had to start again from the beginning, financially. Whether or not he was exaggerating, they were certainly devastated and determined not to take their eyes off the ball ever again. The most industrious member was Bill. He was glued to the telephone, taking care of business, and he probably never received much appreciation for it. Bill may have seemed an unlikely volunteer, but his caring nature, his constant need to look after the rest of the band, was a big driving force. It was a stressful time, and Sabbath had elected to deal with the legal intricacies of their business while also working hard on the musical front. Bill chose to take the weight off the others by liaising with the lawyers hired by Sabbath at great expense to sort out their business affairs after the split with Meehan. Bill was probably as much out of his depth as the rest of the band in all of this, but he did his level best.

Meanwhile, in the Roller, Graham was coming to know Bill and Geezer as human beings rather than the world-famous rock stars that the public saw:

> Bill was the gentleman of the band. He was always concerned that the other members and the crew were OK. He was a worrier, too.
>
> Geezer was the dandy, always dressed well. He came across as quite a deep thinker, although he had a surreal sense of humour and was a football fan. He loved Aston Villa FC and supported them whenever he could get to Villa Park. I was a Middlesbrough supporter, and we would banter about the state of our clubs. Later on, we went to several games together.

Bill was the usual victim of the band's practical jokes, but Geezer was also sometimes on the receiving end. Graham remembers how one good deed of Geezer's backfired on him horribly – thanks to Tony Iommi:

> Geezer invited a fan who lived in his village to come with him to one of the gigs. The kid was in seventh heaven as he wandered

around backstage, and when Tony discovered that he had come in Geezer's car, he set about one of his more imaginative jokes. He sneaked out of the venue with a lump of Gorgonzola cheese and hid it in one of the car's heating vents.

A couple of days later, we asked Geezer how his young friend had enjoyed the concert. He scowled: 'It's the first and last time he will come to a gig with me. He stank that badly I had to drive home with the windows open. And I still can't get the smell out of the car.'

No one is sure if Geezer ever did find out what caused the offending odour.

✝ ✝ ✝

The Osbourne residence was a big, detached cottage at the end of a lane, and its interior furnishings reflected the country setting. There was a spacious kitchen, and the living room was dominated by a huge leather Chesterfield couch and an open fireplace. Ozzy lived here with Thelma, Elliot and Jessica, and they would soon be joined by a new arrival, their son Louis.

The Osbournes were often amazingly normal. Ozzy was a happy, capable father, and Thelma was a loving wife and mother who enjoyed her home and the various household routines that kept everything running smoothly. She cooked, she did the washing, she dropped Elliot off at the Scouts. Sometimes, you could imagine that they were like any other 'ordinary' family. Yet, while Ozzy loved his home life, he couldn't conceal the glint of devilment in his eye when his mates came visiting. Ozzy, like Bill, loved having company.

A couple of weeks into the rehearsals, Sabbath decided on a change of scenery. They moved from the farmhouse to a little place called Weobley, near Norton Canon in Herefordshire, setting up camp in an old vicarage that belonged to a retired executive in the nuclear power industry. He had turned it into a residential rehearsal facility for bands.

He was himself a bit of a character, cooking a full dinner of meat and two veg every night for his beloved Great Dane and serving it on a bone china plate. The first meal he gave the band was roast quail, and they all thought he was serving them sparrows.

The vicarage was eerie and, naturally, was said to be haunted. As usual, Tony Iommi was in his element playing tricks on people. One of his favourites was to sneak up behind unsuspecting members of the entourage wearing a full-face mask of an old man with white hair and a long, warty nose.

Not to be outdone, Ozzy had his own shocks to spring on the company. He cooked a curry one night with some quite extraordinary ingredients. Bill tucked in hungrily, only to spear one of his own old socks, which had disappeared earlier that day. According to Ozzy, it gave the recipe a certain extra zest. Before long, the catering responsibilities were handed over to a local restaurant, the Penrose Court in nearby Lyonshall, which was owned by Monty Python star Terry Jones.

The band were sure they'd been lured into one of Terry's sketches on the day that a Harrier Jump Jet landed in the field next to the vicarage. The pilot disembarked and nonchalantly sauntered over to the house to ask if he could use the phone. Apparently, he had been experiencing communication problems in the aircraft.

✝ ✝ ✝

Black Sabbath decided to call their next album *Sabotage*, exactly what they felt had been happening to their career because of their business problems. They returned to Morgan Studios in Willesden, north west London, for the recording sessions, which took place over February and March 1975.

During this time, the band would stay in town at the Swiss Cottage Holiday Inn from Monday to Friday, travelling back to their country homes for the weekend.

The Holiday Inn had a twenty-four-hour coffee shop, which was unusual for a London hotel in the mid-seventies, and Graham still relishes the memory of one particular visit:

> We had just returned from the studio. It was about 3.00am and the coffee shop was surprisingly busy, but we all fancied a snack, so we took our place in the queue. Ozzy kept teasing Bill about his casual clothes, insisting that he looked like a tramp, but Bill, as usual, refused to be provoked. He waited quietly in line and ordered a sandwich.
>
> Ozzy's turn came to be served, and his eyes lit on a Black Forest Gateau a foot in diameter and at least eight inches high. He asked the assistant how much a slice would set him back, and on hearing the answer, he passed her twenty pounds, declaring, 'I'll have the whole cake.'
>
> She asked if he'd like it sliced into portions, but he said no. She persevered: 'Are you going to eat that all by yourself?'
>
> 'No,' grinned Ozzy, 'I'm going to award it to Bill for his good dress sense!'
>
> With that, Ozzy picked the cake up off the plate and dumped it firmly on top of the drummer's head, where it sat like a big, black, chocolate crown. Without batting an eyelid, Bill turned to Ozzy and thanked him kindly, adding: 'You shouldn't have bothered, though. I'm quite full. I've just had a sandwich.'

† † †

On Fridays, with the week's work over, Graham would first drive Bill to Summerville House and then drop Geezer off at his home in Cleobury Mortimer. Tony would often drive himself, while one of several drivers would take Ozzy back to the farmhouse. Most of these northbound journeys were uneventful, although Bill and Geezer would sometimes want to stop off for a drinking session in a country pub if it was early enough. Since Graham was driving, a couple of shandies was his limit.

One Monday morning, Graham was driving Bill and Geezer down the A40 in the Rolls as usual, on the way back to London. They had just passed Oxford when a white Bentley convertible pulled alongside them, as Graham recalls:

The driver was Led Zeppelin's John Bonham, and his passenger was Robert Plant, their singer. I rolled down the car's electric window and Bill shouted out a big 'hello' to his old mate and fellow drummer Bonzo. Straight away, Bonzo dared us to race him to London, declaring that the roundabout at the end of the A40 would be the finish line.

With Bill promising to pay any speeding fines that we might incur, we zoomed off. Both cars were hurtling along at speeds of over 100 mph. It was neck and neck as we approached the roundabout, and I braked to avoid crashing into it. Bonzo flew across the middle of the roundabout and screeched to a stop in the next lay-by. Miraculously, he, Robert and the convertible came out of it unscathed. We exchanged a bit of banter with the Zep boys and then carried on to the studio.

That evening, Bonzo, Robert Plant and Zeppelin bassist John Paul Jones paid a visit to Morgan Studios, and were soon jamming with Black Sabbath. That really was a remarkable sight. They did 'Long Tall Sally' and improvised some numbers, with John Bonham playing the hell out of Bill's drums. I was worried he was going to break something, but they held up. Luckily, I had got into the habit of nailing them down.

The recording sessions would usually carry on into the middle of the night. Tony Iommi was working really hard on the production side of things with the band's co-producer, Mike Butcher, and he was spending a lot of time working out his guitar sounds. Bill, too, was experimenting with the drums, especially favouring the 'backwards cymbal' effect. He would strike the cymbal, record the sound, play the taping in reverse and then lay it on the track. The band were working towards their most convincing and impressive balance of the grinding, thundering sound with which they had made their name and the more sensitive and unusual elements they had started introducing on *Vol. 4*.

For one song, the band employed the forty piece London Chamber Choir, led by Will Malone, and a female harpist. The whole ensemble trooped into the studio, recorded their piece, asked for their £120 fee and left as quickly as they came. At that time, the track enjoyed the working title of 'We Sell the Worst Chips in the Country', which was quite at odds with the atmosphere created by the choir. They hadn't been 'singing' in the accepted sense, but building a vocal backdrop. It was the sound of a band of demonic angels. The otherwise instrumental track was later given the slightly more appropriate name of 'Supertzar'. Ozzy enjoyed word-play, often using it to deflect from any charges of self-importance – Graham recalls: 'He would often call the band Slack Haddock, and in honour of this, I changed the stencilled name on one of my drum flight cases from Black Sabbath to Slack Haddock.'

Dave Tangye turned up in the studios from time to time with the Necromandus lads while Sabbath were recording the album. On one occasion, Bill Ward recruited Dave, Graham and his brother Jim Ward to clap in time on one of the tracks. Their efforts are immortalized on 'The Thrill of it All'.

The key to the whole album was a song called 'The Writ', Sabbath's expression of fury at the management and legal struggles that had been causing so much worry and anger. Tony Iommi later said, 'That was a terrible period for us, because we were getting bloody lawsuits in the studio. People were delivering us writs and stuff.'

Even the album cover was hijacked.

Graham, an artist who has since presented exhibitions of his work in Britain and America, had been talking to Bill about the sleeve design at time of the sessions. Graham had an idea based on a famous painting by the surrealist artist Magritte, where a man in a dark suit is standing with his back to a mirror. The reflection shows the man's front, not his back. In essence, his image has been sabotaged. Graham explains the concept:

We decided on an image of the band stood along a corridor in an old castle, all dark and gloomy with a stained glass window emitting light at one end. The band members would be dressed in black, and behind each one would be an old, full-length mirror showing the reversed reflection.

This idea was put into the hands of the record company, who announced a photo shoot a couple of weeks later. To my horror, we were told that it was to take place not in some old castle but in a small photographer's studio in Soho. The band were instructed to bring some stage clothes with them for some preliminary photos.

Ozzy threw a kimono and a pair of extraordinary underpants into a bag. Bill brought along a pair of tights. He never wore trousers onstage – only tights or shorts – since he didn't want anything getting in the way of his bass pedals.

When they arrived, no black costumes had been laid on, and someone asked what they wanted to wear. It was obvious then that the original concept had been over-ruled. The designers had no idea of it.

They carried on with the shoot, explaining that they would superimpose images at a later stage and that it would look great, honest. The session was unbelievably rushed, and the outcome was far from what had been originally envisaged. The band were as unhappy as I was, but the whole episode was typical of everything else that had been happening. Ironically, the sleeve design that was intended to illustrate the idea of sabotage had instead become a victim of sabotage itself. By the time they saw it, it was too late to change.

There they were, with Ozzy dressed, as he put it, like 'a homo in a kimono', with Bill Ward squeezed into Ozzy's chequered underpants and an embarrassingly revealing pair of red tights bought for him by his partner Mysti.

✝ ✝ ✝

In the late spring of 1975, with the album in the can, Black Sabbath were making preparations to go to America where they would preview material from it.

Bill had presented Graham with an interesting challenge. He had to find someone who could make a huge fibre-glass clam shell, which would be placed behind the kit to project the drum sound forward and prevent guitar feedback from entering the drum microphones. After phoning dozens of manufacturers around the UK, Graham ended up in Scunthorpe. He had discovered a specialist fibre-glass company that made dinosaurs, giraffes and other animals for theme parks and displays.

They succeeded in creating a clam shell measuring 12 feet by 10 feet, at a cost of £500. Bill was happy, he said it worked for him, and so the band had a new addition to their collection of stage props. They included a huge wooden cross which was suspended over the stage at gigs. It had been made by Les Martin's dad, and was transported around the world in a purpose-built wooden coffin.

The clam shell, the coffin, the snow machines, the amplifiers, the speaker cabinets, the drums and the keyboards – they all amounted to a lot of work for the crew, since they had to load, unload and ensure the safe transit of every item.

The crew flew out to the States a week before the band to get started on the pre-production work, hiring out PA and lighting equipment and getting it ready for the tour. There was no Hollywood jolly-up in the 'Riot House' hotel this time. The guys set up base instead at the Portofino Inn, close to Tycobrahe Sound and Obie's Lighting – the company whose employees had so disastrously tried to smuggle grain alcohol across America in Sabbath's plastic snowflakes.

The Portofino overlooked the Pacific Ocean at Hermosa Beach, and the rooms had balconies with sea views. It was as quiet as the Hyatt was riotous, which suited the crew perfectly. It had become a home from home. They all still fondly remember breakfast times at a small, surfside café affectionately called the 'House of Tits' because of its friendly waitresses.

It was the biggest American tour that Sabbath had tackled since 1972, when they had decided to cut down on long-haul travelling. They felt a new enthusiasm about playing and an impulse to go back out and prove their worth now that they had taken control of their own affairs and had, additionally, recruited a tour ordinator and accountant called Mark Forster. He was well-known in the music industry as a business manager, and had worked on the road with many different bands since the late sixties. He was a gentleman, too, known to be scrupulously fair. Sabbath hired him to look after the financial aspects of their tours, and to collect payments after the gigs.

Over the summer, Sabbath were committed to forty arena dates taking in most of the major cities in the States. It was a massive success, with the band performing brilliantly for sold out audiences everywhere they went. Indeed, there was a full-scale riot outside the one gig that took place in a smaller venue. The Santa Monica Civic Auditorium had been booked by a production company so that the band could be filmed for the prestigious American television series *Don Kirchner's Rock Concert*. The audience was limited to a couple of thousand fans, and it seemed like the whole of LA had got wind of it.

For such a phenomenally popular band, Black Sabbath employed a relatively small crew of about fifteen people. Nowadays, a group touring similarly sized venues would have up to eighty crew members – not the way things were done then, laughs Graham:

In the seventies, we did not have dressing room ambience coordinators and personal chefs. In fact, there was no tour catering at all, and we would know all the best eating places in every major city that we visited regularly.

In Chicago, for instance, Sabbath would play the International Arena, next to the old stockyards. Beside the venue was the Old

Stockyards restaurant, which was supposed to have been frequented by many of the city's most infamous gangsters. You could get the best steak in the mid-west at that very spot.

Another major difference was that we did not use tour buses then. The band flew from city to city, travelling to the gigs by limo.

On this tour, there were no private jets – probably because the band were now managing themselves, and had realized the fantastic cost of such a luxury. Additionally, they no longer felt safe travelling that way. They had come to believe that the pilots were partying harder than they did. Bill reckoned that they wore their dark pilot's glasses all the time to hide their bloodshot eyes.

When the tour began, Spock Wall gave every member of the entourage a book filled with airline tickets for the whole of the tour, and these were guarded carefully. The itinerary called for up to three connecting flights a day, and after a couple of months of this they got to know the hub airports like Atlanta, Chicago and Dallas like the back of their hands.

Sabbath's routine – airport, hotel, interviews, gig, hotel, airport – was as leisurely as possible in the circumstances. They could sleep in a little in the mornings, since they had stopped doing soundchecks and did not have to be at the venues until the evening, although Tony would sometimes turn up early if his equipment had been playing up the night before. The band travelled with Albert Chapman and Mark Forster.

It was a much more gruelling schedule for those members of the road crew who had to pack the equipment away after the gig, load it on to the trucks and leave immediately for the next city. The rest of the crew travelled by plane, staying in hotels close to the airport so they could be up and away at the crack of dawn every morning, as Graham recalls:

This is how it went: Drag yourself out of bed after a couple of hours' sleep. Grab your bags and jump, bleary-eyed, into a hire car, drive like a maniac and drop it off – or if you were running really late, leave it at the kerbside check-in point with a hastily scrawled excuse on a note on the windscreen. Check in for the flight, run for the gate and collapse in your seat as they slammed shut the cabin door.

These early-morning flights were usually full of executives, all suited up and clutching their leather briefcases. We stuck out like sore thumbs, all hairy and unshaven in our denims and T-shirts. We were great fans of the age-old wind-up of sticking a note on the back of some unsuspecting businessman as he disembarked and headed towards the arrivals lounge to meet his clients, unaware that he was telling the world: 'I'm a twat!'

Most of the flights were unremarkable, although there were some spectacular sights to see out of the window, particularly over the western states. The desert and mountain scenery was stunning, and it was easy to appreciate the vast scale of the country. However, as Graham warns:

If you fly often enough, the law of averages decrees that you will eventually encounter the odd brown-trouser jobbie. One flight to Knoxville, Tennessee, on a day off was memorable for all the wrong reasons. The crew had had the luxury of a sleep in and a later flight than usual. We were passengers with Ozark Mountain Daredevil Airways, or something like that, and as we approached Knoxville, we saw the sky turning black.

The captain told us to expect some 'slight turbulence', the 'Fasten your seatbelt' signs flashed on, and all hell broke loose. We were flying into the heart of an electric storm. The plane shook like an old tin can as we were flung about the skies; lightning was striking all around us. The baggage compartments above our heads sprang open and oxygen masks flew down in front of our faces.

The flight attendants strapped into the two front seats had gone deathly white, and they were holding on to each other. Then the captain announced in a southern drawl that he was going to try to get this baby down. We seemed to be going backwards and upside down as we bounced along the runway. Just as we appeared to be skidding to a halt, there was an almighty roar and we careered back up into the black sky for another death-defying, rollercoaster ride. We had run out of runway, and had to attempt another landing.

Mercifully, we did manage to get down in one piece the next time. Relieved but shaken, we stumbled out of the plane, and I overheard one of the stewardesses saying that the pilot had not diverted because he had a hot date that night in Knoxville.

The group returned to England to see *Sabotage* chart at number seven on its release in September 1975. It made number twenty-eight in the USA.

A month later, Dave Tangye accepted the position of right-hand man to Ozzy Osbourne and moved into his home, where he witnessed a variety of bizarre and outrageous exploits from the celebrated 'Wild Man of Rock'.

12

THE TRADESMAN'S
ENTRANCE

Dave's first job with Sabbath lasted for one day. He had joined the crew to help with the equipment, and he humped gear in and out of Southampton Gaumont Theatre with all the typical enthusiasm of a new recruit. The next gig was in Bristol, at the Colston Hall. About fifteen minutes before Black Sabbath were due onstage, Les Martin asked Dave to go to the dressing room and pick up a spare amplifier which Tony Iommi had used during his tuning up.

Dave knocked on the door, apologized for intruding and requested the amp. Tony seemed surprised to see him, asking when he had started working for Sabbath. Dave explained that he was just helping Les on the UK tour. Tony then inquired after the guys from Necromandus, whereupon Ozzy commented, 'What a great shame they folded. They were such a talented band.' Agreeing, Dave left immediately to take the amp to the stage, as he recalls:

After the concert, we were onstage taking the gear down when Spock Wall came over to me and said, 'Ozzy wants to see you. He's in the dressing room.' I asked, 'What's that all about?' He just said, 'You'd better go and see.'

I made my way to the dressing room with some trepidation, wondering if I'd done something wrong or upset someone. It was like going to see the headmaster at school. When I went in, the band were buzzing after the gig, they were high-spirited and jovial. 'Hi, Oz,' I ventured. 'Did you want to see me about something?'

'Yes,' he replied. 'I wanted to know if you were interested in doing a job for me.'

'No problem, what is it?'

'I'm looking for a driver for this tour, and I wondered if you'd like to do it.'

I was gobsmacked. This had come right out of the blue, and I stuttered, 'When do you want me to start?'

'No time like the present,' said a typically practical Ozzy. 'Could you drive me home to Stafford tonight?'

I was anxious about Les. 'What about the gear?' I asked.

'Don't worry about that,' replied Ozzy. 'Go and get your bags out of the truck. You're working for me now.'

✝ ✝ ✝

Dave was born on 11 May 1950 in Cleator Moor, Cumberland. West Cumberland, as it was known then, was a busy, thriving area populated by a diversity of people descended from those who had arrived during the boom time.

Dave left Cumbria in 1973 to work in the engineering and construction industry. He was employed by the Birmingham-based international company Babcock & Wilcox as a coded welder, making precision repairs to ultra-high-pressure boiler systems in power stations. The work was 'seasonal' – in an arrangement called 'home on forty hours', he was paid a retainer while having long periods off between jobs. He worked maybe six months in a year.

This was ideal for Dave, who had met a local band called Necromandus and joined their crew as an unpaid helper. Day job permitting, Dave carried on working and travelling with Necromandus until they split in 1975, and it was during his time with them that he met Black Sabbath. He had been on the road with Necromandus when they so comprehensively wiped the stage with Tony Kaye's band Badger on Sabbath's March 1973 British tour.

Dave had struck up a solid friendship with Sabbath roadie Les

Martin, and had moved into a room in his large house in Erdington, Birmingham. Shortly after Necromandus split, Dave's job with Babcock & Wilcox also came to an end. It was the late summer of 1975, and Dave, aged twenty-five, was on the point of going home to Cumbria to consider his future when Les returned from Sabbath's US tour with an offer he couldn't refuse.

Black Sabbath were touring the UK in the autumn, and Les suggested that he might like to help with the loading and unloading of their ever-increasing amount of equipment. Dave joined the entourage three dates into the tour, at Southampton's Gaumont Theatre on 11 October, as he recalls:

I was very excited at the prospect of working for a band that I had been a huge fan of over the years. It was like a dream come true. We arrived at the Gaumont around 10.30am, unloaded the truck and set the stage up for the band. They arrived in the afternoon, did a quick soundcheck and dashed back out to their hotel. So there wasn't a lot of contact on that particular day, but I remember the show vividly.

Their energy was electrifying, and the audience was in a frenzy. Southampton had a reputation then for being quite a rough town, a busy seaport and a base for both the Royal Navy and the Merchant fleet. You had sailors there who had either just returned from a long tour of duty or were about to set out on one. Either way, these people were hell-bent on getting wasted.

I had never seen so many people so totally off their heads. You could've got high just from the marijuana fumes in the hall. And then there were the drinkers. They were wild – the place was in total chaos and there were fights breaking out everywhere. The security couldn't hope to control this crowd, although Sabbath did – they ruled the roost that night.

Twenty-four hours later, Dave was behind the wheel of a beautiful, metallic green, custom built Mercedes with Ozzy Osbourne as his passenger, driving up the motorway to the singer's home in Staffordshire.

They were not strangers — Dave had, after all, doused Ozzy's jeans with cider to stop him incinerating himself at Clearwell Castle — and alone in the car, their conversation flowed with no awkward pauses, says Dave:

> He was normal and cool, and it was all very cordial. We just seemed to click. We shared the same sense of humour. Ozzy loved telling jokes, and hearing them. I remember one of his was, 'Have you ever been with a queer?' 'No, but I've been with a bloke who has . . .' It was a real seventies thing.
>
> Ozzy was talking a lot about the Mercedes and what it could do, and we chatted about Cumbria and the gigs that Sabbath used to play there. I can't remember a lot more about the conversation because I had never, ever driven such an expensive car, and I was concentrating on the road.

When they finally arrived at Ozzy's farmhouse after driving down a succession of narrow, winding country roads in the middle of the night, Dave was quite disorientated:

> It was in the middle of nowhere. I would never have found my way back on my own in a million years without my 'co-pilot'. I got lost more than once in the first couple of weeks.
>
> When we walked through the door for the first time, I thought, 'Wow, what a great place to live.' But there wasn't a lot of time to take in much else; it was a brief stopover, since I had to be up early to pick up my car in Birmingham and get back in time to drive Ozzy to the band's next gig in Bradford. They had decided to do a soundcheck, and were due at the venue at 3.00pm.

Dave's responsibilities grew as the tour progressed. He was placed in charge of all Ozzy's needs onstage, and had to see that antiseptic throat spray, liquid honey and bottled still water were close to hand. Ozzy never drank alcohol before or during his performance – although he usually made up for it afterwards at the hotel bar.

Sabbath celebrated the last show with an end of tour party in the hospitality bar upstairs at the Hammersmith Odeon on 22 October. Entry to the free bar and buffet was by invitation only, since the band did not want the party gatecrashed by freeloaders or hordes of journalists. They had been getting some rough reviews lately – although this was hardly new. They were never media darlings. Indeed, one American reviewer suggested that his city could have wiped out all its lowlife in one fell swoop by bombing the arena where Sabbath had played. And so the band saw no reason why they should lavish hospitality on the media.

Radio 1 DJ Alan 'Fluff' Freeman and Birmingham rockers the Steve Gibbons Band were among those who were granted entry by Dave, manning the door for the event:

Twenty or thirty people came to the bar without tickets. I declined them entry politely, but I got a bit of flak from some of them. I put on my best 'jobsworth' voice to tell them 'I don't make the rules!'

Three hairy guys approached the door and when I asked for their tickets, they said they were 'with Queen'. I didn't catch on. I said, 'I couldn't give a fuck if you're with the Duke of Edinburgh, you're not getting in here without a ticket.' Luckily, Tony Iommi happened to notice the altercation and immediately recognized Brian May, John Deacon and their road manager. 'Let them in,' he said. 'They're mates of mine.'

Another embarrassing moment had happened earlier in the tour when we left Newcastle City Hall after the gig and found the usual crowd of fans and autograph hunters outside. As I made a path through the crowd to get to the car, someone shouted, 'Better let him through, I think it's Ozzy's dad.' It must have been my receding locks . . . Ozzy called me 'Dad' for a good while after that. I still have a birthday card from him saying, 'Best wishes to Dad, love Ozzy.'

For the most part, Dave had spent the tour keeping his eyes open and his mouth shut:

> I was just taking everything in, making sure that I did my gig right. I was meeting a new circle of friends. I enjoyed the way everyone got on together, band and crew alike. I was keen to show a willingness to work, and to fit in with my surroundings.
>
> Geezer was the quietest member of Black Sabbath. He had an air of mysticism about him, he seemed aloof, and I found him quite difficult to get to know. If I tried to engage him in conversation, he would respond with one-line answers and I started to think that maybe he just didn't want to talk to me. But as time went on, I discovered that Geezer really has a great temperament and a very dry sense of humour. He sees things from a different angle to most people. His commitment to Aston Villa was fanatical. If he couldn't be at a game himself, he always had to find out how the team got on, no matter where he was or what he was doing. He was also devoted to the band and gave it his all. He is a brilliant musician and songwriter.

Tony could also be quiet, and he too was wholly committed to Sabbath, as their unofficial leader. He is a serious musician and a studious type of person. On the road, it was unusual to see much of Tony, except when the band were travelling or playing. He spent a lot of time in his hotel room playing guitar. When he did mix with the rest of the band and the crew, he would be full of devilment, always on the lookout for a wind-up. And if Bill Ward was the usual victim of the pranks, Tony wasn't afraid to take on the authorities either, as Dave remembers:

> He used to like winding up the customs officers at Heathrow. Being with a band, we were subjected to what we thought was over-zealous attention. Tony bought some joke items in a shop somewhere in America which he used to carry through customs in the hope that the officers would investigate them. One was a Bible

that gave an electric shock to the person opening it. The other was a round tin. When you took the lid off, these paper snakes with springs inside them would fly out of the tin into your face.

✝ ✝ ✝

Three days after the UK tour ended, Black Sabbath were off to Europe for a few dates, and Ozzy invited Dave along to help out. They flew into a bitterly cold and frozen Copenhagen, where they checked into the luxurious Plaza hotel next to the world famous Tivoli Gardens.

The first gig, at the Falconer Centre, was not until the next day, and so various members of the band and crew decided to hit the bar. They were joined by John Birch, the guy who made Tony's guitars. Tony had invited John to Copenhagen to sort out an annoying buzzing that had been plaguing his guitar sound throughout the UK dates.

The entourage wanted to sample the best beer Denmark had to offer, and so they asked for the recommendation of the barman. His name was Hans, and so, of course, he became Hans Christian Andersen for the rest of the night. He recommended a local brew called 'Elephant Beer', and at the end of the first round, it was generally agreed that it was indeed an excellent tipple, says Dave:

Hans warned us about the strength of the beer we were drinking and advised us to sip it like wine and to savour it. 'Don't worry about us,' we swaggered, as we knocked back another round like it was going out of fashion. We were joined in the bar by some members of the American band Dr Hook, who were on a Scandinavian tour, and the party soon got into full swing. Tony and Geezer weren't in the mood, and they left early. Bill stayed around for a couple, but he didn't fancy a big session that night. The guys from Dr Hook were enjoying the craic, and Ozzy was up for a bit of fun, as usual.

The barman shook his head every time we called in another

round of drinks. After a few hours, John Birch suddenly fell asleep in his chair mid-sentence. Ozzy, ever the prankster, borrowed a felt-tip pen from Hans, and scrawled in black letters on John's bald head: 'I'm a twat.' John woke up about ten minutes later and carried on talking as though he had been following the conversation throughout.

By midnight we were all wasted. Ozzy and I crawled up to the twin room we were sharing and collapsed in a heap. In the early hours of the morning I was woken by the sound of Ozzy throwing up and the toilet flushing. I fell out of bed and staggered to the bathroom to investigate.

'Get a doctor quick!' he moaned. 'I think I've had my drink spiked.' He was in a right state, and I wasn't much better.

Dave called reception for help and a doctor duly arrived. Finding out what they had been drinking, he diagnosed both Ozzy and Dave with alcoholic poisoning, administered a jab of Valium to calm them down, and delivered a lecture about the perils of 'Elephant Beer'.

'The next morning,' continues Dave, 'we dragged ourselves down to the breakfast area for some strong coffee. And there was John Birch tucking in to a hearty breakfast. Clearly, he still hadn't washed, because the words "I'm a twat" were still loudly emblazoned on his head.'

John Birch guitars are now known worldwide, and are thought by many to be the best on the market.

Travelling on to Germany with Roger Chapman's band Streetwalkers in support, Sabbath played in Ludwigshaven on 1 November, arriving the next day in Dusseldorf – scene of their spectacular punch-up at the Why Not club.

A gig at an American force base in Frankfurt erupted into wild scenes of chaos. For Dave, it was like his first night at Southampton all over again: 'There was trouble from the word go. We had people trying to get over the barriers on to the stage and just ruining the show for everyone. We had guys fighting all over the place. The band just played on through it all. I remember Ozzy appealing to the audience to "Cool it!" more than once, but they paid no attention.'

† † †

Back at the farmhouse, Ozzy had an accident on his trail bike and injured his back muscles, so Sabbath had to call off a short tour of the UK that had been booked for November. He was back in good health in time for a two-week American tour, and the band set off on 1 December 1975. Days later, the band were introduced to a theatrical young band called Kiss, who would be playing with them at a gig in New York state.

Graham was not thrilled by the confrontational demands of the support act. He had never encountered such an attitude and, looking back, he can see it as his first small experience of the music industry's move towards the corporate and ruthless promotion that operates today:

In the morning, we were setting up the Sabbath backline as normal when four semi-tractor trailers, each emblazoned with the word KISS, drew up outside the venue. I was inside at the time, in the empty hall, taking photos of our set-up. Suddenly, a huge security guy came out of nowhere and ripped my camera out of my hand. 'Kiss is in the building – therefore photography is banned,' he snarled, just as I caught my first glimpse of singer and bassist Gene Simmons walking across the stage, without make-up.

It was very unusual for a support band to be laying down the law, and worse was to follow. This band were taking no prisoners. They complained that because of the positioning of our backline, they did not have enough room to set up. We had, rather generously, allowed them twelve feet on this relatively small stage, and so we told them they would simply have to cope. There followed a series of unpleasant arguments and calls to their management, after which Kiss threatened to pull out of the gig and their crew starting packing the gear away. They had just about finished when we informed their stage manager that we had moved Sabbath's backline back by another two feet.

And so the Kiss crew began emptying the truck again, bringing the equipment back into the auditorium – memorably, they were only using half of one of their four trailers – and the gig went ahead. Seemingly, they failed to notice that we hadn't moved our backline an inch.

Kiss were supporting again in Boston a day or two later, and posters had been pasted up outside the venue advertising their appearance but not mentioning Sabbath. This would have been infuriating had it not been for the fact that some bright spark had changed the 'K' in Kiss to a 'P'.

Black Sabbath had already played the most important gig of the tour at the ultra-prestigious Madison Square Garden arena in New York City, supported by Aerosmith. It took place on 3 December – Ozzy's twenty-seventh birthday, and it turned out to be one of Sabbath's most memorable gigs, for better and for worse, as Dave recalls:

> I was setting out the band's refreshments for the performance when I saw this big, black object bouncing off the side of the stage, which was about fifteen feet high. Someone had jumped from the balcony behind the stage area and tried to land roughly where I was standing. He misjudged the distance and broke his neck when he hit the floor, and the last I saw of him, the poor soul was being stretchered out of the hall to a waiting ambulance.

Sabbath were still in their dressing room, and Aerosmith, who had finished their set, were in theirs. There was no interaction of any kind between the two bands.

And then it was showtime. No sooner had Sabbath launched into their first number than Tony Iommi was hit on the head by a full can of beer, lobbed from the crowd. The band stopped temporarily while a doctor put some tape stitches over his wound. Meanwhile, Dave and

Luke – who had returned to the crew now that Patrick Meehan had gone – were down in the audience having a 'sharp word' with the culprit.

Things could only get better, and they did, apart from Ozzy clowning around with 'Black Sabbath', replacing the words, 'Oh no, please God, help me!' with 'Oh no, please God, get that chip pan on!' He always did like his chips, Ozzy.

The New York crowd loved Sabbath, and they went wild when Ozzy was presented with an enormous birthday cake, organized by the promoter Howard Stein. Some stagehands brought it on half-way through the set, and just as they rested it on the floor in front of Oz, the top of the cake burst open. Out jumped a young girl dressed in a devil's outfit with fishnet stockings and a big, black tail sticking out from behind. Black candles flickered around the middle of the tiered cake and as the girl leaped out, she rather spoiled her entrance by burning her backside on one of the candles. Ozzy laughed his head off.

After the show, Howard treated the band to a meal at a posh Indian restaurant, located on the sixth floor of what looked like an office block, remembers Dave: 'It was a wonderful place. As you got out of the elevator, you were greeted by a massive statue of Buddha at the restaurant door. You could watch the chefs working behind glass panels, and the poppadums were puffed up like flying saucers.'

While the band – and Dave – were feasting like kings, the road crew were still trying to get the equipment out of the venue. Graham, Spock and Les had had a difficult and frustrating day, since Madison Square Garden was subject to the authority of the stagehands' union, IATSE as Graham explains:

We couldn't touch our own equipment. We could only supervise the venue's stagehands, who had a different way of doing things. After the show, they immediately took a break and refused to let us load out. To add insult to injury, it was about minus ten degrees that night in New York. It was 6.00am before we got away from the Garden. I should point out that many other venues operated by the union presented us with no problems at all. Soon after this, the rules were relaxed at Madison Square Garden, and our future visits there were always a pleasure.

As the weary crew retired to the hotel, the band were sleeping off their sumptuous meal. 'There was nothing Sabbath liked better than a good curry, although Indian restaurants were very few and far between in America in the mid-seventies,' says Dave. 'No matter what city we went to, we would always go straight to the Yellow Pages in search of a Ruby Murray house.'

Ozzy certainly appreciated his customary vindaloo: America in December 1975 was in the grip of the worst snowstorms and hard frost it had seen for many years. The Ohio River had frozen over and Buffalo, in upstate New York, was officially declared a disaster area. The tour headed south the next day, but even Florida had not escaped the bad weather – it snowed in Miami for the first time in fifty-two years. Somehow, it didn't seem so bad to be returning to the shivery Christmas weather in England.

13

ATROCITY COTTAGE

Ozzy always said he bought the farmhouse because it was near a pub – about 200 m further along the road. He used to joke that it would have been cheaper to buy the pub, but he was wrong there; it would have been cheaper to buy the brewery.

His house was a beautiful, four-bedroom property at the end of the wonderfully named Butt Lane, with a sign on the gates reading 'The End'. Set in acres of idyllic Staffordshire countryside, it was fairly modest by today's rock star standards, although its £25,000 price tag was a great deal of money back then. It had a large conservatory to one side, and with the addition of the studio at the back, it took on a long L-shape. Parked nearby was a traditionally painted gypsy caravan. The extensive rear garden boasted a pine sauna and solarium, and beyond it was a large field known as Oflag 14, which housed the chicken shed. Ozzy owned a second field of several acres about half a mile from the house, where he allowed the local football team to practise and play. At the top of that field was a copse and a big pond, continually replenished by a natural spring.

Ozzy, Thelma, Elliot, Jessica and Louis shared their home with a veritable menagerie. 'It's like Daktari in our garage,' cracked Ozzy, who has recently become legendary as a pet owner and poop scooper in *The Osbournes* television show. 'There's animals all over the place.'

They included two Irish Setters, Gilligan and Shaun. The latter liked nothing better than a doze in the middle of the road outside the house, which was where he met his unfortunate end. The family also had a mynah bird called Fred, whose cage sat on top of the washing machine.

He became expert at mimicking the machine in action, with its worn, screechy bearing.

The house always had a nice vibe about it. It was homely and lived in, and it was here that Ozzy Osbourne, crown prince of heavy metal, became plain John Michael Osbourne, family man. Ozzy loved to be out on tour or recording an album in some exotic location, but he was also a man who loved his home and family and missed them terribly when he was away. He would always look forward to getting back to the farmhouse, and Dave, for one, has seen him sitting in his living room in front of a great log fire with a pipe and slippers. Which is not to say he didn't have his rock'n'roll moments . . .

Ranton had been a peaceful part of the country until 'The Ozzman' arrived. He certainly kept the neighbours in gossip, although he was well liked in the community. Even the local policeman, Peter, would drop by from time to time in his white Mini van for a cup of coffee. Most people were pleased and even impressed to be living so near to a celebrity, and they made no complaints about the regular groups of fans who would turn up in the hope of catching a glimpse of him.

Dave's predecessor had lived at the farmhouse with the family, arranging Ozzy's personal affairs, driving him here and there, taking him to the pub and getting the beers in, and generally being a manservant on call twenty-four hours a day.

Dave met him once while working with Necromandus on Sabbath's spring 1973 UK tour:

He looked like a cross between Jimmy Hill and the American actor and comedian Steve Martin. Oz told me, 'I had to sack him, Dave. He's been wandering around our house bollock naked. I wouldn't mind, but he's hung like a stallion, so I said to my missus, "He's got to go."' Sadly, history doesn't record what the 'missus' had to say about it.

I discovered that this guy had been a disciple of the Maharishi Mahesh Yogi, The Beatles' one-time guru, and had spent quite a bit of time out in India where it was cool to wander about as nature intended.

The end of the 1975 American tour, with all of its breakneck speed and excitement, found the band dropping down about six gears to enjoy Christmas with their families. It was then that Ozzy invited Dave to move into the farmhouse:

I was now Personal Assistant to Ozzy Osbourne, the Wild Man of Rock, the Devil's Emissary and the Prince of Darkness – a nickname that was resurrected by me, having read that description of Vincent Price in *Sounds* magazine. I had entered a jet-set world of first class hotels and flash cars. This was life in the fast lane; I'd been used to the bus lane.

At the same time, there was a great sense of being part of a team. Sabbath had reached the heights of success, they were received with adulation wherever they performed, but they were very much in touch with themselves. They were not prima donnas, and they never treated us as 'staff'. We worked with them, not for them.

Their internal relationships seemed pretty equal, although Ozzy and Bill liked to clown around together, and Tony and Geezer had a close connection through the songwriting. The regular road crew were a great bunch of guys, always on hand if you needed anything. Everyone seemed to pull together, each person doing their bit. We were all professionals; we put the job before anything else. I got on well with everyone, although Graham and I shared a bond in being from the north.

Off the road, the four members of Sabbath kept themselves to themselves for the most part; they did not live in each other's pockets, partly because they weren't next-door neighbours but also because they spent months cooped up together on the road and in the studio, and needed some personal space when they had time off. It was rare for any other band members to visit Ozzy when they were resting, recalls Dave:

If they did turn up, it would be for a business meeting rather than a social gathering. Bill and Ozzy would sometimes meet up socially, and they would all talk quite regularly on the phone. Bill looked on Sabbath as a family and treated everyone associated with them as relatives. He is one of the most caring, sincere people I have ever met. He was a rock for everybody, you could always depend on him, even if he was usually the stooge for everyone else's practical jokes.

His telephone bills were astronomical. Ozzy once said he was going to buy him a gold phone. Bill would often ring to find out if you were in or not – and if you answered, he would say, 'I'll call you back in fifteen minutes now that I know you're there.' This sort of thing was endearing. Bill was never complicated; he was almost fatherly in a funny sort of way. I'm sure his telephone calls were to reassure himself that everything was OK and that his extended family was there for him.

† † †

Life at the farmhouse was rarely dull. Ozzy's voice was just as massive at home as it was onstage. He must have hit a hundred decibels as he paced the rooms, yelling to various members of the family, remembers Dave:

> He could actually change the channel on the TV by shouting at it. He would scream, 'Lamot!' – a brand of lager – and the TV would hop to the next channel. It must have been the pitch or the vibration, but it had to be seen to be believed. I used to be in stitches when he called for Thelma in the style of Fred Flintstone, swapping the 'Wiiiiiilma!' for 'Theeeeeelma!'
>
> I was made to feel part of the family for the whole time I lived there. I normally slept in the studio extension on a big, comfy sofa. On other nights, everyone just slept where they fell. Thelma was very welcoming to me. She was a great cook and a devoted mother. She had to put up with quite a lot because Ozzy liked a drink, and

sometimes when you like a drink, other things get neglected. But Ozzy always missed Thelma and the kids when he was away on tour throughout the early Seventies. He got desperately homesick, and he would regularly call her from America. He never hid anything from Thelma. He was pretty honest in everything he did and, for her part, she realized that he was never going to change. 'He was not a get-out-of-bed-and-roll-a-joint type of character, but he did have a "playroom" at Atrocity Cottage. This was in the studio annexe, well away from the main part of the house and the day-to-day life of the family.'

On one occasion, he had a bag of coke sent up from London. It was probably very pure. After doing quite a few lines, he suddenly started to get paranoid, grabbed the bag and emptied it down the toilet. Ten minutes later, he regretted it and was on the phone arranging a replacement supply. This was typical of Ozzy and his love-hate relationship with the drug. He did have his binges, and yet there were times, especially when he was working, that he wouldn't bother with drugs at all.

Ozzy had a mixed-up lifestyle and his survival technique was quite simple. He created an alter ego, and as the years went by, this character turned into 'Ozzy Osbourne, wild man of rock' as opposed to plain John Michael Osbourne, son of Jack and Lillian. John M. Osbourne was and is a decent, honest bloke who calls a spade a spade and would mix as easily with regular working people and fans as he would with rock celebrities. Ozzy Osbourne, on the other hand, is explosive, in your face, a master of shock and horror who has mellowed not at all over the years; he is still riding the rollercoaster he jumped on in 1968 when he first set out on his journey.

There have been occasions when Ozzy Osbourne and John M. Osbourne have been at loggerheads, and there have been bumpy times when one of the characters is in the process of turning into the other. Thelma had come to expect the unexpected from Ozzy and, for the most part, she handled the situation realistically.

Luke also has fond memories of her: 'Thelma was well-educated, level-headed and friendly when you got to know her. I saw her as an anchor to Ozzy's wayward ways, and someone who gave the kids as normal a childhood as is possible when you're living with Ozzy. She was the most independent of the ladies, and she kept in touch with the friends she knew before she met Ozzy.

Ozzy rounded off most nights at the local pub, the Hand & Cleaver. Locally, it was known affectionately as the Hand & Claypit. He got on really well with the landlord, Richard – unsurprisingly, since he was probably his best customer. He would drink as many pints as he could as quickly as possible and usually fall asleep at the table, or the bar. As usual, Dave was there:

> Another of the regulars was a television personality called Shaw Taylor. He presented a Midlands television show called *Police 5*, which was a forerunner to the BBC's *Crimewatch*. Ozzy and I used to plot to steal Shaw's Jaguar, giggling at the idea of him having to report the theft of his own car. Fortunately for him, and us, we never got past the planning stage.
>
> Sometimes we ventured further afield to an old-fashioned pub called The Anchor, an Ansells brewery house beside a canal where the guvnor, Graham, poured the beer straight from the barrel in the cellar. One night, he sampled too many of his own wares and fell down the stairs into the cellar. He did manage to drag himself back up, whereupon he wished us goodnight, lurched off to bed and left us to serve ourselves. A big mistake.

✝ ✝ ✝

One day, Ozzy decided on the spur of the moment to go to Edgbaston, Birmingham, to catch up with some old friends. Dave drove him, Thelma and the kids to the home of Christopher and Stephanie Sedgwick, and after a while, Ozzy suggested that the guys take a run out to Aston for a look around the old place:

The idea was to have a bit of fun, but we did take the odd detour down memory lane, and Ozzy grew a little nostalgic as he pointed out places of interest. The first stop was 14 Lodge Road, his childhood home. He talked a bit about the cramped conditions in the house, and then he took us to the pub he used in the Sixties. It never took long for a pub to enter the equation.

Its nickname was the Rat Pan, and it did indeed manage to live down to our expectations. The characters we met were a motley crew indeed. One bloke, standing at the bar sporting a woolly bobble hat, had clearly pissed himself. A young lad was on his knees in the toilet, being violently sick into the pan. I asked if he was all right, and he said, 'Yeah, I've just had a bad pint.' By my reckoning, he'd had about a dozen of them.

The pub was filled with the sweet smell of marijuana coming from a bunch of Jamaican guys in their sixties who were laughing, joking and playing dominoes. One was smoking a pipe with a huge bowl. I asked him what was in the pipe. He looked up from the dominoes, eyes rolling in his head, chuckled to himself and said, 'Co-operative Black Twist' [a cheap pipe tobacco].

The pub's nickname harked back to the time when the government put a bounty on rats' tails, due to an explosion in their population. Anyone killing a rat took its tail to the rat pan as evidence, where they would be paid for it.

'We finished our pints,' continues Dave, 'and headed on to a place called the Ickquick Club. We were the only white people in there, and the vibes were so bad that we drained our glasses quickly and left. Aston was a rough place in those days. It would have been an ideal urban warfare training ground for the SAS.'

The good people of Stafford were a more genteel breed, although one of the farmers who lived near Ozzy was an unusual character by anybody's standards. Dave came across him for the first time when he was driving to Stafford railway station to pick up some guests of Ozzy's:

I came round a bend in the Range Rover and saw a huge branch blown into the middle of the road. I jumped out of the motor and started to drag it off the road, and that's when I noticed a tractor parked in the neighbouring field. The driver was standing at the back wheel taking a leak. Nothing especially odd about that, except this person was wearing a floral dress under an anorak and was sporting a floppy hat with a huge feather sticking out of it. If this was a woman, she had obviously perfected quite an unusual trick.

The driver got back on the tractor and headed in my general direction showing, for the first time, a full, bushy beard. I thought I might have been having a hallucination. But just in case I hadn't imagined it, I told Ozzy about the encounter when I got back to the house. He said, 'Oh, I know who you mean. He's a transvestite.'

Although this bloke liked to plough the fields and scatter in a pretty frock, Ozzy was concerned that I hadn't upset him as, appearances to the contrary, he was a tough guy.

Nothing frightened this bloke, but even he would've been taken aback by Ozzy's private arsenal of weapons. He had more guns than the Royal Artillery. His utility room was stacked with pump-action shotguns, crossbows, high-powered rifles, catapults, swords . . . he even had a medieval spiked metal ball on a chain.

'The first time he showed me this array of armaments, I asked him, "Are you expecting trouble?" He just laughed,' says Dave. 'He had a shotgun licence which covered his weaponry – although the spiked ball might have been an exception.'

Despite the heavy artillery, there was a strange tranquillity about the farmhouse. It was as if the local birds knew better than to fly over this Bermuda triangle where they had every chance of being blasted into eternity. No bird had safe passage over this particular airspace. Even Ozzy's chickens would get a warning volley fired over their heads if they refused to lay. The lucky ones were those that had produced a couple of fine free-range eggs by the next morning. Dave would be a witness to the great chicken atrocity which took place in the summer of 1976:

> The chickens had not laid anything for three consecutive days, and Ozzy had fired the warning shots over their heads. I was indoors when I heard the shotgun going off. I stepped outside and there was Ozzy focusing his sights on the chicken run. The next thing I knew, there were blood and feathers all over the place. He shot four chickens, and scared the rest of them shitless. Dennis Armstrong, who lived next door, was in his garden at the time. He famously said to Ozzy, 'Unwinding, are we, John?'
>
> It was then that the farmhouse was christened Atrocity Cottage. It was nothing unusual to be watching television in the living room only to be disturbed by the sound of shotgun fire. I remember one Sunday evening, lazily watching *Songs of Praise* when I heard the bangs of Ozzy's five-shot, pump-action, twelve-bore shotgun. He had sent a wood pigeon to meet its maker prematurely.

Ozzy's gun-lust wasn't sparked by any desire to live up to his reputation as the Wild Man of Rock. He was more interested in cultivating a country squire image, remembers Dave: 'He bought a pair of Westley Richards handmade shotguns, tailored to his own specifications, and he went to Birmingham to have them fitted to suit the length of his arms. These guns cost a small fortune. Every detail on them was unique, and they came in their own leather carry-case.'

But if Ozzy sought to impress his neighbours and generally succeeded, he made at least one mistake. Sabbath's friends the Climax Blues Band, who lived in the area, were rehearsing for a new album in Ranton village hall one day. The local vicar, passing by, heard music coming from the hall and called in to ask the band if they would give a charity concert for the church roof fund.

They were happy to oblige and suggested that the vicar might contact another of his parishioners, singing star John Osbourne, who lived in Butt Lane. The vicar hurried off to the farmhouse but arrived at an inopportune moment. The distinguished, silver-haired gentleman with the dog collar and silver cross around his neck was confronted by the sight of Ozzy blasting at the heavens with a twelve-bore repeating shotgun.

Oz ignored the presence of the clergyman and carried on blazing away. Needless to say, his visitor left the premises tutting and shaking his head, never to return. At any other time, Ozzy would, of course, have agreed to do a charity gig for the community; he was very benevolent that way. But when he was in a gun-toting mood, nothing could distract him, explains Dave:

We arrived back at the house one night after several pints of best bitter at the Hand & Claypit. It was quite late. Oz decided to go shooting in his fields, and I didn't join him because I had an appointment in Birmingham the next morning. Ozzy vanished into the night in full Elmer Fudd hunting regalia – deerstalker hat, tweeds, duck call and a bottle of Famous Grouse Scotch whisky in his jacket pocket. It was freezing, and I was sure he would be back within the hour.

The next morning, when I was making tea and toast in the kitchen, I looked out at the frost on the ground and noticed that the Range Rover wasn't there. I went through to the living room to find Oz stretched out on the couch still dressed in his hunting gear. He smelled of something stagnant, and there was frogspawn stuck on his hat. I shook him and asked where the Range Rover was. He muttered something about the field and promptly fell back into unconsciousness.

I pulled one of the trials motorbikes out of the garage and set off for the field to investigate. Finally, I spotted a glistening roof reflecting in the cold, morning sunlight. The Range Rover was in the middle of the big pond, surrounded by water at least three feet deep. On closer inspection, I spotted the empty whisky bottle on the dashboard. A local farmer called Arthur – thankfully dressed as a man – came to the rescue. He fetched a tractor, and three hours later, we had managed to drag the motor out of the boggy lagoon. Obviously, I had missed my appointment in Birmingham.

I don't think Thelma was around to find her husband with his frogspawn halo, although she would have been used to seeing him slumped in the back of the Range Rover, sleeping off the night before. This happened quite often during the time that the band were having to deal with all their legal and business problems. Ozzy would get a buzz from blagging a bottle of vodka from Sabbath's top-flight solicitor John Wood, and he would drink it as I drove him back up north to the farmhouse, usually demanding several stops on the hard shoulder to relieve his bladder. By the time we arrved at Atrocity Cottage, he would be flat out on tbe back seat and a team of wild horses would not have been able to drag him out of the car.

It was worrying to leave him out there, but there was nothing else for it. If I did manage to rouse him, he would just mumble, 'Get me a sleeping bag,' which I'd throw over him. When he talked to me about this in his sober moments, he'd always say, 'Make sure I'm laying face down, just in case I vomit.' He wasn't convinced that he would be better off forcing himself to get out of the Range Rover and into the house, to bed.

Thelma, for her part, had a great sense of humour, but if she knew there was a heavy session on the cards at the house, she'd leave us to get on with it. Sometimes she took the kids to visit her parents. She was certainly not at home at the time of the great chicken atrocity, or during any of Ozzy's wildlife shoots. He would never have dared to do anything like that in front of his family; they would have given him a very bad time. He burned down the dog kennel a couple of days later and told Thelma that he had discovered rats living in the kennel and the chicken run. This explanation took the heat off the chicken massacre. I always thought that things like this were his way of releasing pressure. In those days, anything could happen.

Ozzy was an extrovert, and he was usually performing. It fulfilled a need in him. Ozzy had to be centre stage at all times. He

Spock Wall stands nervously near the chicken shed at the back of Atrocity Cottage.

Butt Lane in Staffordshire – the home of Atrocity Cottage.

Ozzy getting ready
to 'encourage'
the chickens to lay.

Ozzy and Thelma
at home.

Summerville House
in Malvern, Bill's country
residence.

© David Tangye

Fields Farm, the
roadies' retreat.

© Les Martin

Bill and
Graham Wright.

Author's collection

MIAMI 1976

Bill at the mixing desk during the recording of *Technical Ecstasy*.

Bill makes a rare balcony appearance at the Thunderbird Hotel.

Ozzy says,
'It's party time.'

Ozzy and Graham
celebrate when
fresh supplies
of Newcastle
Brown Ale
arrive in Miami.

Graham and
Ozzy outside
Criteria Studios.

Bill and Graham
chill out at the
end of recording
Technical Ecstasy.

Ozzy back home relaxing.

At the Kansas City Holiday Inn, November 1976. *Left to right:* Albert Chapman,
Bill Ward, Tony Iommi, Geezer Butler, Ozzy Osbourne and Dave Tangye.

Relaxing at the Waldorf Astoria in New York.
Left to right: Dave, Ozzy, Geezer and Luke who was back with the band.

loved having people around him and he was, I suppose, a bit of a show-off in a likeable way. He was quite mad, and I enjoyed his company immensely. We seemed to spark off each other.

There were times, however, when Ozzy's usual high spirits and humour would desert him. He would sink into pensive or gloomy moods, seemingly carrying the whole weight of the world on his shoulders, and he would sit really quietly, as if in a trance. He wasn't normally a miserable twat, and whenever I found him in his sort of state, I'd ask if he was having a full wobbler or just half a wobbler, and he would quite often snap out of it. When you're in your twenties, you're not down for long. He could have real wobblers as well, petulant or angry outbursts, that would subside as suddenly as they'd started.

Black Sabbath was a huge learning curve for Ozzy, and it could seem limiting to him at times. He was and is an instinctively creative person. He used to tell me that, no matter what, he was a 'survivor'. He talked to me about how he would like to do his own album, about the ideas he had for it, how he would like to put them down on tape and record the way he wanted to himself.

Like the rest of the band, he was under a lot of strain at times. The travelling alone could be exhausting, and there were always financial responsibilities to think about.

In other moments, he could be easy-going and great fun. He would take great pleasure in showing you the things that he had, and in sharing the ups and down of his life.

Ozzy sometimes managed to injure himself with his weapons. He once bought a large Bowie knife in a shop in Keswick. Back at Atrocity Cottage, he started showing it off, explaining how the blade was honed on a diamond sharpening machine for the finest cutting edge. Twenty minutes later, we were sitting in the casualty department at Stafford Hospital while a doctor wrapped a turban-sized bandage round Ozzy's thumb.

In a typical act of generosity towards his neighbours, Ozzy once invited a local farmer to sow a crop of barley in one of his fields. There was only one complication: it was the same field used by the football team. Ozzy had previously advised the team that if and when he wanted to plant the land, they would have to take the goalposts down so that the tractor could plough the field. Weeks turned into months and still there was no sign of the goalpost removal squad. One lovely summer's evening after a lavish barbecue, Ozzy assembled a task force to remove the offending items.

'We had no tractor and trailer, not even picks and shovels,' says Dave, 'but we were armed with what Ozzy affectionately called his levelling irons – his twelve-bore, pump-action shotguns. The goalposts crumpled to the ground in seconds in a hail of lead-filled BB cartridges. We blasted them to smithereens; we must have pumped at least a hundred rounds into them.'

Apart from the goalposts and the local fauna, there were no other victims of Ozzy's trigger-finger – except for Eric. Eric was the stuffed bear who stood in the vestibule between the conservatory and the home studio. He was a fearsome-looking grizzly, with huge, outstretched arms that frightened people to death, not least Ozzy. One night, in a blaze of lead, the bear got it. Ozzy gunned Eric down where he stood, claiming that, 'I thought he was a burglar.' Most people around Oz believed he had been meaning to do it for some time.

The threat of gunfire never deterred Ozzy's visitors. There was always someone dropping into Atrocity Cottage for a beer and a chat, and they usually went home with some extraordinary tales to tell. Dave watched it all happen. And as he did, he came to understand more about Ozzy, the man behind the myth, his changing moods and the depths of personality masked by his outwardly exuberant behaviour.

14

TROUT MASK REPLICA

The party went on for three days. It was New Year's Eve and Ozzy had arranged a celebration in his studio at Atrocity Cottage.

Dave had returned from a family Christmas in Cumbria with a posse of pals including the Necromandus lads – Dennis McCarten, Frank Hall and Baz Dunnery – and his best mates Ian Walsh and Geoff Sharpe. Dave and Geoff had worked together with Necromandus. Also in their company was a cabaret singer called Don Mackay. Luke, Spock and Les Martin were present and correct, Led Zeppelin's John Bonham made an appearance, and so did Keith 'Evo' Evans, a roadie with the West Midlands heavy metal band Judas Priest. Thelma Osbourne joined in the party spirit enthusiastically while the kids stayed in the main part of the house with child-minders, safely away from the mayhem and noise in the soundproofed studio.

Ozzy got things going with some home-brewed wine in bottles labelled with a skull and crossbones. He announced that it was elder-berry wine 'with tincture of red Leb [cannabis] matured with Thai stick'. It would have put King Kong to bed. One clever dick fed tequila to the mynah bird. Ozzy said he found it pissed as a parrot, lying on the bottom of its cage singing Mexican love songs.

The revellers shuttled backwards and forwards between the farm-house and the Hand & Cleaver. In those days, there was no such thing as all-day opening; there were very slight regional variations, but in Ranton, the pubs were only allowed to serve between 11.00am and 3.00pm, and then again from 5.30pm to 10.30pm. Ozzy and his guests didn't miss a single session. They were at the doors every time they opened, and they literally drank the pub dry.

Life quietened down for a short while after the great New Year bash, but things never stayed still for long at Atrocity Cottage. Ozzy would leap on any excuse for a party, and on one memorable occasion – for Dave especially – he decided to host a grand Saturday barbecue. This would also give him the chance to show off his latest toy. Oz was into technology, and he had spent around a thousand pounds on a new quadrophonic sound system from one of the high street stores in Stafford.

Dave pointed out to Ozzy that to get the full effect of a quadrophonic sound system, you needed quadrophonic records to play on it. All of Ozzy's records were in stereo format. He waved aside this observation, insisting that it didn't matter – by the time the guests had necked a few glasses of his home-brewed wine, nobody would know their arse from their elbow.

The people from the hi-fi shop arrived at Atrocity Cottage to install the massive sound system in Ozzy's studio. They brought about five miles of cable to hook all the stuff together, there were wires and plugs everywhere, and it took three hours to get it all set up, but it was worth it. The sound was incredible.

On the day of the gathering, Ozzy put speaker cabinets in the garden and loaded up the barbecue with his usual generosity. He never did anything by half. He must have bought a cow, a pig, a sheep and about half a mile of sausage to ensure that everyone had a great feast. Dave agreed, with some trepidation, to be the DJ:

After an hour of head-scratching, I finally worked out how to make this monster hi-fi work. Ozzy brought everyone into the studio for the ceremonial switch on but the only quadrophonic record we had was *Mantovani's Strings*, which had been brought by the installers to demonstrate the system. It was definitely not a party mover.

By 10.30pm, the guests were all well out of their heads on various intoxicants and suddenly the whole sound set-up crashed. I couldn't get a squeak out of it. I was trying frantically to find the fault, leaning over the back of this huge system, when a voice started booming in my ear: 'Oi! Why's the music gone off?'

Without looking round, I said, 'I think a fuse has blown.'

'You think!' thundered the voice. 'You're not paid to think! Just fix the fucking thing.'

This guy was being very unreasonable, but I didn't want to upset any of Ozzy's guests. I turned round to see who was giving me all this verbal and, lo and behold, it was John Bonham. I told him: 'Number one, I'm not an electronics engineer, and number two, I don't fucking work for you.'

He backed off and quickly asked, 'OK, where do I find the home-brew?' I pointed him towards the kitchen. The sound burst back into life as Bonham staggered off purposefully towards the kitchen.

Some of the people who turned up at the farmhouse over the years were much stranger than others. One day, an old friend of Ozzy's phoned to say he was touring the country with a Buddhist monk and asked if they could stay over for a couple of days. Typically, Ozzy said, 'No problem.' The pair of hippies arrived a couple of hours later in a battered old VW camper van. Oz offered them a cup of tea and a corned beef sandwich, and they accepted the tea but not the food. Strict vegetarians and believers in reincarnation, they felt that they could be tucking into dearly departed relatives if they were to eat any meat.

The monk, all kitted out in his robes, introduced himself as Dada. Ozzy promptly renamed him Gaga, and listened as the visitor explained the meaning of life before retiring to the studio to polish off half a crate of Newcastle Brown Ale, recalls Dave:

Eventually, we were all as inebriated as the monk and we turned in for the night. I curled up in the living room, trying to stop thinking about the story Ozzy had told about the ghost of an old farmer who had hung himself from one of the beams in this same room many years earlier. I was unnerved by the living room for ever more. I was sure I could feel something cold and eerie about it.

I had a very fitful sleep until, at about 3.00am, Ozzy burst in to tell me that he could smell food. We went to the kitchen and found Gaga, the committed vegetarian, making himself a bacon sandwich. Ozzy was outraged. 'Vegetarian my arse!' he yelled, as his Buddhist monk visitor cringed with embarrassment.

The embarrassment was all Ozzy's on the day that he took his driving test. He was extremely tense about it. He may have been a star performer at massive arenas around the world, but he was far more worried about taking his test than he ever was about going onstage. He had the Rolls brought out of the garage, and for breakfast he had half a Valium and a cup of tea. That did little to calm his nerves, so he polished off half a bottle of vodka, just to be on the safe side. Of course, it was a fatal error. He arrived at the examination centre so completely relaxed that they would not let him take the test.

But that had nothing on Dave's embarrassment on the occasion that he developed an abscess above one of his teeth. He had tossed and turned all night in agony and by the morning, the side of his face had swollen like a football:

I got out of bed early because I couldn't sleep and went down to the kitchen area, where Ozzy and Thelma were already cooking breakfast. They were shocked by my appearance and upset by the fact that I was obviously in so much pain. Thelma called her dentist in Birmingham to get me an emergency appointment that same morning.

Ozzy was typically thoughtful. He assumed the role of dentist-cum-paramedic, and was trying to sort out a cold compress to reduce my pain and swelling. I heard him shouting to Thelma that there was no ice and that he was trying to find something else in the freezer chest. About five minutes later, he returned with a frozen trout and a bandage from the first aid cabinet. 'This will do the trick,' he grinned as he strapped the frozen fish to my jaw. I looked a right pillock, but I didn't mind because no one else would see me. We weren't expecting visitors at that time of the morning.

Oz said, 'Just get in the car and we'll go straight to Birmingham.' I had no sooner walked out of the front door than the postman appeared in the drive; this was awful timing. He had already seen some peculiar sights during his deliveries to Atrocity Cottage, but they were nothing compared to the vision that confronted him now: half-man, half-trout. I felt like some sort of heavy metal mermaid. To his credit, he showed no surprise, simply asking, 'What's up?'

I said, 'I've got an abscess.'

He looked at me: 'Well, I think its gone septic – it's got a big green head on it.' He laughed uproariously, and I nearly cried.

✝ ✝ ✝

Despite the parties and a short string of UK tour dates replacing the ones they had to cancel in November when Ozzy injured his back, the early months of 1976 were gloomy ones for Black Sabbath. All the talk was about the impending High Court case brought against them by former manager Jim Simpson. Dave remembers numerous trips to the London office of the band's solicitors, where they sat through lengthy meetings.

Simpson was alleging that although he had guided the band from obscurity to stardom, he had not been able to reap the benefits of his hard work when they left his company. He was suing the four members of the group for breach of contract, and was also claiming damages from Patrick Meehan and his partner Wilf Pine, saying that they had poached Sabbath from him. All of the defendants contested the action.

Ozzy, Tony, Bill and Geezer attended the High Court when the five day hearing began on 16 March. Their 'learned friend', the barrister, talked points of law and other fine details to 'M'lud', who was conducting the proceedings. The whole thing rambled on and bored everyone shitless.

It was not to have a happy outcome for Sabbath or, especially, Meehan. The band were ordered to pay Jim Simpson £7,500. Meehan, under the terms of the settlement, had to hand over £27,500. The only 'winner' among the defendants was Wilf Pine; no order was made against him. After the hearing, Simpson said that he had sued for money he could have expected to make had Sabbath stayed with him, explaining that he would invest his total of £35,000 in Big Bear Records, which at the time had a £5,000 overdraft.

Sabbath's solicitor John Wood said the band were now anxious to get out of court and back into the studio. In truth, the payment to Simpson was a drop in the ocean to Sabbath, who were said in court to have earned seven million pounds from their career thus far.

True to their word, Black Sabbath started work immediately on their next album.

They had always liked Wales, and had heard of a rehearsal studio called Glasspant Mansion. It turned out to be an old, dilapidated semi-detached near to Newcastle-in-Emlyn. Sabbath stuck it out there for a week, finally packing their bags when they discovered that the rotten floorboards in one of the rooms gave way to a perilous twelve foot drop.

They moved on to Ridge Farm studios in Rusper, Sussex, which have since been hugely improved. In Sabbath's day, the rehearsal room was just a barn, but the whole place had a reassuring ambience about it, and the accommodation was spot-on. Dave and Graham were sharing a large cottage with Ozzy and Bill in the complex beside the barn.

One day, Bill suggested a Chinese takeaway for the evening meal, and Dave and Graham agreed to go into Dorking to pick it up. The band would be coming out of rehearsal at about 9.00pm. Dave and Graham set off at 6.30pm so they could get a couple of pints in beforehand:

We made our way to a pub called the Star & Garter near the railway station and we got talking to the landlord. He told us that Oliver Reed lived close by, and that he often popped in for a beer or two, or a bottle of Scotch.

He had some great stories about the legendary actor and hellraiser. One day, he told us, Ollie was drinking in the bar and he bet one of the locals £500 that he wouldn't do a streak around Dorking on a Saturday afternoon. The phenomenon of streaking had started a couple of years earlier, when it was immortalized by a singer called Ray Stevens with a smash-hit single called, unsurprisingly, 'The Streak'. The guy jumped at the chance to take £500 off Oliver Reed.

The would-be streaker agreed to strip off and leave the pub at 2.00pm on the dot. Oliver Reed flashed a bundle of ten pound notes as he stripped and shot off round the corner like a whippet. Sadly, he didn't make it back to the Star & Garter to win his wager. He was arrested outside the Victoria Wine store in the High Street, just minutes into his run. Reed had phoned the police to say that a man was planning to expose himself in Dorking High Street just after two o'clock, and acting on this information, they made their arrest.

It was a cheery interlude for Dave and Graham, and a couple of pints later they collected the takeaway and headed back to Ridge Farm. Bill and Ozzy had come out of the studio and were sitting in the lounge of the cottage, watching a western on television. Dave and Graham went into the kitchen and started to dish out the food, but there had been a bit of a mix-up. Bill's meal wasn't the one he had ordered.

Ozzy, Dave and Graham took their plates from the kitchen into the lounge to catch the rest of the movie, leaving Bill in the kitchen, effing and blinding to himself. 'We were getting tucked into the grub,' remembers Dave, 'when Bill came charging into the lounge in a blaze of swearing and threw the chicken curry he had been given at the TV screen.

"'Oh, look Bill," quipped Ozzy, quick as a flash. "Now we're watching *The Good, the Bad and the Curry.*"'

The lounge stank of Chinese spices for a week.

† † †

Dave stayed on at Atrocity Cottage while Ozzy and the band enjoyed a month off before the recording sessions for their seventh album were due to begin in sunny Florida. One day, Dave received a phone call from Bill Ward. Bill wanted wrought iron gates for his house in Malvern, and Dave – who had served his time as an apprentice blacksmith – had promised to make them when he had some spare time:

> When I got to Bill's, I thought it was strange that the Christmas decorations were still up. It was now April. Bill just explained that he liked to see a splash of colour about the house. He didn't have a lot of furniture. There was a nice, big lounge with a leather Chesterfield suite and what Bill described as a 'genuine, reproduction, Louis XIV desk and chair'. I wondered how anything could be both genuine and a reproduction, and I couldn't bring myself to ask how much he had paid for it.
>
> Just as we were making our way to Maude's Morgue for a jar or two before dinner, the dray wagon arrived at Bill's back door with that month's supply of cider. He had it delivered direct from the brewery to cut out the middle man!

Dave thoroughly enjoyed the hospitality offered by Bill and his partner Mysti during his stay. 'Mysti was American, and I believe she had been a model at some time. She cooked for us and was incredibly welcoming. I got on as well with her as I did with Bill.'

Dave's iron gates were a great success. He asked Spock Wall to write out the opening notes of 'Paranoid' as they would appear on a musical score. Dave then constructed five bars across the double gates, fashioned a G clef and welded the notes on to the bars. Bill was so pleased that he decided to treat Dave to a session in the pub, although the journey there turned out to be more memorable than the drinks:

We were half way there, travelling in Bill's four wheel drive Land Rover. Suddenly Bill exclaimed, 'Oh shit, I've got no cash!' I had enough for a pint or two, and so we kept on driving. Closer to the pub, Bill spotted someone he knew and asked me to pull over. He leaned out the window and asked the ruddy-faced farmer, 'Do you want to buy this Land Rover? You can have it for fifty pounds.' The farmer was taken aback. He asked, 'Are you sure? it's got to be worth more than fifty pounds.'

Bill insisted, 'I'm desperate, just give me the cash and you can take it.' We drove the man to his farmhouse, picked up the money and cadged a lift from him to the pub. We never saw the Land Rover again.

Bill's generosity was endless, and there were people who would sometimes try to exploit it. After having the new gates installed, Bill wanted to have his kitchen painted. Graham and Dave recommended Denny, a northern friend who was an accomplished painter and decorator and who would appreciate the work. He was also an out of work bass player. Denny was at Bill's doorstep in a flash, paintbrush in hand. He offered to do the job for a very reasonable price plus bed and board, says Graham:

A couple of weeks later, I received a phone call at Fields Farm from Mysti, Bill's wife, telling me that it was taking Denny a long time to paint the kitchen. I went over to see what was happening. When I arrived at Summerville House, I could see that the kitchen was nowhere near finished, and the only sign of Denny was a one-inch paintbrush, sitting all on its own in a jam jar filled with discoloured turpentine.

My instincts told me to look for Denny in Maude's Morgue. Sure enough, he was propping up the bar dressed more like a rock god than a painter and decorator. As I walked towards him, I could hear him telling two old farm labourers all about his life as a rock musician. He had clearly turned into Denny McStardust. I invited him for a drink in Worcester that evening so that I could have a word with him, away from the locality. Bill kindly lent us his Rolls Royce, and we headed for a pub called the Dirty Duck, which was popular with young, trendy kids.

I went straight up to the bar to get the beers in while Denny scoured the room for a likely 'hippy chick' that he could impress and pull. Amazingly, he found her before I'd even paid for the drinks. She was a goth before 'goth' existed, like Morticia from The Addams Family. Denny glued himself to her ringed ear, whispering sweet nothings.

The way he'd parked, Graham had managed to block in several cars, and it was not long before the landlord loudly requested 'the owner of the Rolls Royce' to move his vehicle. As he walked out to attend to it, Graham saw every head turning towards him. A long-haired hippy with a Roller! Whatever next? He returned to the bar:

I decided after about an hour that I would not be able to talk to Denny about his painting job for Bill. He was too far gone, he was engrossed in the lady, and it was time to leave. Morticia left with us. As I revved up the engine of the Rolls, Denny demanded, 'Driver, would you please drop us off at my new friend's house?' I duly took them to the council estate on the outskirts of Worcester where Morticia lived. I said goodnight to Denny, not forgetting to mention that there was a train leaving Worcester at 10.30 am for the north of England, and that he'd better be on it.

I finished Bill's painting myself.

15

MIAMI '76: THE AGONY AND THE ECSTASY

Why they chose Florida, no one knew. In the mid-seventies, it was far from the tourist destination it is today. Walt Disney World Resort, on the outskirts of a small town called Orlando, was in still in its infancy. The state's main claim to fame was as a winter haven for the 'snow-birds' of the northern USA. Hotel prices dropped in the summer, as most Americans avoided it due to the extremes of temperature and the hurricanes. The crew, with typical 'mad dogs and Englishmen' bravado, scoffed that it would take more than a hurricane to keep them away. They would soon be laughing on the other side of their faces.

The equipment was flown to Miami in a freight cargo plane, while the backline crew – Graham Wright, Les Martin and Spock Wall – travelled separately from Heathrow Airport in a United Airlines jumbo. The flight was delayed for two hours because of tropical storms in south west Florida, although that would turn out to be the least of their problems, as Graham recalls:

After a long flight, we were glad to touch down at Miami Inter-national Airport and see the palm trees and the clear blue skies. We received the usual slap in the face from the tropical heat as we disembarked. Entering the immigration hall, we noticed that the other flights seemed to be coming in from south and central America; ours was the only European arrival. As we stood in line waiting to be interviewed by an immigration officer in a glass box, it seemed almost possible that we had landed in the wrong country.

We were surrounded by passengers and officials speaking only Spanish.

A female immigration officer spoke to us in broken English with a heavy Spanish accent; she asked the purpose of our visit to the United States. We said that we were the road crew for the British rock band Black Sabbath, which brought a worried frown to her face. We had come to Miami to record an album, we explained. She made a quick phone call, and two armed guards quickly appeared. They escorted us not to the baggage claim area but to a secure inter-rogation room. I glanced at Les and Spock with their long hair and droopy moustaches, realizing how much they looked like a couple of Contra rebels.

As we sat in the room, we were informed that we were being 'arrested for attempting to enter the USA illegally with the sole purpose of looking for work'. We were travelling on business visas, and our interrogators seemed to think we should have had work permit visas. They couldn't understand that we were there on business, working for a band.

We were immediately marched off, not to prison, amazingly, but to Miami International Airport Hotel. As far as cells go, this was real five star accommodation. We were banged up in a large room with permanently locked windows, three large beds, a colour television, a telephone, an en suite bathroom and air conditioning. The armed guard made himself comfortable in the corner of the room and within minutes, he nodded off. His understanding of English was poor, which was just as well considering the comments we had been making about him.

After watching the detective series *Get Smart* on the TV for about five minutes, we got bored. We dialled room service on the phone and a voice said, 'Hello, can we get you anything, sir?' Twenty minutes later, a trolley laden with booze and food was delivered to the room. We got stuck into the feast and cleared every plate, while our minder slumbered on in the corner.

The next morning, we were taken to a van and driven downtown with our guards glaring at us, assuring us that we would soon be on our way back home. We were interviewed by a rather stunning blonde American customs officer who stamped our passports and set us free in minutes, apologizing profusely for the mistake. She ordered a cab to take us to our original destination, the Thunderbird Hotel on Collins Avenue, North Miami Beach.

We dumped our luggage in our rooms, went straight to the beach and dived into the ocean. Minutes later, a pretty young girl approached us, realizing we were English, and asked, 'Hi, guys, you wanna party?' Yes, we had arrived. During our stay, she went out of her way to make all of us, crew and band members, very welcome to Miami. And we were amazed by her willingness to party all by herself, to put it politely. Her nickname of 'Chairleg' had nothing to do with the finer points of *The Antiques Roadshow*.

Black Sabbath arrived two days after the crew, on Friday 28 May 1976. They had endured a turbulent flight from London Heathrow, which had done nothing to help Bill's fear of flying. On this occasion, the rest of the band were as terrified as him. There's not much you can do when things go wrong in the skies and your life is quite literally in the hands of the pilot. Dave, travelling with Ozzy, remembers:

The plane was being buffeted about like a kite in a hurricane, and lightning was flashing off the wings. As we neared our destination, Ozzy started winding everyone up, announcing that we had entered the Bermuda triangle and might disappear just like all the other missing aircraft that had flown through this particular air corridor.

The pilot announced over the tannoy that we would be diverting to Fort Lauderdale due to strong crosswinds at Miami International. 'We're coming in too fast!' screeched Ozzy as the plane ploughed down towards the landing strip through thunder, lightning and thick, black rain clouds. Safely disembarking in Miami, we immediately felt the oppressive, atmospheric humidity. 'So this is the Sunshine State,' someone muttered.

The entourage travelled to the hotel in a rented station wagon. It was about 8.00pm when they rolled up at reception, only to be confronted by the hotel manager demanding a guarantee of payment for the final bill. The road crew had met with the same hostility, and had to put their rooms on a personal credit card until the finance was sorted out. After a flurry of frantic phone calls, the local Warner Bros representative saved the day and the rooms were secure for the duration of the stay. But the manager never did become any friendlier. He was probably having trouble getting over all the long hair and crucifixes.

† † †

Max the bartender was a lot more fun. He was serving at the Thunderbird's poolside bar where everyone gathered for a 'pre-recording party' to swap their respective stories of the nightmare journey to Miami. Max looked like Dean Martin. Originally from New Jersey, he had moved south for the sunshine. He shook a wicked cocktail, and he reckoned he made the best Pina Colada in south Florida.

He was a real wisecracker. His favourite saying was, 'Hot? I'll tell you how hot it is – I'm wearing jockey shorts, and I'm sure the jockey's still in them.' He took a big shine to the whole entourage, and in an appropriate cultural exchange, they introduced him to the classic hangover cure of lemonade shandy.

The Sabbath party occupied the best part of the fourth floor. Everyone was sharing rooms to keep the costs down, since this had been arranged as a low budget trip.

Warner Bros had agreed to drip-feed money to the band in weekly instalments to cover the running costs, and Bill Ward would organize trips to the bank to collect the cash. The crew acted as bodyguards, and Bill planned their individual roles to the last detail. The cashiers looked distinctly uncomfortable at these regular hippy invasions, possibly suspecting that Bill and his bodyguards were planning a heist.

Dave was in a twin room with Ozzy, 'the worst person in the world to share a room with'.

He was totally hyper. He just could not sit still for more than five minutes. I remember sharing with him once in Philadelphia. He had bought a music box about four inches square with a string attached. When you pulled the string, it played 'Yankee Doodle'. We spent the night drinking in the bar, returning to the hotel room in the early hours. We had an early flight to New York the next day, so I flopped on to my bed and hoped Ozzy would do the same.

The next thing I heard was the music box. After suffering 'Yankee Doodle' for the tenth time, I looked round to see Ozzy propped up in his bed with a huge grin on his face, wearing a daft American sailor's hat. I asked if I could have a look at the music box. When he handed it over, I smashed it against the wall in proper Laurel and Hardy fashion and got back into bed.

Five minutes later, I woke up to the strains of 'London Bridge is Falling Down'. Ozzy had managed to repair the box, and was now playing the B-side of the plastic disc to death. It went on for about half an hour until he finally fell asleep.

I once shared a room with him in a hotel in Wembley. We were in London on business and we had gone to see the Steve Gibbons Band supporting The Who at the Arena. Back at the hotel after the gig, we brought a few friends to the room, including Gibbons' drummer Bob Lamb, for a few drinks and a smoke.

After a while, we heard a humming, chanting noise coming through the walls. Bob said that he had seen members of John McLaughlin's Mahavishnu Orchestra going into the next room. Clearly, they had all locked on to their mantra. Ozzy promptly called room service and ordered a full crate of Guinness for our next-door neighbours, proclaiming that they sounded like they needed a drink.

Ozzy's unpredictable behaviour in hotels meant that there was always the chance he would need some help from his room-mate at the end of the night. After the first day's sessions in Florida, the entourage headed back to Miami Beach and the Thunderbird. They decided to have dinner in Christine Lee's, a Chinese restaurant that was part of the hotel.

With the meal over, everyone read their fortune cookies and then retired to the comfort of the cocktail bar, where the house special was aptly named the Zombie. It was a concoction of seven different Caribbean rums. Ozzy loved them, and polished off about half a dozen in quick succession. Subsequently, he decided to go to bed on the padded bar top. After several complaints from the bar staff, it became obvious that someone would have to move the comatose singer from the bar to his bedroom. Dave drew the short straw, as usual: 'I took the concierge's baggage truck from the lobby and loaded the loaded vocalist on to it. As I manoeuvred it through the reception area, the duty manager looked up briefly, shook his head and carried on about his business. This was taking room service to new heights.'

The next morning Ozzy woke up feeling groggy, and on Dave's advice went down to breakfast to feed his hangover with bacon, eggs, hash browns and toast. Now, there were many unusual characters hanging around the hotel, but none quite as noticeable as a giant of a man with arms like Popeye who leaned on a walking frame as he shuffled about the restaurant. He sat down opposite Ozzy and Dave, his massive hands dwarfing the breakfast plate as he asked Oz if he was a girl or a boy. 'We are English,' Ozzy replied, oddly. With this, the man snapped: 'I once fought a Limey in London; I beat the shit outta him.' Dave remembers the rest of his story:

> He went on to tell us that he had fought the legendary boxing champion Joe Louis, known as 'The Brown Bomber'. He didn't tell us that Louis had knocked him out in the first round, this great giant sat in front of us. He turned out to be King Levinsky, a heavyweight in every sense of the word, who had been a world-class boxer between 1928 and 1939. He had fought some formidable opponents in his time, including Max Baer and Tommy Loughran. He even squared up to the one and only Jack Dempsey in an exhibition bout.

We bumped into him frequently after that. He had retired to Florida, and often came to the hotel in his spare time. Whenever he passed, he would mutter out of the side of his mouth, 'Limey bastards,' and smile.

✝ ✝ ✝

Sabbath were recording what would become *Technical Ecstasy* at Criteria Studios, beginning on Saturday 29 May. The sessions all began around 4.00pm so that the band could work through the night, when it was cooler. Naturally nocturnal creatures, they would be able to hang off the rafters without anyone batting an eyelid, as Graham explains:

On the first day, as we were setting up the equipment, we all sensed a strange vibe coming from the studio personnel. We discovered that they were terrified of us – rumours of Satanism and devil worshipping had preceded our arrival. That all changed pretty quickly when they realized we were down to earth sorts, and we soon got into a routine.

On the way to the studios, we had to cross a metal bridge spanning a causeway. The sound of the tyres made a distinctive rhythm on the metal surface, and Bill would always pick up his drumsticks and tap along in time on the dashboard. We soon renamed it Bill's Bridge – and we later heard the same rhythm used by The Bee Gees in their song 'Jive Talking'. We often wondered if they had been inspired by driving over Bill's Bridge.

Tony Iommi soon decided that he needed a guitar technician to be responsible for his large range of instruments. He appointed someone in England and arranged for him to fly out to Miami. Graham went to collect this guy from the airport:

I stood in the arrivals hall, looking out for the typical roadie type to walk through. The passengers all walked past, but I could not pick out anyone who was even close to the image I had in my mind's eye. I thought that perhaps he may have missed the flight, and so I walked towards the information desk across an almost deserted hall.

Only one person stood between the desk and me. This guy was dressed in a white suit and platform boots, he was sporting a perm, and he had a Panama hat in his hand. As I passed, he gave me a nervous glance and said, 'Hi, I'm Memphis. I'm from Huddersfield.' I had found my passenger.

During the drive to the hotel, he explained to me that he was into martial arts, didn't drink or take drugs, and had previously worked on a Cliff Richard tour. Something told me that poor Memphis was not Sabbath crew material. Within days of his arrival, he had been rechristened; his new name was taken from a karate kick called mawashigeri and shortened to Mushy.

Early the next morning, I was out on my hotel room balcony overlooking the pool, and there was Mushy, stood on the top diving board. Below him, girls were laying out their towels on sunbeds and the pool attendant was clearing away his cleaning equipment and the various chemicals he used to condition the pool. Noticing Mushy, he started waving frantically and shouting, 'No! No! NO!' Too late. Mushy dived. Until that day, I'd never seen anyone jump out of a pool faster than they'd dived in.

The attendant rushed to the aid of a drenched and screaming Mushy, whose eyes were streaming due to the concentration of chlorine in the water. Needless to say, his female audience was not impressed.

We would soon discover how accident prone Mushy really was. On another occasion, he accidentally electrocuted himself by putting his hand in the back of a live amplifier; he broke the three minute mile, hair standing on end, as he shot off round the studio. He wasn't a bad bloke, old Mushy. He was an oddity and everybody laughed at his antics, but he was out of place. There was nothing down for him with this band.

I guess the final straw came when Ozzy threw a bucket of iced water over him as he slept. He jumped up in shock, and Ozzy immediately apologized and offered him his own bed. Half an hour later, as he dozed off in the warm, dry bed, Ozzy gave him a second dousing. Huddersfield beckoned and, alas, Mushy was homeward bound.

The temperature was in the nineties, and everyone was developing deep tans – everyone, that is, except Bill. He wasn't a sun worshipper, and he avoided the daily swimming expeditions, when the band and crew would enjoy a dip in the sea. After Mushy's experience, they didn't trust the chlorine levels in the pool.

Bill never seemed to leave his room much, and he became almost nocturnal. His rare appearances on the balcony of his room would be met with a round of applause from any of the Sabbath entourage who might happen to be looking up from the poolside bar. The other guests would join in the clapping and cheering, thinking that it must have been his birthday. At the end of his eight weeks in Florida, Bill was whiter than when he had arrived.

'We didn't see much of Tony or Geezer either,' recalls Dave, 'except when we drove them and Bill to the studios and back. They were putting down the tracks to which Ozzy would later add his vocals.

Geezer Butler was the band's main lyricist, but Spock used to enjoy jotting down ideas too. One day he took a walk from the studio and sat down in some nearby gardens. He was minding his own business, enjoying the sun and scribbling some lyrics on a scrap of paper, when two police officers approached him and asked what he was up to. Someone had apparently phoned the station to report a long-haired type acting suspiciously in the gardens. Spock explained that he was with the rock band Black Sabbath, who were using the nearby studio. 'Oh,' said one of the officers. 'Are you looking for divine inspiration? This is a cemetery.'

† † †

The studios themselves were seeing plenty of action. It was a very busy facility, with three separate studios, A, B and C. At the time of Sabbath's residence, some of the other acts coming in and out included Fleetwood Mac, The Eagles, Joe Cocker, Stephen Stills and Neil Young, The Bee Gees and KC and the Sunshine Band.

The Eagles were completing their new album, *Hotel California*, and rumours abounded of major disagreements in their ranks. They certainly didn't seem to be getting on well together; they would travel to and from the studios in separate cars. This was completely different to Sabbath's way of working. 'At that time,' says Dave, 'we were a closely knit bunch, and the working atmosphere was friendly. We had a good laugh among ourselves and with everybody we came across.'

On 4 July 1976, the Independence Day public holiday, The Eagles and Fleetwood Mac were among bands appearing at an outdoor festival in front of 120,000 people in Tampa, Florida. It was being held to mark the American bi-centennial celebrations, which were taking place all over the States.

Graham and Dave went to the festival at the invitation of an old friend, an American roadie called Bob McPhee who was then working for Fleetwood Mac. The Fleetwoods had hired a luxury coach belonging to Frank Zappa. It had a painting along the side like that on a Greyhound bus, including the dog – but the word 'Greyhound' had been replaced by 'Fido'. He had a strange sense of humour, Frank.

It was a great day out for everyone. The Eagles, headlining, were incredible, especially since they had to follow a show-stopping performance by Fleetwood Mac. The whole backstage was buzzing, and so were Graham and Dave, who had made the most of their day off at the hospitality tent, as Dave recalls:

After the show, we all headed back to the Ramada Inn where we were staying that night. Everybody was as high as a kite. We checked into our rooms and made a beeline for the bar, which was located by the pool. We were chatting away to our roadie friend Bob when John McVie, Fleetwood Mac's bass player, came over to join us. After being introduced to him, I told him I was Ozzy Osbourne's road manager. He grunted and sat down. The next thing I knew, he'd thrown a pitcher of beer over me. Now, if someone gives me a beer, I like to give them one back, and I certainly returned the favour to John McVie – right over his head.

Suddenly, his own crew picked up his chair, with McVie still in it, and threw him into the swimming pool, to roars of laughter from the onlookers. He climbed out, shook himself and waddled away to his room to get dried off. He looked like a penguin, which was quite appropriate since he famously believed that he was the reincarnation of one and sported a penguin tattoo on his arm.

To this day I have no idea why he started the altercation. Sometimes I wonder if he'd had it in for all of us ever since the day that Ozzy tried to roll the aeroplane round with Fleetwood Mac in it. Maybe it was just the alcohol. Indeed, we all had sore heads as we travelled back to Miami the next day.

The weeks were flying and we made some great friends out there in Florida, although on one particular night, we bumped into some people we would rather not have met . . .

16

THE BLIZZARD BEFORE
THE STORM

It happened just outside Eric Clapton's old house at 461 Ocean Boulevard. The crew had been given the day off for a spot of sightseeing since the album was virtually finished and Sabbath were beginning to relax.

Graham, Dave, Spock, Luke and Les had spent a riotous evening in Fort Lauderdale, crawling the bars, watching live bands and generally over-indulging. Piling back into the station wagon for the homeward journey, they chose to disregard the 55mph speed restriction, and were soon spotted by a highway patrol. Dave vividly remembers the police driver doing a U-turn, lights flashing, crossing the median in the centre of the road and pulling up behind the wagon. The police always pull you over from behind in America; they don't overtake drivers like they do in the UK:

> He made us pull over just outside the address that Clapton immortalized as an album title back in 1974. We could see the two cops in the rear-view mirror as they sat in the car for a while, making us sweat it out. Soon, another patrol car driven by an officer on his own pulled alongside us and parked on the central median. We could see what looked like a shotgun inside the vehicle.
>
> One of the officers in the first car got out with his hand on his revolver, walked up to the station wagon and asked the driver – Spock – for some identification. He duly obliged. We were then ordered out of the wagon. We had to stand with our hands on our heads by the side of the road while we were frisked and the wagon

was searched. Happy that we, and the car, were free of any guns or drugs, the officer turned his attention to us.

We weren't falling-down drunk, but we'd all had a steady amount of alcohol throughout the day. Spock and then Les were asked to take some roadside coordination tests. First, they had to walk down the single white line along the side of the road. Then they were told to bend over backwards and touch their noses with their index fingers, which is hard enough even if you're sober. Les fared better than Spock and the officer told him that he should take over the driving.

Noticing that we were English, the cop asked what our business was in Miami. We told him we were the road crew for Black Sabbath and were here to record an album. Seemingly impressed, he called out to his buddies and relayed this information to them. He then asked if he could call by the hotel the next day for some autographs and maybe a couple of T-shirts and an album if we had any. Of course, we unanimously agreed to this.

The officer decided that it would be in our best interests to have a police escort back to the hotel. Just before we reached the entrance, he flashed his lights to signify a right turn. Les duly made the turn, but not without demolishing the hotel's 'car parking' sign. We ran to our rooms and hid. We kept a low profile the next day too, and so we never did find out if the cop returned for his autographs.

The band had one week left in this tropical haven, and for some of the entourage there was a chance to visit the Everglades and SeaWorld and all the other touristy parts of the area that they hadn't been able to explore. Some of the guys flew their partners out for a short holiday prior to returning to England. Spock's fiancée Carolyn and Les's girlfriend Jan came too. They had express orders to tuck a few cans of Newcastle Brown Ale into their luggage, and they kindly obliged. It's amazing what you miss when you've been away from home for a while.

It was July, and the heat and humidity of the Miami summer were rising on a daily basis. Tony Iommi, Spock Wall and album producer

Robin Black were to stay on for a while, to work on some final additions to *Technical Ecstasy*. Graham and Les were moving on to California with the band's equipment.

The rest of the band, Dave and Luke were looking forward to going home. They knew the UK had been enjoying one of its hottest summers on record, although without the hurricanes and monsoons that had been such a dramatic part of the Sabbath experience. Back on English soil, driving through the countryside, they were stunned at the sight of parched grass in the fields. Even the motorway banking was scorched.

† † †

Graham remembers Ozzy strolling around Miami in a T-shirt bearing the legend 'Blizzard of Ozz'. He also remembers the singer stating that if he ever made a solo album, that would be its title. Graham didn't think anything of it at the time although, in retrospect, it was the first sign of something new and different entering Ozzy's vision for the future. Dave was receiving the same signals. Ozzy disclosed to him that he wanted to get a solo band together when he returned from Miami, just for the experience of working with different musicians and trying out ideas that might not fit into the Black Sabbath framework.

Like Graham, Dave saw nothing ominous in this and suggested that Ozzy could invite the former members of Necromandus down from Cumbria to Stafford. They would be ideal – they had played together for a long time, and they and Ozzy knew and liked each other. They were all accomplished musicians, too. Ozzy liked the idea and asked Dave to make the arrangements. The Necromandus lads were all quite keen to give it a shot, and Dave agreed to collect them.

Three days after he returned from Miami, Dave left Atrocity Cottage for his hometown of Egremont. First, of course, he called on his mum. Then he rounded up guitarist Baz Dunnery and drummer Frank Hall. Bassist Dennis McCarten was the final pick-up, since he had moved to Birmingham:

174

We got the studio ready for the rehearsals. Ozzy had loads of speaker cabinets and amps, Frank brought his drums, and I set up the Revox tape recorder through the PA system to make sure we had a record of what went down. The sessions went well for a couple of days, but everything soon began to fizzle out in a blur of alcohol. I think the Necromandus guys were in awe of Ozzy, and whatever he suggested they went along with. This included visits to the Hand & Cleaver for a pint or ten on every occasion that it was open. Ozzy was up to his antics, and the whole project turned into a huge piss-up.

At some point, Ozzy's wife Thelma decided that it would be a good time to go and visit her family. She was right. The shenanigans carried on for days, as Dave remembers:

We came back from the pub one night and Ozzy said he would make us all something to eat. He looked in the fridge to see what he could rustle up, but ruefully reported back, 'There's fuck all in there. I thought we had some chicken pieces.' Seconds later, he was out in the garden with a huge, scimitar-style sword, running straight for the chicken coop, which always meant trouble. Within twenty minutes, he had beheaded, disembowelled, plucked and cut up two chickens. The pieces were still warm when he tossed them into the frying pan, and when they were cooked, they were so tough no one could eat them. Even Gilligan and Shaun, the Irish Setters, wouldn't look at them.

We had a run out in the car one day and ended up in a town called Eccleshall. As usual, we went for a pint or two while we were there. As we drove along the High Street, Ozzy spotted two young kids with the words Black Sabbath on the back of their leather jackets and shouted, 'Stop!', which I did. He jumped out of the car and dashed over to these youngsters. 'What the hell's that on the back of your jackets?' he demanded. 'You want to grow up and act your age . . .' The kids, obviously Sabbath fans, were totally gobsmacked. They stood there, half-thrilled and half-bewildered, as Ozzy jumped back in the car and we roared off.

The great Necromandus bender ended with a flour and egg fight in Atrocity Cottage. Typically, the mayhem started after a night in the Hand & Cleaver, remembers Dave:

> We had congregated in the kitchen to make some supper. Ozzy went to the window sill next to the sink where Thelma kept the eggs. Dennis McCarten was standing with his back to Ozzy, waffling on about something or other, when Oz suddenly smashed an egg over his head. Dennis was stunned, standing there with yellow yolk running down his face as the rest of us dissolved into fits of laughter. Ozzy scored a direct hit on Frank Hall with the next one, and suddenly it all kicked off. We were chucking bags of flour and rice at each other and when there was nothing left to throw, we went to bed. Nobody thought of clearing up the mess.
>
> Thelma picked the wrong morning to return to the farmhouse. She walked in to find eggs spattered all over the walls and floor of the kitchen, which looked like a snowstorm had hit it with pounds of flour strewn everywhere. She took one look at the devastation, told us we were like a bunch of overgrown school kids, ordered us to 'Get that bloody mess cleaned up before I come back,' turned her car around and drove away again.
>
> It took all day to restore the kitchen to its normal state, and we made several phone calls of apology to Thelma before she decided to come home.

The artists formerly known as Necromandus realized it was time to leave.

Graham and Les, meanwhile, were living out the dreams of boys who had grown up in the fifties. They had not returned to the UK with the others when the recording sessions in Miami had finished. The next Sabbath tour was due to start in America in October, three months later, and it was decided that Graham and Les would hire a truck and drive the band's equipment to Los Angeles, where preparations for the tour were already being made and a completely new stage set was being built.

Both Graham and Les were thrilled at the prospect of the 2,759 mile road trip. They had a leisurely two weeks to complete the journey, and they had exciting plans. Driving over the Texas border, across New Mexico and on to Arizona, they were careful not to mention Black Sabbath at truckstops since this was redneck country and, in those days, anyone even vaguely suspected of devil worship could have been suspended on a blazing cross for the entertainment of the local community. At the very least, there was a certain hostility towards long-haired, hippy Englishmen travelling the highways and byways of the Bible belt.

In Arizona, the pair took an unforgettable detour, as Graham explains:

We were heading for Tucson but on our way, we noticed a sign for Tombstone and could not resist taking a look. This was the home of the OK Corral, Wyatt Earp and Boot Hill! As we drove into the main street, we realized we had stumbled upon a genuine western town.

We parked up, checked into the old Tombstone Hotel, dropped our bags and went straight to the Golden Nugget Saloon. It was like being in an old cowboy movie. There were no gunfights in the bar, and there was certainly no Mae West wiggling her voluptuous way down the staircase, but after a few drinks, we did fall into conversation with a couple of local girls who were more than happy to show us the sights, including the nearby border town of Bisbee. It had been a virtual ghost town, now peopled by a community of hippies and artists.

Later, back at the hotel, we discovered that our new friends were related to the sheriff and the mayor. We didn't fancy being strung up at dawn, or even shot, for whatever misdemeanours we may or may not have committed with the young ladies, so we tiptoed out to the truck under cover of darkness and set off at full speed.

Arriving at their final destination in LA, they knew they had been paid to make the trip of a lifetime.

Graham returned to the welcome of an empty house. Fields Farm was deserted, with Malcolm Horton and his friends having moved on to pastures new during his absence. This could have posed big financial problems for Graham, but luckily, he had friends who wanted to rent the vacant rooms – Terry Lee, an up and coming stage lighting designer, and Keith 'Evo' Evans, the Judas Priest roadie. They set about redecorating and improving the farmhouse, exposing all the old timbers. The parties that they subsequently held in the house became legendary in the Bishampton area, with all four members of Black Sabbath putting in appearances from time to time. One memorable gathering was enlivened by the presence of two local girls. During the party, the girls began an erotic performance on the living-room floor.
Graham:

Suddenly there seemed to be hairy buttocks everywhere as some of the men joined in. They were interrupted when Ranger, the farm's labrador dog, trotted into the room and over to the action where he started licking bare arses. 'Oh,' one of the guests joked, turning round to see what was happening. 'This is different. I quite like it . . .'

✝ ✝ ✝

October 1976 was an eventful month. The release of *Technical Ecstasy* marked the group's return to the Vertigo label from Nems, which had released their last two albums in the UK.

It was also time for Sabbath to return to America, with the latest tour due to begin in Tulsa, Oklahoma, on 22 October. The band were required to fly over early for production rehearsals at an old Columbia studio in LA. They decided to travel by Concorde for the first time. The supersonic jet, a triumph of British and French engineering, had gone into service in January that year. Originally, it flew only between London and Bahrain, and Paris and Rio de Janeiro, but in May 1976, it introduced services connecting London and Paris to Washington's Dulles International Airport. Sabbath would break the sound barrier on their way to Washington and then take a conventional connecting flight to LA.

Ozzy was very excited by the prospect of this new adventure and he talked about it for days. The people who used Concorde back then were mainly well-heeled businessmen whose appearance reflected their wealth and social standing. Ozzy intended to make a statement of his own – he dressed down for the occasion in a pair of Levis and a short-sleeved, salmon pink shirt with an iron-shaped scorch mark right between the shoulder blades.

This was a big tour for the band, especially Bill Ward, who was now the proud owner of his most extravagant drum riser yet. It was a huge box containing a powerful array of spotlights and strobe lighting effects. Also built into it was a dry ice machine, which could be operated from the side of the stage. The drum riser sat on top of a stained glass pedestal, and above it hung a giant chandelier with flaming gothic torches attached. The backdrop curtain was painted with designs from the *Technical Ecstasy* album cover, and the whole effect was stunning. Bill was delighted with his new toy.

With bands like Boston, Ted Nugent and Bob Seger and the Silver Bullet Band booked as support to Sabbath, the tour was selling out fast – although *Technical Ecstasy* was not. It charted respectably in Britain at number thirteen, but in America, it staggered to a halt just outside the top fifty. Sabbath were not surprised it was savaged in the press, but had not expected such poor sales. Hardline Sabbath fans were disappointed with the album, since the band had gone for an experimental approach featuring keyboards and strings, at the expense of their familiar heavy, dark and sinister metal.

Graham feels that it was perhaps a little over-produced and was not as good as *Sabotage*, although he still likes it. Dave agrees: 'It was a huge shift away from anything they had done in the past. It took a while for me to get over the change in the band's sound, but it does have some really great tracks and I can hear a positive interaction between Tony, Geezer and Gerald Woodroffe, who played the keyboards.'

Fans of the traditional sound were not so open-minded. Gerald, joining the band on tour, took a lot of flak as the man held responsible for their latest attempts at diversity. When the tour arrived in the UK, an audience member on one of the balconies threw a bag of chips at Gerald's head.

Due to the complexities of the tracks they were now including in the live set, they needed Gerald's help to play them properly. However, he was never invited to be a full-time member of the band, and his keyboards were set up behind the stage right PA stacks, not on the stage but on the floor.

It was on this American tour that Bill Ward decided once and for all to stop flying between gigs. Bill couldn't get on a plane without a bag of medication to calm his nerves, and he was also interested in the American countryside rather than looking at the clouds above it. He would see plenty of scenery from the windows of his hired Winnebago truck as he travelled through the states by road.

In many ways, this was a time of great change for Black Sabbath.

17

'WE HAVE A POSITIVE
ON THE SHIT!'

Bill's incredible drum riser caused problems immediately. Sabbath had to hire an extra truck for its transport, and the vehicle broke down on the way to the first date in Tulsa. The panic-stricken crew hired a semi-tractor unit to tow it to the venue so that the band would not miss show-time.

There were no such traumas for Bill himself, cruising the highways in the Winnebago camper van with Mysti's brother Dave Strait at the wheel. After three gigs in Texas, Ozzy and Dave Tangye decided to hitch a ride cross-country with Bill. It was an intensive two day journey of around 700 miles from Dallas to Des Moines in Iowa, scene of the next gig on 28 October. The two Daves shared driving duties, stopping off en route to pick up supplies of fast food and alcohol for their passengers, as Dave Tangye recalls:

> We called at one place in Hicksville USA and, as a joke, asked if they had any 'White Lightning' for sale. Looking at us with a raised eyebrow, the shop assistant asked where in the world we were from. Hearing 'England', he vanished to the back of the store and returned with a jar shaped like a honey pot, which he passed discreetly over the counter. 'Don't drink it all at once,' he warned. Back in the Winnebago, Ozzy took the lid off the jar, and I swear you could see the contents evaporating in front of your eyes.

The two Daves left the two musicians to get on with it and can safely say that Ozzy and Bill felt no pain for the rest of the twelve hour journey.

Finally arriving at the Ramada Inn in Des Moines, everyone was desperate to crash out, but the American military had other ideas. An hour after slipping into a welcome sleep, Dave Tangye was woken by a deafening roar. The hotel was right beside an airforce base, and the jet fighter pilots were out on night exercises. The sound was awesome, and Dave's bed physically vibrated as the aircraft skimmed the top of the motel. He, for one, had no further rest that night.

Regardless of *Technical Ecstasy*'s undistinguished sales the faithful flocked to the gigs in their thousands – as always. Sabbath had a hard-core following in America, as in Europe. And so to Hallowe'en, and a bewitching gig and fancy dress parade at McNichol's Arena in Denver, Colorado. The audience were the real stars. They dressed for the occasion in a variety of ghoulish, grotesque and downright outlandish costumes. Several people were chosen to be brought up onstage and properly applauded. A zombie towered almost seven feet high, holding his head under his left arm. Another contestant climbed the steps with a giant anaconda wrapped around his neck, although no one dared go near enough to give him a congratulatory hug. The winner bounced across the stage in the guise of a seven foot penis, spurting like a great whale. The audience went wild, and they stayed wild until the lights went down on a sensational Black Sabbath set.

But it didn't have to be Hallowe'en for the weirdos and freaks to turn up at Sabbath shows, especially in America. Despite the band's long-standing contention that their 'black' imagery was not to be taken seriously and their genuine efforts to disassociate themselves from the occult, it was something that returned to haunt them again and again. Many of their most famous songs – 'War Pigs', 'Paranoid', 'Iron Man', 'Snowblind', 'Killing Yourself To Live' and 'The Writ', to name but a few – are clearly focused on other subjects, and Geezer's 'After Forever' is interpreted by many to have a Christian theme. Of those songs which do roam the underworld, most warn against Satanic involvement. Apart from anything else, the fact that devils and demons appear in various lyrics doesn't mean that the band, in their private lives, were scampering around naked at black masses. The Dark Lord Geezer Butler was more likely at the football.

The people who chose to believe in Sabbath as hell's own messengers were oddly obsessive, and they liked to stalk the band. Ozzy once walked out of a lift in a hotel in Atlanta to be confronted by several characters dressed in black coats and pointed hats, chanting and holding flickering, black candles aloft. Calmly, he walked among them, blowing out each flame as he passed, and sang a spirited rendition of 'Happy Birthday' as he took his leave.

On another occasion, the band were driving out of Houston, Texas, to the next gig, 350 miles away, when they noticed that they were being followed by a car containing three guys in their late twenties or early thirties. Says Dave:

Luke was driving, and Ozzy, Geezer and I were his passengers. We pulled off the Interstate a couple of times, just to see if the other car would stop too, and it did.

After the long drive, we checked into the hotel while our followers hung around in the car park. We stayed in our rooms, waiting for showtime, and travelled to the venue in limos.

When Sabbath finished the gig, we dashed back to the hotel to catch the bar before it closed, and we felt very uneasy to see that the three men in the car were still lurking around. Albert Chapman and I approached one of them and asked what he was after. Did he want an autograph? A T-shirt? We wanted to know why his company had followed us from Houston.

The guy was totally out-of-it, but not drunk. His pupils were dilated, and he seemed unable to comprehend what we were saying to him. I told him that the band were not too happy with him and his friends, and suggested they should leave. With that, he started yelling, 'Sabbath are the true Messiahs! Satan lives!'

We returned to the bar and carried on drinking until about half past one. Turning in for the night, I had just settled into the room

I was sharing with Ozzy when I heard a knock at the door. But there was no one there. Ten minutes later, the phone rang and it was Albert Chapman, asking me to come to his room because he could hear mumbling and chanting outside the door.

As I approached his room, I came across our friends again, but seeing me, they disappeared down a stairway at the end of the corridor. Albert and I gave chase and found ourselves in reception. We asked the night porter to phone the police and shortly afterwards, two cops rolled up. We told them that some guests were being harassed by weirdos and asked if it would be OK for us to sort them out ourselves if they came back. 'No problem,' said the officers.

A short while later, the men returned. Albert and I cornered them and spoke to them in a universal language that they obviously understood, since they left the hotel at great speed and did not bother us again.

Sabbath also received the attention of people from the other side of the spiritual divide.

Graham remembers:

One night, after a gig in the Ozark Mountain region of Arkansas, we were on the stage packing up the gear when we suddenly realized we'd been surrounded by a group of people brandishing Bibles and placards denouncing Sabbath as sinners who should repent and be saved by Jesus. The band had already left, so they picked on the crew instead, which was a huge waste of their time. We saw them off quickly and easily.

We didn't get a lot of hassle from religious fanatics and when we did, it would usually be in the southern states – the Bible Belt – or at airports. There, we would sometimes also be stopped by Krishna followers. Dave and I did not feel that we should have to defend ourselves or enter into conversations with strangers, and so when anybody asked if we were members of the Sabbath entourage, we would simply say we were welders, checking out the American cross-country pipelines.

Sometimes, the stalkers would be without any religious agenda but were still distinctly unsettling.

Graham: 'One fan who kept on appearing during the American tours between 1975 and 1978 looked and dressed exactly like Tony Iommi, and would hang around the lobby of the band's hotel. He never made a nuisance of himself but he would be lurking there with an unnerving smile on his face. We named him Tony's Twin.'

Dave: 'There was one couple who would turn up at every gig Sabbath played in New York State. They never approached anyone or announced their presence, but they would always appear in the backstage area during the afternoon when the show was being set up and just loiter around. The crew wondered what it was they wanted or got out of this wordless experience.'

✝ ✝ ✝

The tour was split into three parts. The first leg finished in Seattle in mid-November, and the band and most of the crew flew home to England for a ten day break. Graham and Dave decided to stay on for a short vacation in LA and booked into a two-bedroom apartment at the Grand View Hotel on Hermosa Beach. It was cheaper than the Portofino and nearer to the bars – both important factors since the pair were paying for themselves and were determined to make the best possible use of their days off.

They became regulars at Stan's Liquor Store, the only shop in LA where it was possible to buy imported English beer. They quickly stocked their fridge with cans of Newcastle Brown Ale, and settled on a place called Shenanigans for their nightlife. Shenanigans was a bar and club with live music from local bands. The guys from Obie's Lighting would hang out there and go back with Dave and Graham to their apartment for a few more drinks, so the social side of things was chilled and happy, says Dave:

> One night in Shenanigans, we got pretty wasted on mezcal and we just about managed to stagger back to the Grand View with an Obie's guy called Dave Cavelli. We carried on drinking into the early hours and then went to bed. At about 5.00am, I felt a violent shudder, shot upright in bed and opened my eyes. The first thing I looked at was the corner table; the empty beer cans were dancing along the table top and falling on to the floor. I remember saying to myself, 'That's the last time I drink tequila,' before falling back into an alcohol-induced coma.
>
> When I got up later that day, Graham told me that he'd seen the same thing, but we still both thought we had dreamed it. We only later discovered from the television news that there had been a severe earthquake in the Santa Monica area during the night, registering about six on the Richter Scale. It caused a lot of damage in the neighbourhood.

† † †

David Strait was unable to come back for the second part of the tour because of family commitments. And so when Sabbath returned for the next spate of dates, starting in Knoxville, Tennessee, on 23 November, Bill was accompanied by his brother Jim, who took over the driving responsibilities. This time they were travelling not in a Winnebago but another state-of-the-art mobile home, a GMC Palm Beach camper van.

Jim had been taking care of business for Bill in England during the summer and autumn. He had harvested Bill's raspberry crop and looked after his horses, Snowy and Silver. Now he was faced with a new challenge. The weather was rapidly becoming very wintry indeed and the driving conditions were hazardous.

All sorts of things were going wrong. The band flew into Kalamazoo, Michigan, to discover that one of their trucks had ground to a halt, its fuel frozen in the lines from the tank to the engine, in the middle of nowhere – and the sound and lighting equipment was on board. There followed a frantic dash to hire a lighting rig and sound system locally so that in the grand traditions of showbusiness, the show could go on . . . after a fashion. The replacement lights were like something you'd see at a school disco.

Sabbath and their old friends the Climax Blues Band took to the stage that night wrapped up as if they were going on an Arctic expedition. Bill got behind the kit in a parka, and Ozzy was wearing a pair of woollen mittens that Dave had found in the dressing room. It was minus thirty degrees outside. And it wasn't much better indoors, since the venue was an ice hockey rink.

The whole of the eastern seaboard was suffering from the adverse weather, the authorities started closing the freeways, and Jim swore he had never known anything so hair-raising in his years of driving.

Even worse lay ahead. The toilet got bunged up and filled the camper with a stomach-churning stench. Jim stopped at a gas station to empty it and pulled the release lever. It wouldn't budge, no matter how many times he tried. Returning to the driving seat, he started the engine while Bill took over on the lever. Seconds later, Bill cried loudly, 'We have a positive on the shit!' Jim turned round to see his brother, Sabbath's famous drummer, standing at the door of the camper with the contents of the toilet all over his clothes. 'How come it's me that always ends up in the shit?' quipped Bill, with remarkable good humour.

Somehow negotiating the icy conditions of the northeast states without any missed gigs, the tour descended on the Big Apple – and a day off. Graham picked up a paper and noticed that Dr John was playing a gig that night in the Village. He asked if anyone was interested in going. No one from the band responded, but Graham made a call and arranged for the crew members to see the show:

We were given a table in the VIP section. Being typically English, I went to the bar to order a round of drinks rather than wait for table service. As I stood there waiting to be served, I noticed a guy on the bar stool next to me. He looked familiar, and I asked him if he was from Middlesbrough. He replied, 'No, I'm from Liverpool, but I went to Middlesbrough once.'

We chatted on and he told me he was living in New York. He'd nipped out to catch Dr John and have a few drinks because his missus had been driving him up the wall. I said goodbye to him with a casual, 'See you later' as I returned to our table with the drinks, and Spock jumped on me straight away: 'So how come you know John Lennon?' I was kicking myself, but not as much as Ozzy and Bill were the next day. Lennon was one of their all-time heroes.

✝ ✝ ✝

Madison Square Garden in New York was always the big one. Sabbath played there on 6 December, with support act Ted Nugent rampaging round the stage like Tarzan on speed.

Sabbath were introduced on stage by American guitarist, singer and satirist Frank Zappa, who was a friend of Ozzy's and a great fan of the band. Originally, there were plans for Zappa to play a guitar duet with Tony Iommi and although Frank's equipment was set up onstage, the idea was called off. They tuned their guitars differently and were not sure of finding a way that they would sound good together.

After the concert, the promoter took the band to the Time Life building for a slap-up meal. Zappa came along with his bodyguard, an ex-Marine called Smothers who was built like the proverbial brick shithouse, remembers Dave:

Smothers had a metal, telescopic cosh secreted in the collar of his jacket. He could whip this extended cosh out in a flash and have it touching the end of your nose before you had time to blink. During dinner, a bunch of grid-iron football players from the New York Giants tried to crash the party. They were big guys but they were no match for Smothers and Albert Chapman, who persuaded them to leave with a quiet word in their ears.

Appearing in New Haven, Connecticut, on 11 December 1976, Sabbath were delighted to add a famous name to the guestlist. Linda Blair, star of 1973's occult horror movie *The Exorcist*, arrived with her brother to see the gig, and Ozzy took a particular shine to her.

They met backstage, where he drooled over Linda outrageously. He was, of course, playing to the audience and giving everyone a good laugh. It was a perfect photo opportunity – the Prince of Darkness and the face of demonic possession; truly a friendship made in hell. Indeed, the whole crew had found it quite disturbing to see her sitting on the left-hand side of the stage during the show, since the film was still horribly fresh in their memories. One photograph which emerged from this meeting shows Ozzy cradling Linda in his arms, one arm around her back and the other holding up her legs. For ages afterwards, he would perform his *Exorcist* party piece, proclaiming in a throaty, demonic snarl that 'Your mother knits socks in hell!'

It was typical of the atmosphere around Sabbath at the time. Any individual worries or dissatisfactions they may have been harbouring did not disrupt the general light-heartedness of their daily routine, with all of its jokes and pranks.

'Tony Iommi and Albert Chapman had their moments on that tour,' declares Dave. 'On one occasion, we were all drinking in a hotel bar which was separated from the swimming pool by a panoramic glass wall. You could look straight through into the water. Tony and Albert left the company, and the rest of us carried on boozing. We nearly choked on our beer when we happened to glance over at the pool. Tony and Albert were swimming around completely starkers, in full view of everybody in the bar.'

After a Christmas break back in England, Sabbath returned for their third and final month-long batch of dates, touching down in Boston, Massachusetts, on 15 January 1977. Like Ozzy on the Concorde journey, Bill Ward flaunted his fame in a perversely modest fashion, arriving in the United States with his belongings crammed into two Tesco carrier bags. That was the extent of his luggage. He was wearing an old, black coat that he had bought at a jumble sale. He looked like a tramp, albeit a jet-setting one.

By now, Sabbath had obviously abandoned any hope of keeping their Stateside gigging to a minimum, despite their earlier pledge. They needed to make a substantial comeback in America. And since they were managing themselves, in conjunction with their business representative Mark Forster, they were more aware of their financial situation and the need to keep earning.

The stage production was changing again, and they turned not to their old LA allies Obie's and Tycobrahe, but to a Dallas firm called Showco which was offering an all-in-one package – sound, lights, trucking and technicians. This was obviously more convenient, it streamlined the operation, and Forster had undoubtedly negotiated a good deal with Showco.

Sabbath held their rehearsals at a college theatre close to the company's warehouse and factory, and then they went back on the road, where they met a man who knew Elvis.

They were in Memphis, Tennessee, on 27 January, talking to the local Warner Bros representative – a guy called Mike, who had previously worked for Elvis Presley. He said that 'The King', remarkably, was a fan of Black Sabbath and might appreciate an invitation to their gig the next night at the Mid-South Coliseum.

He also declared that if the band would like to take a run out to Graceland in the afternoon before the gig, he could probably arrange for them to have a 'meet and greet' with Elvis. It wasn't really Tony Iommi's sort of thing; he liked to keep himself to himself, and he wasn't a 'starry' person at all. Bill Ward, for whatever reasons, was also unavailable for the trip.

On the other hand, Ozzy, Geezer, Albert and Dave Tangye were fantastically excited by the prospect of meeting one of the world's greatest rock legends, and the next day they set off in a limousine bound for Graceland. 'It was 4.00pm when we pulled up at the gates to the mansion,' remembers Dave. 'We were met by a guard who asked us to get out of the limo and into an army-style jeep. The driver of the jeep broke the sad news: "Elvis is asleep, and is not receiving any guests right now." We were all very disappointed, and I asked, "Can you not get him up? I've come all the way from Egremont to see him." The guy just laughed, but he did give us a guided tour of the grounds as a consolation. Needless to say, Elvis didn't show up at the gig that night.'

The tour carried on and in Norfolk, Virginia, Mark Forster arranged a special dinner for a high-flying American accountant called Donald Schaut. He wanted to have a chat with Schaut about the band's finances in the States. Dave takes up the story:

Mr Schaut arrived at the hotel with his wife, and we all took our seats in the restaurant. There were nine or ten of us around the table, and the whole affair was very cordial and informal. At one point, Bill asked a particularly nonsensical question. Ozzy summoned the wine waiter, asked for a cigarette lighter, leaned over towards Bill and set his beard on fire with the lighter. It was like a burning bush. A huge, copper-coloured flame shot out from Bill's chin before he managed to stifle the fire. He then leaned back, inhaled the fumes and remarked casually, 'Not a bad smoke at all, that.'

Mr and Mrs Schaut were gobsmacked, but everyone else around the table carried on as if nothing had happened. Ozzy has since accused Tony of being the fire-starter on this occasion, but he may have been getting mixed up. Bill had been set on fire more than once.

✝ ✝ ✝

Things weren't so easy back then, before the European Union. Tours were troubled with all sorts of red tape at the various borders, and the tour bus, with its tables, lamps, lounge, bunks, kitchen, toilet, TV, video and sound system, had yet to become a regular part of life on the road. Cars and trucks were still the staple transport, and rock'n'roll catering was an undeveloped art form. In Germany, you were lucky to get a bratwurst sausage from the promoter for lunch, and this posed perennial problems for Geezer, the vegetarian.

The dash for food would usually take place between the afternoon soundcheck and the point at which the venue opened its doors. This was fine in big European cities where the band and crew had identified the decent restaurants and would seek them out immediately. The smaller German towns were more problematic in the seventies when there was a great trend towards pigs' trotters and other equally meaty dishes. It's amazing that Geezer didn't starve to death. He only ever seemed to eat French fries.

Sabbath's love for playing great British cities such as Glasgow, Birmingham and Newcastle had never waned, but their feelings about Europe had changed enormously since they first got on the ferry as excited kids going to the Star Club in Hamburg. In Germany, the American GIs could be relied upon for a wild response, but elsewhere in Europe, the audiences could be hard work. The Swiss were unfeasibly well-behaved, the Dutch were too stoned and the French were . . . well, French. The band would often blow out gigs and, on one occasion, cancelled their last few European tour dates just so they could go home.

However, one of the great joys of the April 1977 European tour was the support band, AC/DC. Since Sabbath's first encounter with them in Australia in 1974, they had moved to London and had been working non-stop, paying their dues in every pub and club which would book them. Unlike the majority of British rock bands posing in silks and satins with beautifully tangled flowing hair, AC/DC took to the stage in workaday T-shirts and jeans – except for the precocious 'schoolboy' guitar genius Angus Young – and they rocked like there was no tomorrow. The highlight of their show was the moment that singer Bon Scott hoisted Angus on to his shoulders and strode into the auditorium with the guitarist still playing like a demon, pulling faces and lolling his tongue around at various members of the audience.

Tragically, Bon died two years later after a drinking session in London, and Geordie singer Brian Johnson took over the microphone. The next AC/DC album, *Black in Black*, was released as a tribute to Bon. It established them as a major force, and they remain one of the world's most popular rock bands.

AC/DC worked non-stop during that European tour. They would often play two shows a night – one with Sabbath and one in their own right at some club or other. On Sabbath's days off, they would usually be gigging. When they did have a free day, Bon Scott liked to have a drink and a game of pool with the crew. He was a gem. He had no airs and graces, he liked a laugh, and he was a great performer.

In Switzerland, an incident occurred between Geezer Butler and AC/DC rhythm guitarist Malcolm Young. It was something and nothing, all over in a flash – until the press sensationalized it. According to some reports, Geezer had threatened to stab Malcolm with a flick knife and Sabbath had then kicked AC/DC off the tour. None of this was true. A small altercation occurred after a gig at the Zurich Volkshause on 14 April. Both bands and crew members were in the hotel bar, and Geezer was messing about with a comb that had been designed to look like a flick knife. Malcolm thought it was a real knife and got annoyed with Geezer, shouting 'Don't point that at me!' He calmed down when he realized it was a comb and Geezer was only larking about. No blows were exchanged, and it was forgotten as quickly as it had happened.

Both bands continued to Scandinavia, finishing the tour in Sweden on 22 April. They returned to England together by ferry from Gothenburg. The crew members decided to hold an end of tour party on board the ferry as it crossed the North Sea. Despite the rough waters, the celebration quickly escalated into a serious drinking session. Everyone got totally ripped during the twenty-three-hour journey, and a couple of the Colac hire company guys were locked in the brig, on Captain's orders, for their own and everyone else's safety.

It was a fitting send-off for Dave Tangye. He was about to leave the band because they were going off the road for what turned out to be more than a year. In the beginning, Ozzy had paid Dave himself to be his right-hand man, since the rest of the band weren't convinced that the singer needed a personal road manager and assistant. As time went on and Dave proved his worth to Ozzy and all of Sabbath, he went on to the group's payroll.

Now Mark Forster had decided that since there would be no more touring for some considerable time and there might not be a lot for Dave to do, it would not be cost-effective to keep him on. Mark was doing his job; he was saving the band money. He explained the decision to Dave in a letter, which was also signed by the band members. Ozzy was unhappy about it, but did not offer to reinstate the original deal whereby he dipped into his own pocket for Dave's services.

Dave was not offended, because he had begun to see storm clouds gathering above the band, Ozzy in particular, and in any case, he fancied a change.

'I had a sixth sense that things were just not right, and a foreboding that some dam or other was about to burst,' he recalls. 'There were no huge arguments: the band had been together since they were little more than kids, they were like brothers, and they had spent so long in each other's company that they were more likely to suppress any problems or tensions than to confront each other or to create angry scenes in front of other people. This close familiarity and unwillingness to offer criticism was probably their main problem.

'I knew that some sort of breakdown was happening. I could just feel that the fun was going out of it all, the good-time atmosphere had gone, the conversations were becoming shorter, and Ozzy was having more than his fair share of depressive moods. He had confided in me on a few occasions that he felt left out of the big musical decisions.

'None of the crew asked any questions. We just went ahead and did what we were paid to do to the best of our ability. Sabbath were great guys to work with and they had always created a family atmosphere, but we knew our place – we were on a wage . . .'

Dave was right – Ozzy's demons would shortly emerge with a vengeance. He knew something else too: 'If things picked up for Ozzy, he would have me back. We kept in touch, and I visited him at Atrocity Cottage when he was at home. I returned to work with him at his invitation when he formed his own band, Blizzard of Ozz.'

† † †

Staggering out of the uproarious ferry party into Harwich, Dave spent a couple of days at Fields Farm with Graham before returning to Egremont. As a farewell outing, at least for the time being, they set out to spend some money at the Cheltenham Races on Gold Cup day. Remarkably, one of the horses in the first race was called Black Sabbath. It was owned by none other than Patrick Meehan. 'Dave and I saw this as an omen,' says Graham, 'since we'd just finished a tour with the band, and we both had a bet on the horse to win. It went like a bolt to the first fence, and crashed into it.'

The real omen, unknown to Dave and Graham at the time, was that of life imitating sport. Sabbath were heading for their own spectacular crash – but at least they'd made it well beyond the first fence.

Some famous faces turned up at Fields Farm during this period. With Britain in the grip of punk rock and the new, young breed kicking hard against the likes of huge rock bands like Sabbath, two of the most likeable visitors to the house were Joe Strummer and Mick Jones of The Clash. They were friends of Terry Lee, whose fledgling company Light and Sound Design was really starting to take off. He'd lit the Sex Pistols' notorious 'Anarchy' tour, and went on to work with The Clash on their 'White Riot' outing.

Graham remembers their visit well:

I woke up one morning, looked out of the window and spotted Mick Jones prodding the giant mushroom we had planted in the garden. We had rescued it from the *Land of the Giants* set at Shepperton Studios during production rehearsals for the European tour with AC/DC. Joe was staring at the chickens roaming freely around the grounds. I went down to the kitchen to make a bit of breakfast for us all. Joe was raving about the countryside and how much he liked it. He told us that one of his ambitions was to leave London and get his own place out in the sticks, which, eventually, he did.

Joe and Mick stayed for a couple of days, and they were entertaining and thoughtful guests. I was especially struck by Joe's offer to cut the grass for us, and I was saddened to hear of his death from a heart attack at the age of fifty.

Another visitor was AC/DC guitarist Angus Young. He had come to see Graham's housemate Evo Evans, who was now working for his band. Graham liked Angus a lot. They got on well because of their mutual passion for art and painting. 'While he was at Fields Farm, he mentioned that he wanted to buy a new pair of jeans,' says Graham. 'I took him to a department store in the nearby town of Evesham and steered him towards the men's section. "What are you taking me here for?" demanded Angus, an admittedly tiny figure. "I always buy my clothes in the kids' department." He strode off to the kiddie rails and picked out a pair of jeans. Of course, they fitted perfectly.'

**Rockfield Studios,
1978**

Above. Rehearsing
around the fire.

Right. Bill wears his
birthday cake!

© Les Martin

Newcastle City Hall, 1978

Left. Ozzy gets in the mood, backstage.

Below. Geezer and Tony going on stage.

Opposite. The City Hall audience.

Opposite, bottom. Bill in interview mode.

© Alistair Smith

CALIFORNIA STAR TRAVEL, INC.

914 So. Robertson Blvd. Los Angeles, California 90035   213·659·3065

BLACK SABBATH CREW (Revised 11/1)

DATE	CITY	FROM / TO	AIRLINE & FLIGHT	DEPT.	ARRIVE	HOTEL
Fri. 11/10	Memphis, Tenn.	Nashville Memphis	NL 13	10:43a.	11:18a.	Ramada Inn SouthEast 3896 Lamar Ave. Memphis, Tenn. 901/365-6100
Sat. 11/11	Cincinnati, Ohio	Memphis Atlanta Cincinnati	DL 949 DL 720	9:24a. 12:11p.	11:27a. 1:27p.	Holiday Inn Downtown 8th and Linn Cincinnati, Ohio 513/241-8660
Sun. 11/12	Atlanta, Ga.	Cincinnati ~~Atlanta~~ NASHVILLE AA143	~~AA 897~~	~~1:00p.~~ 9·15AM	3:10p. 9·04	~~Marriott Courtland St. at Ivy Blvd.~~ Atlanta, Ga. 404/659-6500
Mon. 11/13	Atlanta, Ga.	NASHVILLE to ATLANTA	EA 299	10·38	12·25	Same as above HILTON COURTLAND & HARRIS ST.
Tues. 11/14	Mobile, Ala.	Atlanta Mobile	EA 699	10:53a.	10:54a.	Sheraton Motor Inn 301 Government St. Mobile, Ala. 205/438-3431
Wed. 11/15	Amarillo, Tex.	Mobile New Orleans Dallas Amarillo	NA 479 DL 535 Bn 31	12:30p. 2:15p. 4:40p.	1:02p. 3:27p. 6:10p.	CivicCenter Travelodge 321 S. Polk Amarillo, Texas 806/372-4101

A Subsidiary Of

STARFLIGHT TRAVEL CO. OF NEW YORK

Six days on the road – the crew's itinerary.

Geezer on stage, 1978.

Bel-End, the house on the hill. Bel-Air, LA 1979.

© Graham Wright

Ozzy in his 'Billy Smarts' jacket in his Le Parc apartment.

Ozzy eyes things up at Le Parc.

© David Tangye

© David Tangye

Graham, Bill and Dave at a
Black Sabbath reunion gig,
NEC Birmingham,
4 December 1997.

Tony, Dave and Ozzy meet up again at the Academy in Birmingham, a warm up charity event in aid of the Children's Hospital, 2001.

© David Tangye

18

PEDIGREE CHUMS

The old mill house was situated beside a tranquil stream where Tony and Ozzy would sometimes sit quietly, fishing. Sabbath had put their feet up for a while after touring intensively throughout America and Europe, and they were back in Monmouth, Wales, to rehearse for another album.

They had heard that the Rockfield empire had recently expanded with the acquisition of the mill house, converted into a rehearsal studio with accommodation. There were further plans to turn it into a recording facility. (Indeed, as Monnow Valley Studios, it has since become one of the UK's most popular and picturesque recording centres, and was sold on by Charles Ward only a couple of years ago.) It's about half a mile along the road from the Rockfield complex, at the end of a secluded drive, and Sabbath liked it so much that it became their favourite rehearsal spot.

They had the gear set up in a large back room with French windows leading out into the gardens, and their dartboard took pride of place in the dining room. This was the scene of many marathon darts sessions stretching well into the night. Tony Iommi was the keenest and best player, and Bill Ward was the Jocky Wilson of the band – not because he could throw an arrow but because he enjoyed a drink while he was throwing it.

There was a self-catering arrangement at the mill house, and while Ozzy and Graham made the tastiest curries, Oz would sometimes be tempted to take things too far. He liked to sneak into the kitchen and stir jars and jars of hot vindaloo paste into the curry, and then get Les to sample it. Tony Iommi was worse, according to Graham: 'On one occasion, I caught him taking the filling out of meat pies and replacing it with dog food. He watched avidly as his unwitting victims tucked into their pie and peas. Later, I found him lying on the studio floor, hysterical with laughter.'

Mealtimes were at the centre of many wind-ups during this period, and everyone quickly learnt to approach their food with caution. Other pranks were planned for their surprise value and, as usual, Bill Ward was a perfect victim, says Graham:

One night we sneaked into Bill's room while he was asleep, lit a candle next to his bed and held a large mirror inches from his face. We quietly woke him. He half-opened his eyes, let out a terrifying scream and seemed to pass out immediately. We made our escape and ran down the stairs.

The next morning, a few of us were having breakfast when Bill came into the room shaking his head and looking very pale. We asked him if he was all right. He replied that during the night, he'd had the worst nightmare of his life – the Devil himself was hanging over him while he was in bed. Ozzy just about pissed himself laughing.

The boys had parked an impressive array of cars outside the mill house. There were Mercedes, Rollers, Ferraris – and Graham's Hillman Minx. One day, after a weekend at home, Les turned up in a Lamborghini Espada sports car, which he'd bought with his savings.

Heads certainly turned as Les drove Graham up and down the main street in Monmouth on their daily shopping runs. The local butcher was particularly impressed. After a few teatime pints in the local pub, Les would offer him a lift home. In return, Les would receive a large pork pie. He had found a new best mate.

The local pub in Monmouth was rife with rumours of the goings-on at the studio. Once, a helicopter landed in a field next to the main Rockfield studio complex. The grapevine started buzzing immediately – helped in no small way by Sabbath and their crew – and within days, the whole town was convinced that John Lennon had flown in to work on his next album. The less glamorous truth was that the helicopter pilot had landed to take a break during a day of crop-spraying.

It was in the same field that Ozzy held a football match which ended in disaster for Graham. Ozzy had been upset one night watching a music programme on television. Meat Loaf was making an early appearance on British television (he wouldn't release a record until the next year) and someone in the room joked, 'That band have a fat singer too.' Ozzy was conscious of his weight. He was, after all, Sabbath's frontman. On one occasion, he was pictured on the cover of *Sounds* magazine stripped to the waist and showing a bit of a belly. 'Sabs Fight the Flab,' blared the headline, and it needled Ozzy into one of his irregular keep-fit campaigns. They didn't usually go on for longer than a day or two, but he would be full of enthusiasm while they lasted.

The day after the Meat Loaf incident, Ozzy announced that it was time for everybody to get fit, especially him, and decided on a game of soccer. The entourage duly trooped to the field and started the match as soon as the cows had been herded out. They laid jackets on the ground to act as goalposts, and Oz temporarily abandoned his usual snakeskin platforms for a pair of hobnail boots hastily borrowed from a local farmer.

Bill was definitely not a sporty type, and he didn't want to invite any injuries which could affect his drumming, so he elected not to take part. But he entered into the spirit of the occasion as a supporter on the imaginary sideline, and his presence was appreciated by Graham more than anyone:

Within minutes of the kick-off, I slipped on a huge cowpat and went face down into another. Covered in shit, I tried to get back up, only to realize that I had damaged my foot. Whether it was sprained or broken I could not tell. Bill came running over carefully, so as not to spill his cider. After a hearty slurp, he declared that I would have to see a doctor. Bill and Les Martin helped me into a car and whisked me off to the nearest hospital.

Arriving, I was put into a wheelchair. Bill pushed me towards the casualty department using my extended and very sore foot as a battering ram to negotiate the swing doors. My yells of pain cut no ice with Bill, who simply kept on swigging from his bottle. Luckily, I was rescued by a nurse who took over the wheelchair and escorted us to a room to wait for a doctor. Les passed the time by talking about the hospital he had worked in when he first left school. Spotting a thermometer sticking out of a jar on a shelf, he announced that he was an expert at taking temperatures, grabbed the thermometer and placed it under his tongue. At this point I noticed a label at the back of the jar, and pointed it out to Les. It read, 'For anal use only.' Les spat out the thermometer, which shot through the air like a miniature Cruise missile and smashed to pieces against the opposite wall. He then began to cough and spit as he lunged for the sink to wash his mouth out.

Of course, the doctor walked in at this precise moment. With Les hacking over the sink, Bill slumped against the wall in a state of considerable inebriation and me lying on the bed in hysterics, the doctor cast his eyes around the scene and calmly asked, 'Who's first?' Eventually, he ascertained that I had not broken my foot. He bandaged me up, gave me some painkillers and sent the three of us packing.

So much for getting fit.

✝ ✝ ✝

Ozzy had been threatening to leave the band for quite a while, but no one believed he would actually do it. Like many clowns, he would be high as a kite one minute and down in the depths the next, and he had been like that throughout the whole of Sabbath's career.

After rehearsals at the mill house one day, he announced that he needed a break, got into his Mercedes and drove home – illegally, because he didn't have a licence. He never had passed his driving test after that first, abortive effort. He later phoned Bill to say he was not coming back to the band. Nobody took it that seriously – they reckoned it was just Ozzy playing up again, and Tony carried on working on new riffs. But as days passed and the singer didn't return, Sabbath realized they really were Oz-less in Monmouth.

They decided to hire a replacement. At the very least, they would have the opportunity to find out what it was like to work with a different vocalist. And if Ozzy did turn out to be serious about quitting the band, they would be able to stay in business. But Graham, for one, believes that they were actually calling Ozzy's bluff. Dave Walker, an old mate of Bill's and an ex-member of the Savoy Brown blues band, arrived at the mill house, tentatively joining Black Sabbath as their new lead singer. He was accompanied by his wife, who liked to have him tucked up in bed by eleven o'clock at night. From the outset, then, alarm bells were ringing loudly. And although Dave Walker did contribute to the songwriting and even filmed a BBC TV appearance with Sabbath at Birmingham's Pebble Mill studios, there was a general feeling around the band that this was a pointless exercise.

Ozzy, meanwhile, was trying to make sense of his problems. He was not feeling good about himself. He was disappointed and disturbed by the way things had been going for Sabbath over the past couple of years, with falling album sales and management difficulties undermining their previously effortless ascent. He was confused too, wanting to go in a new direction of his own while still not ready to cut his ties with Sabbath.

But the major issue was his musical conflict with Tony Iommi. Ozzy believed passionately in the original Sabbath blueprint, the enormous, insistent, spine-chilling heavy metal that had made their name. He was miserable about the way the music was going and he had disliked *Technical Ecstasy* since he was not – at that time – interested in experiment or exploration. Ozzy grumbled later: 'It seems to me that the names Black Sabbath and *Technical Ecstasy* were diametrically opposed to each other.' He hadn't felt reassured by the rehearsal sessions for the next album either, and his reaction had been to retreat from the creative process, subsequently alleging that he had been made to feel his opinion was unimportant.

Tony Iommi, on the other hand, was keen to expand the Sabbath sound, and he had been exasperated by Ozzy, declaring that he wasn't pulling his weight. Tony had really wanted Ozzy to change, which is treading dangerous ground in any relationship. People only change because they want to. At the same time, Tony claims to have been feeling the strain of the responsibilities placed upon him by the other band members, who largely relied upon him to be the leader, come up with song ideas and represent their interests in the studio.

Graham believes that something else was troubling Ozzy immensely: 'He was always saying that he was going insane, and I came to think that John Osbourne from Aston was cracking under the pressure of having to be Ozzy Osbourne, rock star, the Prince of Darkness.'

Ozzy has said of this period of estrangement: 'I missed the family atmosphere of Black Sabbath. I had a rest but knew in my heart that I was making a mistake and I just had to get back in there.' The rest of the band felt the same. The experiment with Dave Walker hadn't worked out too well, and he left the band without any great fuss.

'There was no screaming or shouting,' says Graham. 'He just left. He was there one day and he wasn't the next. From the moment he walked in, he'd seemed more like a substitute than an alternative to Ozzy. Someone may have had a little chat with him; I don't know. But everybody, including Dave Walker, knew that Oz needed to come back. It was a very strange time. Bill and Oz were good mates, and I'm sure it must have been Bill who phoned him to say, "Why don't you give it another go?" Eventually, we all heard that he was on his way back.'

Shortly after his reinstatement, Ozzy described his absence: 'It's been like a holiday. It's given me a lot of time to think, and although I'd been trying to work with other musicians, it was very difficult. After nine years with the same people, you get used to things. When they rang up to ask if I'd come back, I knew there was only one answer.'

Graham remembers a certain element of surprise about Ozzy's return to Wales:

It was about 10.30am at the mill house. I was in the kitchen, and I heard a gun going off. I thought, 'That'll be Oz back, then.' He knew we would all realize it was him. He'd been away for a few weeks and now he was announcing his return, blasting his shotgun outside Bill's bedroom, and suddenly things were back to normal. Bill was still in bed. Oz, having pulled up in his car to see Bill's curtains closed, stood under his window and fired five times.

Everybody was pleased he was back. Now Black Sabbath could get down to work properly. Ozzy seemed happy too; he said he was looking forward to a fresh start.

He explained he'd needed a break to sort his head out, and the band accepted that. He seemed to have recovered his enthusiasm, and the atmosphere between Ozzy and the rest of Sabbath returned to something approaching normal. But there was always the nagging worry that, one day, he might do the same thing again.

Going back into rehearsals, Ozzy would remain disapproving of the way the music was heading. The songs were not flowing in the way that they used to. Sabbath's creative juices were drying up, and it was only a matter of time before the volatile singer would walk out again, this time for good.

December 1977 was the beginning of Sabbath's winter of discontent.

The band moved the rehearsals from the millhouse in Monmouth to a room in Fields Farm, where Graham was living. With Bill's drums and the guitar stacks set up, it was crammed in there. The Aga cooker in the kitchen and the open fire in the living room were well stoked up to keep everybody warm, but the Aga developed a tendency to belch out rancid smoke, and before long the whole house was constantly filled with a black fog. Ozzy announced that he had contracted a new ailment, Aga Throat, and he prescribed his own treatment, a liquid remedy served in pints at the local pub.

It was during this time at the farm that Ozzy's father, Jack, died after a long battle with cancer. The rehearsals came to an abrupt end, and everybody felt for Oz, who was totally distraught. After the funeral, Ozzy drove straight back down to Fields Farm. Graham and his housemates Terry Lee and Evo Evans were at home when Ozzy walked into the living room, stripped off his suit and threw it on to the open fire, declaring that he needed a drink. 'We told him that he couldn't go to the pub in his underpants,' says Graham. 'With that, he dashed into the kitchen, grabbed a bin liner and put it on, tearing holes in the bag for his head and arms. We all piled into a car and drove to the Dolphin, our local, where we ignored the disbelieving stares at Ozzy's appearance and got royally pissed. Ozzy was obviously very upset, but we did our best to try and cheer him up at this impromptu wake for the late Jack Osbourne.'

✝ ✝ ✝

Toronto in January was freezing cold at the best of times. In 1978, Canada was enduring a particularly harsh winter. 'It's probably warmer at the North Pole,' said Ozzy, bitterly.

The band had chosen the city's Sounds Interchange Studios for the recording of their next album, *Never Say Die!* It was a very hip facility, and Sabbath also liked Toronto as a city, although it would have been a lot more pleasant in the summer. Regular weather warnings were being broadcast on television advising people not to venture outside because temperatures were heading down to minus fifty degrees Centigrade. There were rumours of people's eyeballs freezing, and to take a leak out in the open would have been inviting catastrophe. The blizzards pummelling the city were blowing people along the street like pieces of paper. 'Even Nanook of the North would've frozen his bollocks off in this place,' huffed Ozzy. The whole band hated it.

The local Warner Bros representative arranged for them to relocate from their hotel into an apartment block just off Younge Street, a main thoroughfare in the downtown area of Toronto. On the corner of the street was The Gasworks, a bar that would become their local. The apartment building came to feel like a prison. It was impossible to go out for a walk because of the weather, but if you ran, you could just about make it to the doorway of The Gasworks without getting frostbite.

Ozzy spent more time in his room than the other members of the band. He was being pursued by two especially persistent groupies called Abracadabra and Silver. He would lock himself in his apartment and pretend to be out because they were, he decided, 'bloody Radio Rental' – mental.

Before the recordings began, Sabbath spent some time rehearsing in an icy cold, old cinema. They were limited to mornings and afternoons, and the mighty sound of Sabbath in action often found itself in competition with an old lady who would roar around the cinema with the loudest vacuum cleaner anyone had ever heard, cleaning the floors before the evening programmes started.

Another inconvenience presented itself when the band moved on to Sounds Interchange Studios. They decided that the acoustics in their room were too 'dead' and that they would have to customize the studio. 'We had to try and liven it up,' says Graham, 'so we imported sheets and sheets of plywood to place on the floors and to cover up the acoustic padding on the walls.'

In the light of their sliding record sales in America, the band were trying to get back to basics on at least a few of the tracks, but many fans would complain that they didn't go far enough. Elsewhere, they again ventured beyond the tried and tested Sabbath formula, bringing in decorative instruments such as brass, harmonica and keyboards, this time contributed by Don Airey.

Graham says of the recordings: 'Personally, I thought some of the songs were not strong enough, although I liked others. But I would have preferred to hear the band going back to the real heavy stuff. The sound they had on early albums such as *Black Sabbath* and *Paranoid* was their trademark. I thought that, with this album, maybe they were trying too hard.'

Still, the band seemed to have shaken off everything that had happened in the previous few months. Ozzy was firmly back in the fold, and the flirtation with Dave Walker was a forgotten episode. Sabbath never washed their dirty laundry in public, not even in front of the crew. Neither Graham nor Dave ever heard raised voices or any kind of serious argument, and whatever disputes or complaints there may have been among the band were voiced quietly behind closed doors if they were spoken at all.

And so it was only later that anyone realized the unhappiness behind the scenes in Toronto. Tony Iommi has since told author Steven Rosen that the recording sessions were a nightmare: 'We were all into silly games . . . and we were getting really drugged out . . . We'd go down to the sessions and have to pack up because we were too stoned. Nobody could get anything right. We were all over the place. Everybody was playing a different thing. Particularly, it was very difficult for me to come up with the ideas and try putting them together that quick.'

Geezer Butler was experiencing something similar with his lyrics, later asserting: 'I used to hate doing it towards the end of the Ozzy era. He'd say, "I'm not singing that." So you'd have to rethink the whole thing.'

Bill Ward simply remembers that, 'I was getting ill all the time with my drinking.'

And as for Ozzy, he later reported a whole catalogue of frustrations. Chief among them was that he loathed the tracks the band were recording, claiming that they embarrassed him and amounted to 'the biggest pile of horseshit that I've ever made in my life'. Clearly, this re-opened the rift between himself and Tony, the musical director.

Ozzy also objected to the multi-tracking and other studio effects that made the songs impossible to recreate onstage, he was outspoken about the huge amounts of money spent to keep the band recording in Toronto, and he contended that they could have used an impartial producer rather than again attempting the job themselves. Of course, Ozzy has since talked at great length about his drug abuse during this period.

There were other reports that Ozzy was at loggerheads with a couple of the road crew, not including Graham, who says: 'I was aware that Ozzy wasn't too happy about Albert Chapman, just because he was one of Tony's best friends from school. Ozzy thought that Albert was always batting for Tony, and he took the piss a little out of Oz. Les was also very friendly with Tony. But I don't believe that any of this was relevant to Ozzy's problems at the time.'

The real source of Ozzy's continuing dissatisfaction was the music, and that in turn made impossible any hope of a true reconciliation with Tony Iommi.

Some might say that Ozzy had done the wrong thing by rejoining the band, but he would stick it out for long enough to celebrate their tenth anniversary with a big, international tour – which would really only prolong the misery.

19

VAN ALIEN!

The fresh English spring felt like a sub-tropical paradise after the big freeze they had endured in Toronto. The band and crew took a couple of weeks off to thaw out before the tenth anniversary tour, named after the forthcoming album, *Never Say Die!*

The tour opened on 16 May 1978 in Sheffield, where Black Sabbath met the group who would support them throughout most of the UK dates and then across America and Europe. Van Halen were from Pasadena, California. At the time, no one in the Sabbath camp knew much about them, only that they'd recently had a hit in the States with a cover of The Kinks' 'You Really Got Me'.

Van Halen weren't the only newcomers to Sabbath circles – an American guitar tech named Barry had joined the crew. He sat in with Graham and Les as they took turns behind the wheel of the 7.5 ton truck that transported the backline from town to town, while the rest of the equipment travelled in a 40 foot artic. Barry was a great lad, very jovial. It was his first visit to the UK, and he was keen to see some of the countryside. As the tour got under way, moving from Sheffield to Glasgow, he was amazed at how green the landscape was – but the grass wasn't the only thing that was green, recalls Graham:

We were heading up the A1 through Northumberland when we realized the extent of Barry's naivety. He was ripe for his initiation – a massive wind-up. Ten miles from the Scottish border, we asked him if he was sure his visa and work permit were in order to enter Scotland for the next few gigs. He looked at us in horror: 'Work permit? Visa?' After feigning dismay at this oversight, we informed him, gravely, that the London office had obviously forgotten to do the paperwork, since we usually had an all-English crew who did not need such documentation to travel around the UK.

There was only one thing for it, we announced. We would have to have to smuggle Barry into Scotland. We pulled into the nearest lay-by and opened the back of the truck. Barry climbed in and we sandwiched him between two large speaker cabinets, explaining that we had to do everything possible to conceal him from the eagle eyes of the Scottish border guards.

As we drove off again, Les and I could not look each other in the face. We were in tears of laughter, so much so that we nearly crashed the truck. Heading towards Berwick-upon-Tweed with our illegal alien hidden in the cargo, we stopped off at a pub for a couple of pints and some pie and chips for lunch. We ate, we drank and we returned to the truck, talking loudly to imaginary border guards and assuring them that there was no need to inspect the back of the truck since we were only carrying musical equipment for Black Sabbath.

We were still in hysterics as we crossed the Scottish border. We carried on for another three miles, just to compose our faces, pulled into another lay-by and opened the back of the truck. I told Barry that we were now safely in Scotland. 'Thanks, guys,' he replied. 'But I think I should stay in here for another few miles, just to make it safe.' When we finally set him free from his hiding place, he was jubilant to have made it across the border.

Of course, we had to warn Barry to watch his step in Scotland. He shouldn't mention the escapade to anyone he met, because there was a hefty bounty on the heads of illegal aliens there. After completing the Scottish gigs, we smuggled him back into England, and arriving for a gig at Newcastle City Hall, he immediately told a bemused Geordie crew about his daring exploits. Sabbath thought the whole thing was hilarious, but it didn't even end there.

We continued south to Manchester for the band's Apollo Theatre show on 22 May, and while we were getting things ready in the venue, the local bobby paid a visit. We knew him; he'd often pop in for a cup of tea backstage. We told him all about the wind-up and managed to talk him into going onstage, where Barry was working, to 'arrest' him. The cop marched straight over to Barry, asked for confirmation of his name, and stated: 'We have information from Strathclyde Police that you illegally entered Scotland and were then illegally smuggled back into England. I have no alternative but to arrest you for . . .

Barry immediately flew into a panic, protesting his innocence and blaming everybody he could think of for not providing him with a visa or a work permit, or even telling him that he needed them. Sadly, the policeman couldn't keep up the charade, and he soon confessed that the whole thing was a joke. Barry chased me up and down the length of Manchester Apollo yelling, 'You bastards!' – words he probably still repeats to this day when he thinks of Black Sabbath and their road crew.

The Apollo is situated in the Ardwick district, close to the city centre. The crew always enjoyed working there since there was a pub, the Aspley Cottage, next to the stage load in.

On this visit, they had arrived earlier than usual to set up the back-line because Sabbath had decided to carry out their own soundcheck. They usually did one at the start of every tour and left it to the crew thereafter. But on certain occasions, if Tony's guitar had started buzzing, for example, then it was all hands on deck, says Graham:

It was a beautiful, sunny morning. We were all busy at the back of the venue when a bloke in a greasy blue boiler suit appeared at the loading dock and said, 'Eh-up, lads, I've got this bloody big power transformer for some Dutch bloke called Van Haling or something. Where do you want it sticking?'

Positioned on the back of his flat-bed truck was a massive industrial transformer. After much scratching of heads and mutterings of,

'Over the top, man,' we cleared an area where this huge contraption would not be in the way. The man in the boiler suit craned it off and left. It was Van Halen's first European tour, and judging by the size of the transformer they had now had delivered, they were going all-out to impress.

The band were proving to be every bit as enthusiastic as their new piece of equipment suggested; they couldn't wait to play, even before the doors had opened. When Sabbath had finished their soundcheck and retired to the Apollo dressing rooms, Van Halen's crew set up their backline. Shortly afterwards, the band hit the stage and started to play Sabbath tunes. It was their way of paying tribute to the Sabs, but Tony Iommi was strangely annoyed by it. He may have misinterpreted the gesture as a piss-take, which it certainly was not. Van Halen were in awe of Sabbath, and their ingenious lead guitarist, Eddie van Halen, was a big fan of Tony. The unwitting faux pas was soon forgotten. The two bands came to get along very well together, and Alex van Halen would often sit next to Graham behind Bill's drumkit, watching and listening to him play onstage.

The UK shows were a great success. Sabbath's loyal audience was back in force, with every gig sold out, and Van Halen went down a storm. The band had been formed by brothers Eddie and Alex Van Halen. Together with bassist Michael Anthony and flamboyant frontman David Lee Roth, they swept in with a cool new take on metal music, but Sabbath more than met their challenge, triumphing every night with all the authority of the rightful headliners. Heavy rock was definitely alive and well in the summer of '78.

It was a long and topsy-turvy kind of tour. One of the most illogical decisions involved an invitation for Sabbath to appear on *Top of the Pops* to promote their new single, 'Never Say Die', which was released ahead of the album. The crew heard about this new engagement late one night after a return visit to Glasgow Apollo, while they were loading the equipment out of the venue. They were suddenly instructed to drive straight to London for the recording at the BBC TV studios in Shepherd's Bush.

Unfortunately, someone had stolen the radiator cap from the truck and the crew had to stop periodically throughout the journey to fill the radiator with water, stuffing the top with socks and anything else that came to hand to try to prevent it from boiling over. The killing joke was that there was no need for the backline to be taken to London at all. The band knew they would be miming, and the only possible reason for the last-minute motorway dash was that Bill simply wanted the British public to see his drumkit. He didn't even bring the giant clam shell.

✝ ✝ ✝

The two bands then embarked on the US leg of the tour, recalls Graham:

> We were somewhere in the Midwest. As usual, shortly before the band were due onstage, I took Bill's snare drum into the dressing room and handed him a pair of sticks so that he could tune it.
>
> I needed the toilet, so I nipped into the nearby locker room and underneath one of the cubicle doors, I couldn't help noticing a pair of red, stiletto shoes next to a pair of men's boots – all of which I recognized. The shoes belonged to a groupie, who had come to the gig as a guest of the band. The boots belonged to someone who worked for the promoter.
>
> I sneaked out, rushed back into the dressing room and told Oz: 'You have to come and see this.' Ozzy grabbed a huge ice bucket and we crept into the toilets, whereupon he tipped the contents over the top of the cubicle door. The guilty pair emerged seconds later like drowned rats, and the red stiletto lady ran off screaming. We never did see her again.

The gigs were selling out all over America. Van Halen's presence had a major influence on ticket sales since they were a much bigger draw at home than they were in the UK. The tour had opened in Chicago on 14 August 1978, taking in the Midwest and the east coast before heading west to finish in Seattle at the end of September.

When the show rolled into Van Halen's home turf of California, they gave Sabbath a real run for their money – even when David Lee Roth welcomed the audience in Oakland, just outside San Francisco, with the immortal, 'Hello, Los Angeles!' The audience fell silent, but the instant Eddie van Halen struck up the first deafening chord on his guitar, all was forgiven.

Black Sabbath and Van Halen flew back from the States at the end of September for a string of European gigs, prior to tackling the second part of the US tour. On one memorable night in Germany, Sabbath ended up hiding from their own audience. It was a disastrous day from the beginning. They had thought they were playing in Nuremberg that evening. The crew got up early and drove into town to set up the gig. In those days, tour itineraries were not the detailed works of art they are now; you were lucky to get a list of cities, let alone the names of the venues. In most places, an experienced crew would know the regular halls and would drive there automatically. However, in Nuremberg, the crew discovered that the band were not booked to play anywhere locally.

Graham had to drive around, scouring the buildings for advertising posters before he finally discovered that Sabbath were actually playing in a small town called Neunkirchen Am Brand, nestling in the forest some thirty miles north. The venue was a reasonably sized sports hall – the Hemmerleinhalle, recalls Graham:

As we were setting up, we noticed a lot of GIs congregating in the parking platz next to the gig. It was incredible. They were coming in armoured cars and all sorts of military vehicles, even helicopters. The local crew explained to us that the American soldiers had just finished six weeks of manoeuvres and were looking to celebrate, big time. The German promoter had kindly over-sold the show and by the time Van Halen took the stage, the hall was crammed with thousands of extremely stoned, drunk and rowdy GIs, all ready to rip.

Van Halen earned a tumultuous reception, and as the audience waited for Sabbath during the changeover, they started chanting loudly and excitably. They went wild when the band finally walked on and launched into the heavy drone of 'Black Sabbath'. But three songs in, Tony Iommi stormed offstage. His guitar stack was buzzing, he couldn't get rid of the problem and he wasn't prepared to put in a sub-standard performance. He stalked off to the dressing room, beneath the stage. Sabbath couldn't possibly have struggled on without the lead guitarist, and when they saw that Tony wasn't coming back, they stopped playing, left the stage and joined him in the dressing room. Ten minutes later, the crew were locked in there with them.

Realizing that Sabbath really had quit the gig, the American army went into battle, instigating a riot in which they wrecked the hall and flung bottles and every other missile they could lay their hands on at the stage. Eventually, we were rescued by the riot police, who arrived to find us under siege in the dressing room. The band were finally able to make a quick getaway while we spent the rest of the night looking over our shoulders as we hauled the equipment back into the trucks.

One of the regular stopovers on the German touring circuit was at Nuremberg's Grand Hotel, overlooking Hauptbahnhof and the city square. It wasn't Ozzy's favourite place, says Graham:

In the early hours of one morning, Ozzy called me and said he couldn't sleep. He complained that he was getting weird vibes from his room and asked me to come up for a beer. He was in a large corner room with a huge bed and French windows opening on to a balcony. I walked out, noticing the pock-marked masonry surrounding the windows.

It was said that when the Americans took possession of Nuremberg during the war, they took pot-shots at this hotel and, specifically, at this very same balcony.

'No wonder you can't sleep, mate,' I remarked to Ozzy. 'I think they've given you Hitler's old room.'

✝ ✝ ✝

In October 1978, *Never Say Die!* was released to indifferent or critical reviews, which was not unusual, and, more seriously, to a public who were clearly voting with their wallets. As a live act, Sabbath were still a top-flight international attraction, but their popularity as recording artists was on the wane. *Never Say Die!* produced their worst ever showing in the American albums chart, peaking at number sixty-nine, although they just about kept their heads up in the UK where it registered at number twelve, one place higher than *Technical Ecstasy*.

Still, they kept on pounding away at America, returning in November for the second leg of the tour. No one who was around Black Sabbath in Nashville, Tennessee, will forget the events of 16 November.

The Municipal Auditorium was packed out, and Van Halen were going through their paces to storms of applause. Backstage, Sabbath were arriving for the gig. Bill and Geezer turned up first, followed by Tony, and they were sitting around the dressing room when Albert Chapman, now officially the tour manager, walked in with some worrying news.

He had gone to collect Ozzy from his hotel room, but the singer wasn't there. His luggage was stacked on the floor unopened, the bed was fully made and the sanitary paper band was still in place across the toilet. Ozzy had not even checked into his room. Albert then searched the hotel – the large Hyatt Regency in downtown Nashville – to no avail. The rest of the band were unruffled at first, assuming that he would wander in at any moment. But time marched on, and there was still no sign of Oz as Van Halen finished their set.

Tony started tuning up, Bill was banging on the snare drum in his usual pre-gig ritual, Geezer was combing his hair, and Albert and the promoter were screaming, 'Where the fuck is Ozzy?' In a panic, they reported his disappearance to the police, and contacted the local radio station which immediately broadcast an appeal to the people of Nashville: if anyone is with Ozzy Osbourne, or sees him, please tell him to go to his gig, or bring him yourself if you have to.

Sabbath's showtime came and went, and the fans were becoming impatient. Their mood was getting ugly. Backstage, speculation was reaching fever pitch. He's been kidnapped! He's flipped again and gone home! He's holed up in a bar somewhere pissed out of his mind! After an hour, Tony, Geezer and Bill were ushered out of the arena and back to the hotel, out of harm's way. The promoter then announced that Sabbath would not be performing that night. Predictably, all hell broke loose and the fans did whatever they could to trash the Municipal Auditorium.

Much later, Sabbath and crew assembled in the hotel bar. Ozzy was still on the missing list, and it looked as though the rest of the tour was in serious jeopardy, remembers Graham:

The next day, I went down for breakfast and bumped into Albert. He wasn't a happy man. He had received a call from Ozzy at 6.30 am 'Hi Albert, I'm ready for the gig.'

Albert went ballistic. 'What do you mean? Where the fuck have you been?' he demanded. Ozzy told him he'd been in bed. He'd slept right round the clock, woken up, seen that it was six o'clock, and thinking that it was still the evening before, had got ready for the show. Even more incredibly, he'd been sleeping in the wrong room.

When Ozzy had arrived at the Nashville hotel and headed for his room, he took the wrong key out of his pocket. It was the one belonging to his room in the last hotel he'd stayed in – another Hyatt. Reading the room number from the key in his hand, he set off to find it. The door was open and a maid was finishing the maintenance man and a cook, a lovely woman called Rachel who would serve up real American fare, thick steaks and sweet potatoes with corn. Sadly, she didn't stay around for long because Sabbath were not a band for regular mealtimes; their sleeping patterns were all over the place.

'So here we were in Bel-Air, still cooking for ourselves,' laughs Graham. 'We would often take a run out to the nearest supermarket and bring back about a hundred dollars' worth of food to fill up the enormous fridge. We'd cook up our usual curries and traditional English comfort food such as shepherd's pie.'

The band soon converted the carport into a rehearsal room, and everything seemed perfect, but 'I couldn't help wondering if it really was going to be heaven – or hell,' says Graham. Despite the idyllic setting of the house, Sabbath were only a few minutes' drive from the temptations of Sunset Strip, with the Rainbow, the Roxy, the Whisky A Go-Go and Barney's Beanery among the potential distractions.

The Rainbow Bar and Grill on Sunset Boulevard stands on the site of the former Villa Nova restaurant, where Marilyn Monroe first dated her future husband Joe DiMaggio in 1953. It was also the place where Judy Garland became engaged to Vincente Minnelli, Liza's father, in 1945. In the early seventies, the Rainbow became a favourite watering hole for the rock community. Upstairs was a VIP bar, Over The Rainbow, which contained an elevated platform with a table and chairs. Known as the Fox's Lair and reached by a wooden ladder, it was here that John Lennon, Keith Moon, John Entwistle and Ozzy Osbourne would engage in their legendary drinking sessions.

The Whisky A Go-Go at 8901 Sunset is world famous as a live venue and an important port of call for bands starting out on their careers in America. In 1966, The Doors were the house band, and since then such luminaries as The Who, Led Zeppelin, Jimi Hendrix, AC/DC and Black Sabbath have graced its stage. George Harrison, visiting the Whisky with John Lennon at the height of Beatlemania, caused a sensation in the media when he threw a glass of water over the Hollywood starlet Mamie Van Doren. George, who had been having a stressful evening due to press attention, had actually been aiming at a photographer.

cleaning. She then left and Ozzy, who was shattered that day, went to bed for the longest nap of his life.

Tony, Geezer and Bill took it all in their stride. They were annoyed, but they weren't surprised at Ozzy's explanation, and they were relieved that no harm had come to him. Albert told him, 'You're a twat,' but Oz laughed it off and so, eventually, did everybody else.

The cancelled show finally went ahead a few days later. It had been scheduled as a travel day – a day off for the band, if not the crew – and the show was held in the afternoon so the trucks could leave in enough time to make the next gig. 'The band were pissed off at not having their day's break,' remembers Graham. 'Especially since the one person who did have a day off was Ozzy.'

As the tour wound up in Albuquerque, New Mexico, on 11 December, Sabbath had completed more than a hundred gigs with Van Halen. Van Halen had probably won out as the stronger band in many American cities, but their journey was just beginning. Sabbath were commemorating their ten-year anniversary. And having done that, they would not play live with Ozzy again for another seven years – although nobody knew that at the time.

† † †

The 'Van Halen Effect' stirred Sabbath into action. The sheer energy of the young Californian band had served to emphasize Sabbath's own loss of passion and purpose. At the same time, British groups like Queen were taking showmanship and spectacle to new, pioneering heights with huge stage productions.

Sabbath were also uncomfortably aware of a whole new generation of punk rock heroes led by the Sex Pistols, The Clash and The Damned, who had been snapping at their heels for the past two years, especially in the UK. The punks and their audiences revelled in attacking the existing musical establishment, with Sabbath and their like condemned as 'dinosaurs' and 'boring old farts'.

The irony was that even in this climate of huge musical extremes, one band was very much like the next, no matter how different their ages or musical angles. Underneath it all, they were just a bunch of blokes getting up on a stage to do a gig, and that's entertainment.

Nevertheless, January 1979 saw Sabbath take a long, hard look at their career: it was time for a new start and a new direction. After several years of trying to manage themselves, they decided that enough was enough. They announced that they had signed a management deal with Jet Records boss Don Arden. They'd spoken to Arden on and off in the past, and had approached *him* this time. Arden – father of a woman called Sharon – vowed to revitalize their career. Plans were made for an album and a tour which would boast a dynamic new stage show.

Sabbath had been impressed by Arden's management of the Electric Light Orchestra, fellow Brummies who were enjoying huge success in both the UK and America with their dextrous melodies and harmonies and extravagant stage productions. They were setting an example of transatlantic staying power that Sabbath hoped to follow.

Jet Records was based in LA, and it was decided that the band should rent a house there to start rehearsals for the next album. They were all in high spirits about this, since they had happy memories of the mansion in Stradella Drive. On 3 March 1979, Sabbath and crew flew out to Hollywood and moved into a beautiful, spacious house in the hills. It was in the exclusive, private estate of Bel-Air, soon renamed, a little irreverently, Bel-End.

20

THE HOUSE ON THE HI
IN BEL-END

Before they left, Ozzy had renewed his transatlantic friends
Frank Zappa.

In February 1979, he organized an outing to one of two
Zappa was playing at the Birmingham Odeon. After the show
invited Frank and his wife, a beautiful Japanese woman, to the
rated Koh-I-Nor restaurant in Bristol Street. 'You could have hea
drop as our fellow-diners suddenly realized that there were stars
midst,' says Graham. 'Ozzy ordered his usual vindaloo. In thos
Indian restaurants also offered an English selection on the men
Frank opted for a less exotic steak and chips. As he chewed on hi
Ozzy asked him, "What's it like, Frank – old boots?"

"No", came the reply. "It's like new ones . . .""

† † †

1950 Bel-Air Road was typical of the houses in the area, painted
and surrounded by gardens with a large swimming pool and par
views of the valley descending into Beverly Hills and west Holl
It had eight bedrooms and an open-plan living room. To reach
drove past the homes of movie stars and the mega-rich of L
interesting local property was the mansion used as the local
the American television comedy series, *The Beverly Hillbillies*. N
had the Birmingham Hillbillies moving in up the road.

It was all very luxurious, with a staff including gardeners

Barney's Beanery, on Santa Monica Boulevard, had been a gathering place for creative types since the twenties, with writers, artists, actors, actresses and rock stars among those regularly calling in for one of the restaurant's celebrated chillis, or maybe just a drink or a game of pool. Janis Joplin had the last drinks of her life – two glasses of vodka and orange – at Barney's.

The hotels of Hollywood were, similarly, a playground for bands like Black Sabbath. The Riot House had featured regularly in their history, and they also liked the Beverly Wilshire and the Sunset Marquis, which is built around a pool. Bill, however, preferred the Chateau Marmont, a big, old, Gothic structure which was at that time slightly run-down and living on its former glories. Actor John Belushi later died there from a drugs overdose.

'I remember Marty Feldman, the British comedian, sitting at the bar in the Rainbow one evening,' recalls Graham, 'saying that he had walked out of his room at the Chateau because it was full of people he didn't know. He was filming in Hollywood at the time, and he reckoned the studio had laid on a party and rented a crowd of extras to keep him company.'

Eventually, it would not be the drinking dens, rock clubs or flesh-pots of the Strip that would prove the undoing of Sabbath: it would be the band themselves.

✝ ✝ ✝

Everything seemed to be going so well at first. The rehearsals were in full swing, and the atmosphere was positive.

'I remember Ozzy asking me to write down some lyrics for him,' says Graham. 'He wasn't embarrassed about it – it was widely known that he was dyslexic. He was working on the album's title track, "Heaven And Hell". It was good to see Oz getting involved in the writing rather than sitting back and leaving it all to Geezer.'

But after a few weeks, their concentration started falling off. This was to be their ninth studio album in ten years, and the creative force that had at one time seen them knocking out three great albums in eighteen months had plainly diminished. They were now struggling to produce one album over two years. The years of working and living on the road were taking their toll.

The band have since blamed drugs and booze for the situation that was developing at the house on the hill at Bel-End. But while those temptations were never too far away, and there were certainly times when everybody went on binges, individually or together, they were not a daily occurrence. No matter what their legend, and no matter how much they themselves contributed to building it, Sabbath had always been able to sober up and straighten out for long periods of time, especially when they were busy. The real difficulty, as far as Graham could see, was a serious case of familiarity breeding contempt. A rift was opening up between Ozzy and the rest of the band, and it was becoming wider every day: 'We could all feel that the tension between Ozzy and Tony in particular was reaching breaking point.'

The fundamental problem between the singer and the guitarist hadn't gone away. Ozzy was frustrated by Tony's musical ambitions and willingness to spend extended periods in the studio. He believed that Sabbath had lost their direction, were well on the way to becoming another Foreigner, and needed to return to the purity, spirit and spontaneity of their fire and brimstone heavy metal. He also felt belittled by Tony's continuing disregard for his point of view. Iommi, for his part, was livid at Ozzy's apathy, his lack of commitment and contribution to the next album, which was supposed to be a brand new start for Sabbath.

Bill, as ever, tried to be the peace maker, he encouraged debate and they would all discuss the various issues, but Ozzy and Tony could never seem to find any common ground. As usual, it was all talk. There were no full-blown shouting matches or fights, but the bad blood kept on pumping just below the surface. Geezer and Bill simply ran out of ideas; they didn't know how they could hope to patch things up and get the band back on track.

Privately, some of the Sabbath members had recently suffered family bereavements and illnesses – Bill had lost both his parents in 1978, and Geezer was worrying about the health of some of his family. Three members of the band were also going through marital difficulties. Tony had split up with his wife Sue, Geezer was separating from Georgina, and although Ozzy was still officially with Thelma it seemed their relationship was also under pressure. The band had always put Sabbath and the music before anything else in their lives, they rarely brought their wives to gigs, parties or any other social events, and now they were paying the price. Ironically, the group in which they had invested everything was also disintegrating, almost inevitably, at 1950 Bel-Air Road.

Something, somewhere, was bound to snap soon. But even in these dark days, the schoolboy humour that had always bound the band together would burst, briefly, into life, as Graham recalls:

We did have some laughs at Bel-End, which was a great escape valve. And that's why I hoped and believed that Sabbath would be able to overcome their differences in the end. One day, we heard that Demis Roussos, the huge, Greek, kaftan wearing warbler had an appointment to come and view the house. He was looking for a property in the area, and if he liked it, he would take over the rental when Sabbath had left.

Les Martin bore an uncanny resemblance to Demis and on the day of the viewing, he put on a dressing gown to answer the knock on the door. Demis' face was a picture; it was priceless. All of us – including the four members of Sabbath – ran off together to hide in a room, laughing hysterically as the two gentlemen wandered around the house in their long robes. Our visitor drove away again looking puzzled and shaking his head; we never did find out if he liked the mansion.

On another evening, the Hollywood movie star Tony Curtis turned up at the door with a couple of girls, saying he had come for the party.

'The only trouble was, there wasn't a party that night,' says Graham, 'and Tony Iommi and Les were too wired to make small talk with an A-list celebrity. So I turned him away, insisting that I had no idea who he was, and he looked every bit as confused as Demis Roussos as he was driven away.'

A more welcome visitor to the house was Andy Gray, the Scottish soccer player who was turning out for Aston Villa FC at the time. He had made friends with Tony and Geezer, Sabbath's resident Villa fanatic, and they had invited him over for a two week holiday in the luxury of Bel-Air while the English football season was closed, recalls Graham:

> Andy seemed like a fish out of water, since these were mad days at the house on the hill, but we set up a routine of sorts. Quite often, we would go down to the Rainbow Bar and Grill for a pizza and a few drinks. One evening, a couple of groupies came to join us at our table. They were typical Hollywood types, checking out any newcomers in the hope of a fresh conquest. Andy explained that he was not in a band; he was a footballer. Disbelievingly, they concluded that this was impossible since he was too small. They make 'em big over there.

✝ ✝ ✝

The rehearsals ground to a near-halt, the members of Black Sabbath started avoiding each other, and Tony Iommi went into hibernation in his bedroom. You would hardly see him. Occasionally, he would come down during the night to cook a meal, usually steak smothered in Lea & Perrins Worcestershire Sauce.

The atmosphere in the house was terrible; you could have cut it with a knife. The place was a tip. The home furnishings were gradually being removed, the Mexican gardeners disappeared, and the pool maintenance man no longer visited. Don Arden, who had rented the house and was paying the staff, had obviously realized the band were on the verge of splitting, and was cutting his losses, just in case the worst happened. As events would show, he had no interest in Black Sabbath without Ozzy Osbourne.

Then the road crew started leaving. Les Martin quit the band, after all those years, to go and live with his girlfriend at Hermosa Beach. Roy Lemon, Tony's latest guitar tech, flew back to England. Left on his own, Graham saw the whole house of cards collapsing around him:

> To escape the house, I would drive out to Santa Monica and go to a pub called the King's Head. It was owned by a chap called Phil who was from Birmingham, and it had become a home from home for a lot of expatriate Brits. Many had come over on Freddie Laker's Skytrain, an airline offering cheap flights to America in the seventies and eighties; you could fly from London to Los Angeles for £100 at a time when the big, corporate airlines were charging fantastic amounts of money for the same journey.
>
> The King's Head was populated by all sorts of ordinary, working people – carpenters, plasterers and brickies – and it was a relief to get back down to earth in their company, when life with Black Sabbath was increasingly surreal. The airline crews would bring the English daily papers to the King's Head, and it served the best fish and chips outside the north of England.

It was Friday afternoon, 27 April 1979, and the Birmingham Hillbillies had been in Bel-Air Road for two months when it suddenly happened. Ozzy left the house – and the band. Graham was shocked:

> Oz said that Bill Ward had told him he was sacked. At first I thought he must have misunderstood since Bill had been Ozzy's closest friend in the band, and had tried his hardest to calm the troubled waters. They were true soul brothers. It took a while for the news to sink in.

For his part, Bill has agreed that he volunteered to break the news to his friend, stating: 'Ozzy was in really bad shape at that time. We were not accomplishing a whole lot . . . I reluctantly pitched in and agreed that we would need another singer . . . It was the right thing to approach him directly and talk to him.'

Ozzy later described his last days with the band as 'a real bad mess', a sad and depressing time which ended with him and Tony not speaking at all. He added, 'Black Sabbath was as black as its name at the end of the day.' Pinning much of the blame on drugs and alcohol as usual, he has also complained that the former friendships and loyalties had broken down, that the social side of the band had crumbled as decisively as their musical unity, that it had become 'bitchy and catty' and that he had actively disliked the last two or three albums he made with Sabbath, especially *Never Say Die!*

Ozzy told *Circus* magazine: 'Sabbath was a walking disaster, you know. Everything it touched – in one hand was gold and in the other was a big piece of shit.' Stating that the band had been 'ripped off ruthlessly' over the years, he said: 'It got to the point where I wasn't putting my heart and soul into it. I hated being part of it. I was killing the band, and the band was killing me. I finally needed to make a move for my own life.'

However, he added: 'It was the greatest thing in my life. Sabbath was a fucking phenomenon. There'll never be another band like that again. I don't care if you could resurrect Elvis Presley. I remember the thrill it was to come from the back streets of Birmingham in England to Madison Square Garden in New York . . . it's like playing on Mars. You can't buy that.'

Tony Iommi has also since looked back on the Ozzy era with affection, suggesting that, as young men, the band had been quick to make mountains out of molehills. He traced his own actions and reactions back to his perpetual grievance that he had been placed in the unpopular position of band leader and was always under pressure to come up with ideas for the albums – because no one else did.

Graham was filled with sadness:

I was devastated when Ozzy left. Even after everything that had happened, I couldn't believe it. I hoped that it was a temporary thing and that he would be back. I don't think that, deep down, the rest of the band wanted to get rid of him. Yet again, they might have been praying for a miracle, that he would change, which in retrospect was stupid and impossible. But I think they all realized that this time was different, that things had gone too far for Ozzy to stay with Sabbath. They were all very sad about it, Bill and Geezer more than Tony, although they didn't say much about it in my hearing. As usual, they kept their private business to themselves. They just seemed to want to get on with the recording of *Heaven and Hell*.

Anticipating Ozzy's departure, Sabbath had called on the services of a new singer, the American Ronnie James Dio, who had previously fronted Rainbow and Elf. He'd been waiting in the wings before Ozzy even left, ready to take the microphone, says Graham:

> I think Ozzy might have got wind of something going on. Tony had met Ronnie Dio in the past, and someone at Jet Records had suggested the new arrangement. There hadn't been any special friendship between him and Sabbath that I was ever aware of.
>
> Within days of Oz splitting, in walked Ronnie. The thought of this small guy having to sing 'Iron Man' on stage made me cringe, and it probably made Ronnie cringe as well, although he told me he was a long-time fan of the band. He really wanted to do a good job for them. But he couldn't hope to be a Prince of Darkness, or even a Prince of Daftness, as we used to call Ozzy. He was a different character completely.

Ozzy pithily remarked: 'Ronnie James Dio is going to have to have a bullet proof vest.'

Wihout Ozzy, Sabbath went back into rehearsals with a renewed enthusiasm – or so it seemed. But out of the blue, in another body blow, Geezer walked out of the band and returned to England. He had a couple of serious domestic issues coming to a head at home, not least that he was finally splitting with his wife Georgina, having fallen in love with another woman – his second wife Gloria – in St Louis on the 'Never Say Die' tour. The recent traumas in Sabbath had undoubtedly compounded his problems; at a time of great change, Geezer probably decided that it was the end of an era and an appropriate time to cut out. Luke was among those who was shocked at Geezer's marriage break-up. He says, 'I pictured him and Georgina staying together for ever.'

Practical as ever and none too sentimental about the bass player's departure, Tony quickly contacted an old Birmingham friend, Geoff Nichols, and asked him to fly out to join the band. Geoff arrived in LA shortly afterwards, but rather than taking up bass duties he became the keyboard player – and he still is. As a musician and as Iommi's right-hand man, he has never been a full band member, although his contributions have been credited on Sabbath albums.

As for the vacant bass job, that went to an American musician brought in by Ronnie Dio. Craig Gruber was another ex-Rainbow member. The band, to all intents and purposes, had become Black Rainbow.

✝ ✝ ✝

Immediately after leaving Sabbath, Ozzy went to stay with the girl-friend of a guy who worked for Don Arden's Jet Records. She lived in the San Fernando Valley on the north side of the Hollywood Hills. Keeping Oz company was an old mate called Geoff Sharpe, who was from Egremont, Cumbria. He had been tight with Dave Tangye and Necromandus, and he remained a trusted friend, as Graham explains:

> Geoff had flown out for a holiday with some friends in Philadel-phia, and he called me saying that he would like to come and see us in LA, never dreaming that he would find the band in such a state of upheaval. Ozzy was more than pleased to hear about his visit, and we both went to pick him up at LAX airport.

Ozzy and Geoff stayed at this girl's house for a couple of weeks and I took it upon myself to visit them every day. Despite the fact that Oz was seriously upset by what had happened with Sabbath, it was not all doom and gloom. Whenever he was in the building, something hilarious would usually happen. One day, the girl held a wedding reception at her home for one of her friends. After a few drinks, the guests were invited into another specially decorated room where the table was laden with trays of food arranged around the wedding cake.

They all walked in and milled around the table, and no one could have failed to notice that the once-magnificent centrepiece, the cake, was lying squashed in pieces all over the table. Geoff had had his wicked way with a wedding guest over the table. Ozzy was surprisingly shocked when he found out Geoff was the guilty party – the next day they both moved out of the house.

They took apartments at a hotel called Le Parc in Hollywood. Geoff went back to England soon afterwards, but Ozzy remained at Le Parc for quite a while longer, planning his next move. He has since described his stay at the hotel; how he sat, suicidal, alone in his room with the curtains drawn for weeks on end, smoking endless cigarettes and ordering deliveries of fast food.

'In fact, after Geoff left, Don Arden's daughter Sharon came to see Ozzy at Le Parc,' says Graham. Her brief as far as Ozzy was concerned was to look after the managerial side of his solo career on Don's behalf. She did this so efficiently that Ozzy later raved about her business capabilities and about the encouragement and respect she showed him.'

After Ozzy's marriage to Thelma ended, it was Sharon he turned to. They married in 1982 and history has proved that she has been looking after Ozzy very well ever since.

✝ ✝ ✝

The Bel-End experience was over. Sabbath relocated to Miami and Criteria Studios, scene of their *Technical Ecstasy* recording sessions, and checked into the Coconut Grove Hotel.

Bill, predictably, had elected not to fly, so Graham rented a one-way truck, loaded all of the backline into it, and drove Bill coast to coast from LA to Miami:

> I was the only roadie left by then, and it was up to me to take care of everything. It was difficult, but Bill gave me a hand. On the way along Interstate 10, I stopped and telephoned to check that the rest of the band had arrived safely at their hotel. I discovered that a raging hurricane had hit Miami and Sabbath were literally boarded up in the hotel, prisoners until the storm passed.
>
> Bill and I, on the other hand, had started out on a seven day journey, and as we drove across the various states, we knew that we were leaving behind the Sabbath we had known and loved, and that it was irreplaceable. Bill was very sad about the split with Oz, we were both worried about him, and we hoped that he would have success with his own band – or maybe even come back.
>
> The road trip was therapeutic for both Bill and me, and we made the best of it, stopping off at every place that took our fancy. In San Antonio, Texas, a favourite spot, we caught a gig by Sabbath's former support band Black Oak Arkansas, who were surprised to find Bill Ward travelling the country in a truck.

With Bill and Graham arriving safely in Miami, Sabbath and crew rented out a house owned by The Bee Gees' Barry Gibb. Two weeks into the sessions, Geezer returned to the fold, remembers Graham:

> There'd been a general feeling in the band that he would come back once he'd sorted out his personal problems, and so there was less drama around his departure than there had been around Ozzy's. Similarly, there was no huge sense of surprise when he flew into Miami to rejoin Sabbath, although everyone was really pleased to

see him back. I don't know how Craig Gruber felt. One minute he was in Black Sabbath, and the next he wasn't. I expect Ronnie Dio talked him gently through the situation.

The sessions for *Heaven and Hell* went really well, with Martin Birch brought in to produce it. Released by Vertigo in April 1980, it would restore Sabbath's commercial fortunes to some extent, entering the British top ten and recording an encouraging number twenty-eight in America, the best US result they'd had in some time. It wasn't a classic Sabbath album – there would never be another classic Sabbath album – but it was a good, solid rock effort, despite the opinions of many reviewers who could not accept the absence of Ozzy.

Things had changed for Bill Ward: 'After I got sober, I realized that I lied to Tony, Geezer, Ozzy and myself. I didn't want to be in a band without Ozzy.' And so Bill and Graham reached the end of the road with Black Sabbath. The brave new world that both they and Don Arden had envisaged when they signed on the dotted line to his management company had not materialized.

By the summer of 1980, Black Sabbath had parted company with Arden, who had opted to stick with Ozzy, both as his manager and label boss. Sabbath signed to Blue Öyster Cult manager Sandy Pearlman, and the two bands found themselves out on a co-headlining tour of America, with Sabbath promoting *Heaven and Hell*, as Graham recalls:

It wasn't the same any more. When they played live, they were really pretty good, but there was a different vibe because Oz wasn't around. Ronnie had come in with a lot of ideas and he was up for it; the whole band had taken on a more serious approach.

One night, I had set the equipment up at McNichol's Arena in Denver. Bill's brother Jim Ward had come back, and they had been travelling together in a camper van. Jim arrived backstage to say that

Bill was outside in the van but was adamant that he would not be coming into the gig. He had finished.

I went out to talk to him in the camper van, and I saw a relatively young man, very tired, very drunk and very confused who was nevertheless certain about one thing: he wanted to quit and he did, there and then. I tried to talk him into staying, but it was no good. He went to live in Seal Beach, LA, and he's been there ever since.

With what seemed like indecent haste, only a matter of days later Black Sabbath had found a replacement for Bill and were back onstage at the Aloha Stadium, Hawaii, with Vinnie Appice on drums. It was one insult too many for Graham. He stayed around for as long as it took to collect his paycheck, and headed back to LA.

EPILOGUE

Ozzy Osbourne finally left his apartment at Le Parc to launch a successful solo career, aided and abetted by a host of different musicians over the years. Memorable among them have been guitar aces Randy Rhoads, who died tragically young in a plane crash in 1982, and Zakk Wylde, who came in at the end of the decade.

He married Sharon on a beach in Hawaii on 4 July 1982. She manages Ozzy's career to this day and is mother to their three children, Aimee, Kelly and Jack. In 1996, Ozzy brilliantly reinvented his career when he established the Ozzfest, headlining a series of heavy metal festivals which would also feature the most hip and happening young bands of the genre.

Now, he's a household name across the world, having laid bare his unique presence to a mass audience with the reality television show *The Osbournes*, negotiated by Sharon. Ozzy continues to muddle his way through life in the family chaos of his Hollywood mansion.

✝ ✝ ✝

Black Sabbath carried on in a variety of line-ups with Tony Iommi at the helm, but none of the albums they released throughout the eighties and nineties would bring the kind of rewards the band had known with Ozzy at the microphone.

In 1985, the original Sabbath reformed to appear at the Philadelphia leg of the international fund-raiser Live Aid. It was great to see them back together, and many people among the television audience of millions must have hoped that they had buried the hatchet. Unfortunately, they hadn't. Ozzy admitted that he only joined the reunion because if he hadn't, he'd have been criticized for failing to help the Live Aid effort. He later insisted that, 'I will never rejoin Black Sabbath,' and on another occasion, said of the reunion that: 'This whole black cloud has followed us again . . . the cement was on the fucking box.'

There's no confirmation of reports that Ozzy had wanted to help the starving millions of Ethiopia by playing 'Food Glorious Good' – but it sounds suspiciously like his sense of humour.

Geezer Butler had made his peace with Ozzy by 1988, when he played bass on one of Oz's tours.

Finally, in 1992, Sabbath enjoyed what seemed like a genuine reunion, performing at the end of an Ozzy Osbourne solo gig in California. They regrouped for the 1997 Ozzfest and have since played various special concerts and tours, proving that the old bonds between them may have been tested but were never really broken.

Ozzy later said: 'We gave each other space and respect, and it worked. All the juvenile shit-slinging, slagging and petty jealousies have finally gone . . . There's this invisible fucking magic that just happens when we're up there.'

His former foe, Tony Iommi, added: 'It was great to get back together. We were all in the right frame of mind . . . We've got a unique sound that none of us have been able to recreate with other players.'

Bill Ward commented that he 'felt fantastic' about the touring, and Geezer simply paid tribute to Ozzy as 'the craziest person I've ever met'.

Geezer still lives on the outskirts of Birmingham, closely follows the ups and downs of Aston Villa FC and works on various musical projects. Tony Iommi lives not far away from Geezer, still plays guitar and drives around in sports cars. Bill has remained on the west coast of America, south of Los Angeles, and has released several solo albums.

Dave Tangye returned to 'real life' after leaving Black Sabbath in 1977:

I decided to go back to the job I had prior to my excursion into the world of heavy metal. I felt that the sudden shock would get my feet back on the ground after flying so high during the Sabbath years, and it certainly worked.

However, this turned out to be a short respite, I was soon back in the rock'n'roll circus. I had kept in contact with my old boss Ozzy Osbourne, making several journeys to see him at his farmhouse, and he in turn came up to Cumbria to see me. Late in 1979, he was auditioning musicians for his solo career and he asked for my help. He wanted me to look out for people who might be suitable for his band. Subsequently, he invited me to look after security on his first UK outing, the 'Blizzard of Ozz' tour, in September 1980, and then on his 1981 American dates. I was present when he recorded *Blizzard of Ozz* and *Diary of a Madman*, arguably the two most creative albums of his solo career.

This was just short-term employment for me. I left the Blizzard of Ozz band in 1981, having decided to go back to my trade in engineering and construction. The golden days of rock'n'roll were behind me. I no longer felt the thrill of the music business. I'd been there, seen that, and got the T-shirt to prove it.

Over the past twenty years or so, I have worked my way around the globe again. With the eighties boom in the global construction industry, particularly in nuclear, petrochemical and pharmaceutical fields, I have been gainfully employed on projects too numerous to mention, on a worldwide basis.

Looking back at my days with Black Sabbath, and Ozzy in particular, my fondest memory is the camaraderie, the way that everyone pulled together, even when things were tough. I'm sure that the close bond of friendship between them has somehow survived everything life threw at them.

Dave has recently started a Sabbath website at: www.blacksabbath.co.uk.

† † †

Graham Wright returned to LA after quitting Sabbath and settled in Laurel Canyon, where he rented an old garage and turned it into an artist's studio. He stayed there for a couple of years painting large-scale canvases and enjoyed some success exhibiting and selling his work, a selection of which is on view on his website at: www.stagewright. freeserve.co.uk/ graham_frank_wright1.htm.

In 1982, he returned to North Yorkshire and held exhibitions at York City Art Gallery and Middlesbrough Art Gallery but art was not all life had in store for him:

> I thought I had left the music business for good until I bumped into Ozzy and Sharon in London. After joining them on a hilarious visit to Ireland, I found myself on Ozzy's 'Speak of the Devil' tour as a bass guitar tech. 'Getting back into the business, I teamed up with Les Martin again. We toured with a Birmingham band called Shy as they supported Gary Moore and Twisted Sister around Europe, and then went on to work with UFO. On tour with them in 1986, I met my future wife, Mikki, in Austin, Texas, and stayed on there with her for six months. We married in January 1988 and now have two sons, Daniel and Bryan.
>
> I became a stage carpenter with Dio's band, then The Scorpions and Tina Turner amongst others. Returning to my roots, I got back behind the wheel for some rock'n'roll truck driving, ferrying equipment for everyone from The Rolling Stones to the housewives' favourite Julio Iglesias. Over the past couple of years, I have taken time out to co-write this book with Dave, but I have squeezed in tours with AC/DC, Kylie Minogue, Jamiroquai, Gomez and those relentless heavy metal rockers The Tweenies.
>
> Looking back over my life and career, I can see what a fantastic

privilege it was to have spent so much of the seventies working for Black Sabbath, or Slack Haddock, as we called them. Heavy rock was in a period of development, and we wouldn't be wrong to see ourselves as pioneers, laying the foundations for the huge arena shows that became a vital part of the rock itinerary in the eighties.

I speak to Bill Ward a couple of times a year, and Dave and I met all four original members of Sabbath when they played at the Ozzfest at Milton Keynes in 2001. We were welcomed backstage, where we chatted to Ozzy, Tony, Geezer and Bill as though it was only the day before that we'd all been on the road together.

Dave takes up the story:

We sat out in the sun in the hospitality area next to Ozzy's trailer. At one point, Ozzy walked out and beckoned me over to his palace on wheels. He invited me in, sat me down on a plush black leather suite and played me his new album, *Down to Earth*, which was still unreleased. We reminisced for a while, and I told Ozzy that Graham and I intended to write this book. 'Great idea,' he enthused, immediately giving his blessing.

As I sat with Ozzy listening to the album tracks, a sense of déjà-vu came over me, but the mood was broken with the entrance of his right-hand man, Tony Dennis. 'It's showtime, Oz,' he declared, ushering in a doctor who had arrived on site to give the singer a vitamin injection. In my day, it was honey, a bottle of mineral water and a Choloroseptic throat spray.

Yes, some things had changed, but some things never would. Minutes later, the Prince of Darkness was on the stage with Tony, Geezer and Bill, and Sabbath sounded just as black as they ever did.

GEORGE JACOBS AND WILLIAM STADIEM

Mr S: The Last Word on Frank Sinatra

PAN BOOKS

An insider's account of life with Sinatra during the heady years . of the Rat Pack that's as cool, original and dazzling as the man himself

Generally considered 'the last of the Rat Pack', George Jacobs was Sinatra's valet and confidant from 1953, when Ava Gardner had just left him, until the end of his short-lived marriage to Mia Farrow in 1968. In *Mr S*, George describes one of the longest and most outrageous midlife crises ever.

'I doubt you'll find anything as memorable . . .
so wittily and stylishly written that it goes straight
to the top of my showbiz memoir league'
Lynn Barber, *Daily Telegraph*

'A unique, gossipy perspective on Sinatra's relationships
with some of the glossiest women and dodgiest
men mid-century Hollywood has to offer'
Observer

'Juicy tidbits concerning the Mob, Marilyn, the Kennedys
and other cool stuff Robbie Williams can but dream of'

Q

J. RANDY TARABORRELLI

Madonna

An Intimate Biography

PAN BOOKS

The massive bestselling biography of this international diva – updated with three new chapters

Whereas other books about Madonna have been based on previously published material, this biography is the result of ten years of exclusive interviews with people who are speaking publicly for the first time, including close friends, business associates and even family members. Bestselling author J. Randy Taraborrelli has also interviewed the star herself on numerous occasions and he draws on these first-hand experiences to bring Madonna to life as not merely a tabloid delight, but as a flesh-and-blood woman with human foibles and weaknesses, as well as great strengths and ambitions. This paperback edition includes three new chapters that discuss the 'Drowned World' tour, marriage and motherhood.

This is as close as you can get without being Guy, Rocco or Lourdes!

'A thoroughly professional job . . . makes her more,
not less, fascinating'
Lynn Barber, *Daily Telegraph*

'A book you will find yourself "just dipping into"
for hours at a stretch'
Evening Standard

J. RANDY TARABORRELLI

Michael Jackson: The Magic and the Madness

PAN BOOKS

**By the bestselling author of *Madonna: An Intimate Biography*
– the acclaimed biographer on his greatest subject**

So much has now been said and written about the life and career of Michael Jackson that it has become almost impossible to disentangle the man from the myth. The truth may be stranger than any fiction; such is the uniqueness of the world in which he lives, and his vision of the world. Recent revelations are of course only the latest instalments of a saga that began decades ago, and simply add more twists to an already-tangled family epic.

This book reveals the behind-the-scenes story to many of the landmarks in Jackson's life: his legal and commercial battles, his marriages, his passions and addictions, his children. Objective and revealing, it carries the hallmarks of all of Taraborrelli's bestsellers: impeccable research, brilliant storytelling and definitive documentation.

'I feel I can learn more about Madonna and Michael Jackson by talking to Taraborrelli than by talking to the artists themselves . . . When there's so much misinformation about celebrities, which they often plant themselves, the restless perfectionism of Taraborrelli is the only reassurance we can have that we have any chance of understanding these people. Already I feel closer to the unreachable, thanks to his work'
Tom Payne, *Telegraph*

CYNTHIA TRUE

American Scream

The Bill Hicks Story

PAN BOOKS

The first ever biography of the cult anti-hero comedian

*You know who's bugging me these days? The pro-lifers . . . if you're so
pro-life, do me a favour – don't lock arms and block medical clinics.
Lock arms and block cemeteries.*

*A lot of Christians . . . wear crosses around their necks. Nice senti-
ment, but do you think when Jesus comes back he's really going to want
to look at a cross? . . . Ow! Maybe that's why he hasn't shown up yet.*

It is this kind of humour that made Bill Hicks 'an exhilarating comic
thinker in a renegade class all his own' (*New Yorker*). But it also led
to the notorious censorship of his entire twelfth performance on the
Late Show with David Letterman. Hicks's response was typical: 'Why
are people so afraid of jokes?'

Bill Hicks died of pancreatic cancer in 1994, just four months after
the Letterman incident. He had been selling out theatres all over
Britain and at thirty-two was on the brink of becoming a major voice
in America. His popularity has mushroomed since his death, with
the video and CD legacy of his anarchic talent consistently occupy-
ing the comedy bestseller lists.

'Conscientious, perceptive and affectionate . . .
[True] understands her subject perfectly'
Independent

'The future, past and present of stand-up comedy'
Sean Hughes, from the Foreword

RUSTY YOUNG

Marching Powder

PAN BOOKS

A darkly comic, sometimes shocking account of life in the world's most bizarre prison

When Thomas McFadden was arrested trying to smuggle five kilos of cocaine out of Bolivia, he was thrown inside the notorious San Pedro prison. He found himself in a bizarre world, where corrupt politicians and major-league drug smugglers lived in luxury apartments in one wing while the poorer sections of the prison were too dangerous to enter after dark. To survive in San Pedro you needed an income – and so prisoners turned to the trade they knew best: manufacturing cocaine. Even the prison cat was addicted to crack. After spells as a drug dealer, shop keeper and Mormon pastor, Thomas hit upon the idea of giving guided tours of the prison, and as a result became legendary on the South American backpacking circuit. But behind the show he put on was a much darker reality, where brutality and death were common currency, and sometimes even the strongest did not survive.

'Awesome. Astonishing real-life story of a Brit drug smuggler banged up in Bolivia's most notorious jail. Another world seen through the terrified eyes of a likeable Englishman'
***FHM* (5 Stars)**

'All the staples of the prison memoir are here: sadistic guards, an attempted break-out, the terrors of solitary confinement, the joys of freedom . . . The result is a truly gripping piece of testimony'
Sunday Telegraph

OTHER PAN BOOKS

AVAILABLE FROM PAN MACMILLAN

GEORGE JACOBS AND WILLIAM STADIEM
MR S: THE LAST WORD ON   0 330 41229 9   £7.99
   FRANK SINATRA

J. RANDY TARABORRELLI
MADONNA: AN INTIMATE BIOGRAPHY 0 330 48164 9   £7.99
MICHAEL JACKSON: THE MAGIC   0 330 42005 4   £8.99
   AND THE MADNESS

CYNTHIA TRUE
AMERICAN SCREAM: 0 330 43806 9   £7.99
   THE BILL HICKS STORY

All Pan Macmillan titles can be ordered from our website,
www.panmacmillan.com, or from your local bookshop
and are also available by post from:

Bookpost, PO Box 29, Douglas, Isle of Man IM99 1BQ
Credit cards accepted. For details:
Telephone: +44(0)1624 677237
Fax: +44(0)1624 670923
E-mail: bookshop@enterprise.net
www.bookpost.co.uk

Free postage and packing in the United Kingdom

Prices shown above were correct at the time of going to press.
Pan Macmillan reserve the right to show new retail prices on covers
which may differ from those previously advertised in the text
or elsewhere.